The Satyr

The Satyr

An Account of the Life and Work,
Death and Salvation of
John Wilmot,
Second Earl of Rochester

CEPHAS GOLDSWORTHY

Weidenfeld & Nicolson
LONDON

First published in Great Britain in 2001
by Weidenfeld & Nicolson

© 2001 Cephas Goldsworthy

A CIP catalogue record for this book is available from the British Library.

ISBN 0 297 64319 3

Typeset by Selwood Systems, Midsomer Norton
Printed and bound by Butler & Tanner Ltd,
Frome and London

Weidenfeld & Nicolson
The Orion Publishing Group Ltd
Orion House
5 Upper Saint Martin's Lane
London WC2H 9EA

To my wife Lindsay, my daughters Claudia, Flavia and Francesca,
and to my niece Kate for all their Herculean labours

CONTENTS

INTRODUCTION

'Death, I defy thee!'
The Hobbesian Flux

Nay, the two nearest ways to enter the closet of the gods, and lie
even with the fates themselves, are fury and sleep. Therefore the
fury of wine and fury of women possess me waking and sleeping.
Let me dream of nothing but dimpled cheeks, and laughing lips, and
flowing bowls. Venus be my star, and whoring my house, and Death,
I defy thee!

Duke Nemours (Rochester), in Nathaniel Lee,
The Princess of Cleves, 1681

In 1660 England saw the end of eleven years of Puritanism. Throughout
that time secret police and religious fanatics had controlled the state.
Dancing was condemned. The maypoles had been torn down, the
theatres were closed and singing was permitted only for hymns. Drink
and sex were frowned on and, wherever possible, punished. John
Wilmot, the second Earl of Rochester, was brought up and formed
by this cold world. In 1660, when John was thirteen, Charles II was
suddenly restored to the throne. The monarchy and sin were acclaimed.
An undercurrent of Thomas Hobbes's philosophy, based on Lucretius,
stimulated both Charles II's natural tendency to pleasure and the
reaction of his subjects – not least, in time, John Wilmot – against the
chill of the last decade.

Hobbes, now a venerable seventy-two, had been born in 1588,
prematurely, due to the shock his mother suffered when the Spanish
fleet entered English waters. He used to say that his mother brought
forth twins at once, 'both me and fear'. His father was a 'choleric'
vicar who had fled after a brawl with a parishioner at his own church
door, leaving his children to be brought up by his brother. Thomas
became a classical scholar and philosopher. He evolved a set of
precepts based on the assumption of underlying human folly, depravity

I

and ambition, and on the belief that society's sole purpose was the securing of wealth, security and glory. All human behaviour was driven by fear towards pleasure or mere self-preservation. Where mankind was left in a state of nature, there was a 'war of all against all', during which there could be no civilisation, and human life became 'solitary, poor, nasty, brutish and short'. The answer that he proposed was the 'Social Contract'. Men had to give up their right to injure others in return for the right not to be injured by them. These reciprocal rights had to be surrendered to the sovereign, who might be a single person or an elected legislature that Hobbes called the 'Leviathan', after a gigantic sea-monster. In addition, he believed that the cause of all things lay in motion and that all people and things were in a constant state of flux. Only the present existed in nature. Things past had existed in the memory only. Things to come did not exist at all, the future being but a figment of the imagination inspired by the past and the present. His doctrine led to a general delight in the ephemeral. In the words of John Dryden,

> Happy the man, and happy he alone,
> He who can call today his own:
> He who secure within can say,
> 'Tomorrow do thy worst, for I have lived today.'
> Be fair, or foul, or rain, or shine,
> The joys I have possessed in spite of fate are mine.

Rochester subscribed to Hobbes's belief that the Christian soul did not exist except as part of the body. Hobbes rejected conventional morality and propounded the theory that man's behaviour was, and should be, governed by his senses, desires and passions, a position now sometimes called 'psychological hedonism'. God, the supreme creator, had now become incidental. Since everything was in perpetual motion, sensual atheism gave free licence to every appetite. Priests and others who condemned pleasure had a vested interest in maintaining power through superstition. *There was no supernatural punishment or reward.* These precepts, especially the last, dominated the young Earl's life and work, and ultimately framed his death.

While Charles, then Prince of Wales, was in exile in Paris in 1646, Hobbes had been his tutor in mathematics. It was at this time that the young prince became imbued with the philosopher's ideals. It later became a popular philosophy among those at his Court who had endured the austerity of the Commonwealth or the privations of exile. Very few had actually read Hobbes. If they had, they would have found a less cheering philosophy than they expected, for it had no place in it for love. As it was, Hobbes was the excuse for ungoverned loose behaviour and merriment. In 1675, in *The Character of a Town Gallant*, the anonymous author described 'The Courtier' thus:

His religion (for now and then he will be prattling of that too) is pretendedly Hobbian, and he swears *The Leviathan* may supply all the lost leaves of Solomon, yet he never saw it in his life, and for aught he knows it may be a treatise about catching sprats, or new laws regulating the Greenland fishing trade. However the rattle of it at the coffee-houses has taught him to laugh at spirits and maintain that there are no angels but those in petticoats.

During the Commonwealth, Hobbes had attached himself to the Parliamentarians for the purpose of self-preservation. After the Restoration the generous Charles forgave him and allowed him to remain at Court with a pension of £100 per annum. He enjoyed the old man's wit. He loved to laugh and could forgive anyone who amused him. Equally he enjoyed scandalising his Lord Chancellor and his bishops. Furthermore, the philosopher's views offered such persuasive support for the King's absolutist ambitions and for the self-aggrandisement and indulgence of his followers that the pursuit of pleasure became almost a scientific duty. However, the price to be paid for the old man's sanctuary was silence. Parliament was investigating blasphemy and taking a close interest in the *Leviathan*, and a gag was the only way to keep him alive. But the damage was done. His observations, though heretical, were now thoroughly fashionable with the Cavaliers. Rochester's views were fuelled by the modish tenets of Hobbes, and the philosopher's influence can be detected throughout his startling poetry and his wayward life. His early years were pure extract of Hobbes. 'Good' and 'evil' were mere words, supported by no sort of authority. Hobbes said, 'Every man calleth that which is delightful to himself, "good"; and that, "evil", which displeases him.' Every man might differ in which of these was which. There were no absolutes. A direct result of that teaching was Rochester's utter recklessness, but the sweet elixir of depravity curdled, as time passed, into misanthropy and destruction.

Rochester's life was governed by his own unpredictability. It was not a studied characteristic assumed for others to applaud. It was the inevitable result of his determination, in accordance with Hobbes's and Lucretius' teachings, to act solely for the moment. For centuries students have quarrelled and wrangled over who wrote which of the poems; if it was Rochester, when did he write it, and why? They have striven to find some sort of unifying thread to compile 'Rochester's canon'. It does not exist. His only consistency lies in inconsistency. His poems are sometimes good, sometimes not. His thoughts are sometimes base, sometimes elevated. His opinions are constantly contradicted in his own works, sometimes within the same poem. His work comprises what has been described as 'a kaleidoscopic series of reversals, in which no sooner does the poem settle on a dominant note than it undermines it in an endless and recursive movement'. The past was dead and the future did not exist. What he did or said was based exclusively upon the desire or feeling or whim of the moment. It is impossible to be sure which poem or which part of a poem is a joke and which is not, or who is the speaker and why. There are works that were long thought to be expressions of his own opinion, only for it then to appear that they were written through the mouth of his most hated enemy, Lord Mulgrave; yet many of the attitudes placed in the mouth of his enemy were his own. So much that he wrote was irony that one cannot be sure that he genuinely meant any of it.

He did not shrink from adopting the same view twice if necessary. However, like many intelligent minds, his was capable of holding two diametrically opposite beliefs at the same time. An added complexity is that many of his writings went up in flames when he died and it is impossible to complete a jigsaw with half the pieces missing. He was, of course, throughout his adult life consistently or inconsistently drunk, but the contradictions in his work are generally deliberate. He was a diligent poet who worked hard at his craft. He spent months in the country polishing his 'libels' and had abundant time to reflect on what he was saying in the light of comparative sobriety. On the other hand some of his work was clearly impromptu or written after little preparation and left unrevised. A French critic, Emile Forgues, wrote in 1857 of Rochester's 'bizarre individuality, the contradictions of his character, the caprices of his vanity, his mixture of scepticism and indignation, of insolence and cowardice, whose incoherence seems at times systematic, as if premeditated'. The random philosophy was reflected in his behaviour and in his mercurial relationships.

Rochester's friend Sir Charles Sedley wrote 'In Praise of Constancy':

> Not, Celia, that I juster am
> Or better than the rest,
> For I would change each hour like them,
> Were not my heart at rest.
>
> But I am tied to very thee
> By every thought I have,
> Thy face I only care to see,
> Thy heart I only crave.
>
> All that in woman is adored
> In thy dear self I find,
> For the whole sex can but afford
> The handsome and the kind.
>
> Why then should I seek farther store,
> And still make love anew?
> When change itself can give no more,
> 'Tis easy to be true.

It was a charming thought, and must have brought tears to its recipient's eyes. It was, of course, humbug. Sedley was described by Samuel Pepys as 'one of the lewdest fellows of the age, only worsened by Lord Vaughan [the Lord Chief Justice]'. Fidelity was no more in his nature than in Rochester's.

Rochester's version of the sentiment was 'Against Constancy':

> Tell me no more of constancy,
> The frivolous pretence
> Of cold age, narrow jealousy,
> Disease, and want of sense.
>
> Let duller fools on whom kind chance
> Some easy heart has thrown,
> Since they no higher can advance,
> Be kind to one alone.

Old men and weak, whose idle flame
   Their own defects discovers,
Since changing does but spread their shame,
   Ought to be constant lovers.

But we, whose hearts do justly swell
   With no vain-glorious pride,
Knowing how we in love excel,
   Long to be often tried.

Then bring my bath, and strew my bed,
   As each kind night returns.
I'll change a mistress till I'm dead,
   And fate change me to worms.

Maureen Duffy, in her biography of Aphra Behn, suggests that Rochester was the model for Willmore, the rake in Aphra's play *The Rover* and, more particularly, *The Rover, Part II*, who announces:

I wish I were that dull, that constant thing
Which thou would'st have, and nature never meant me:
I must, like cheerful birds, sing in all groves
And perch on every bough,
Billing the next kind she that flies to meet me...

One of Rochester's greatest works, 'A Satyr against Reason and Mankind', denounces reason and consistency and sets out with all the weariness of twenty-seven years the essential absurdity of a creature that supposes itself lord of the earth. It is fundamental to understanding the mind of the poet:

Were I – who to my cost already am
One of those strange, prodigious creatures, man –
A spirit free to choose for my own share
What case of flesh and blood I pleased to wear,
I'd be a dog, a monkey, or a bear,
Or anything but that vain animal,
Who is so proud of being rational.
His senses are too gross; and he'll contrive
A sixth, to contradict the other five;
And before certain instinct, will prefer

Reason, which fifty times for one does err.

Reason, an *ignis fatuus* of the mind,
Which leaving light of nature, – sense, behind,
Pathless and dangerous wand'ring ways it takes,
Through Error's fenny bogs and thorny brakes;
Whilst the misguided follower climbs with pain
Mountains of whimseys, heaped in his own brain;
Stumbling from thought to thought, falls headlong down,
Into doubt's boundless sea where, like to drown,
Books bear him up awhile, and make him try
To swim with bladders of Philosophy;
In hopes still to o'ertake the escaping light;
The vapour dances, in his dazzling sight,
Till spent, it leaves him to eternal night.

The deluded follower of reason discovers his folly too late:

Then old age and experience, hand in hand,
Lead him to death, and make him understand,
After a search so painful, and so long,
That all his life he has been in the wrong.

Worse still, 'His wisdom did his happiness destroy, Aiming to know
that world he should enjoy'. The poet is filled with scorn: ' 'Tis this
very reason I despise, This supernatural gift that makes a mite Think
he's an image of the infinite'.

Rochester continues his assault against rationality, and begins to
outline its proper use:

'Tis this exalted power whose business lies
In nonsense, and impossibilities.
This made a whimsical philosopher
Before the spacious world his tub prefer,
And we have modern cloistered coxcombs, who
Retire to think – 'cause they have nought to do.

But thoughts are given for action's government;
Where action ceases, thought's impertinent:
Our sphere of action is life's happiness,
And he that thinks beyond thinks like an ass.

This is, in other words, a satire against the misuse of rationality:

> Thus, whilst against false reasoning I inveigh,
> I own right, reason which I would obey:
> That reason which distinguishes by sense
> And gives us rules of good and ill from thence;
> That bounds desires with a reforming will,
> To keep 'em more in vigour, not to kill.

Or, more succinctly, 'Your reason hinders, mine helps to enjoy, Renewing appetites yours would destroy,' and again, ''Tis not true reason I despise, but yours.'

Rochester now turns from reason to mankind:

> Thus I think reason righted, but for man,
> I'll ne'er recant, defend him if you can.
> For all his pride and his philosophy
> 'Tis evident: beasts are in their degree
> As wise at least, and better far than he.
>
> Those creatures are the wisest who attain,
> By surest means, the ends at which they aim.
> If therefore Jowler finds and kills the hares
> Better than man supplies committee chairs:
> Though one's a statesman, th'other but a hound,
> Jowler in justice would be wiser found.

The poet offers the test, 'Which is the basest creature, man or beast?'

> Birds feed on birds, beasts on each other prey,
> But savage man alone does man betray:
> Pressed by necessity, *they* kill for food;
> Man undoes man, to do himself no good.
> With teeth and claws by nature armed, *they* hunt
> Nature's allowance to supply their want,
> But man, with smiles, embraces, friendship, praise,
> Inhumanly his fellow's life betrays...

It is the lust of power alone for which man dares be brave, 'To which his various projects are designed, Which makes him generous, affable, and kind'.

8

Look to the bottom of his vast design,
Wherein man's wisdom, power, and glory join:
The good he acts, the ill he does endure,
'Tis all from fear, to make himself secure.
Merely for safety after fame they thirst,
For all men would be cowards if they durst.

And honesty's against all common sense.
Men must be knaves, 'tis in their own defence.
Mankind's dishonest: if you think it fair
Among known cheats to play upon the square,
You'll be undone —

Nor can weak truth your reputation save,
The knaves will all agree to call you knave.
Wronged shall he live, insulted o'er, oppressed,
Who dares be less a villain than the rest.

Rochester reaches an appropriately cynical conclusion:

Thus sir, you see what human nature craves,
Most men are cowards, all men should be knaves;
The difference lies, as far as I can see,
Not in the thing itself, but the degree;
And all the subject matter of debate
Is only, who's a knave of the first rate?

Man is by nature dishonest. Anyone who aspires to a lesser corruption than the rest will be cut down. He cannot restrain himself from pointlessly attacking his fellows simply because of his own insecurity. Mankind is moved only by fear for its reputation and the desire for power, even sometimes to feats of courage, *'for all men would be cowards if they durst'*. In his *'Addition'*, he qualified his all-embracing disgust:

All this with indignation have I hurled
At the pretending part of the proud world,
Who, swollen with selfish vanity, devise
False freedoms, holy cheats, and formal lies,
Over their fellow-slaves to tyrannise.
But if in Court so just a man there be,

(In Court, a just man! – yet unknown to me)
Who does his needful flattery direct
Not to oppress and ruin, but protect;
Since flattery, which way soever laid,
Is still a tax on that unhappy trade.
If so upright a statesman you can find,
Whose passions bend to his unbiased mind,
Who does his arts and policies apply
To raise his country, not his family;
If upon Earth there dwell such god-like men,
I'll here recant my paradox to them,
Adore those shrines of virtue, homage pay,
And with the rabble world their laws obey.
If such there are, yet grant me this at least,
Man differs more from man than man from beast.

His fundamental statement is his dismissal of logic. It is an *ignis fatuus* of the mind, a will o' the wisp. To Rochester, philosophers, the 'cloistered coxcombs, who Retire to think – 'cause they have nought to do', are objects of contempt. They waste their lives asking themselves pointless and unanswerable questions, only to discover in the end that all their lives they have been wrong. Their 'reason' exists to condemn pleasure; Rochester's 'reason', that is 'sense' (sensuality, as well as common sense), exists only to provide pleasure. Rochester was not always truthful, but he was true to his own beliefs.

I

'There were many that did not like him'
Henry Wilmot

Henry Wilmot was a man of haughty and ambitious nature, of a
pleasant wit and an ill understanding, never considering above one
thing at once and incapable of being contented. Danger was something he commonly prevented and warily declined. He neither valued
his promises, professions or friendships according to any rules of
honour or integrity.

    Edward Hyde, Lord Clarendon, Lord Chancellor, on Henry Wilmot,
        first Earl of Rochester and father of John

John Wilmot, Henry's son, was born on 1 April 1647 at 11.07 a.m., a
day heavy with portent. The notorious astronomer Gadbury later
published his horoscope. With the authority of fifty-one years' hindsight
and the wrong date of birth (he thought it was the 10th) he revealed
that John 'was endued with a noble and fertile muse'. The sun governed
the horoscope and the moon ruled the birth hours. 'The conjunction
of Venus and Mercury in M. Coeli, in Sextile of Luna aptly denoted
his inclination to poetry. The great reception of Sol with Mars and
Jupiter posited so near the latter, bestowed a large stock of generous
and active spirits, which constantly attended on this native's mind, in
so much that no subject came amiss to him.'

Thus the astronomer explained the rare conjunction of the planets
at the time of his birth. No power could ever explain the extraordinary
conjunction of his parents at the time of his conception. There were
those indeed who refused to believe that a union could have been
consummated between two such opposite people. Anthony Wood, a
poisonous Oxford antiquary, put it about that he had been 'credibly
informed by knowing men that John was begotten' by Sir Allen Apsley
MP, who became one of Rochester's trustees on his death. Sir Allen
was Lady Rochester's cousin by marriage, but there is no evidence of

any such misdeed. Little is known about him. His most noteworthy appearance in the pages of history was in 1664 when he and Sir Allen Broderick entered the House of Commons drunk and simultaneously addressed the outraged Members for half an hour, despite forcible efforts to prevent them. In about 1679 he was falsely accused of plotting to murder Lord Shaftesbury and raise an army against the King, but nothing came of the charge, and he was available to act as trustee of Rochester's estate on his death the following year.

There was no physical resemblance between Henry and his putative son, apart from their tired eyes. John's face was lean and long, Henry's was round; John's nose was long, Henry's snub. Their eyebrows were differently shaped and so were their mouths, the son's full, sensual and feminine, the father's small and grim. They were as different as a greyhound and a pug. For most of his life, Henry was in exile in Europe with Charles II. He commemorated the birth of his son by fighting a duel with his enemy Lord Digby in Paris. On the only recorded occasion when he had a clear opportunity to meet the boy, he disappeared for nine months and did not reappear until his wife had lost heart and returned home to England with her sons. 'Honi soit qui mal y pense,' however. Despite the miasma of doubt, John's life unfolded as though Henry were indeed his father. The son grew into a man so contradictory in every facet of his character that, when after his death Nathaniel Lee wrote a play based upon him, everyone knew that Rochester was the subject, but no one has ever been sure which character. The answer is that he was probably two of them. He was kind and he was cruel; he was sober and he was drunk; he was loyal but treacherous; he was an honest liar; he was vain, but deeply modest; he was a coward who was brave. He was wise and he was foolish. He loved women and he hated them. He was masculine but epicene. He loved and hated himself. He loved the King and satirised him brutally. He was an unbeliever and a believer. He was never completely serious and he was never completely frivolous. There was no aspect of his character that was not in direct conflict with some other.

One thing is clear: he was not a 'nice' man and, though capable of irresistible charm, was quite indifferent to the esteem of any but the few whom he respected. In his early years he went out of his way to be as much disliked as possible by those for whom he had no regard.

He frankly admitted his self-centredness, and any other fault of which he was accused, whether justly or not. He admitted to the misdemeanours of others, not for any noble motive, but simply *pour épater le bourgeois*. He was a misanthrope, and wanted the world to know it. He was a rake.

His parentage and background were as improbable as his character. His mother Ann had already been widowed once. Her father had been Sir John St John, of Wiltshire, one of the oldest and most respected Puritan families in England. Her first husband, Sir Francis Lee, had been an eminent Puritan too. She was starched hard and ramrod backed, immersing herself in the grave religious literature of divines like Simon Patrick and Richard Sibbes, whom her son later lampooned. Little is known about her. Despite her lifelong disapproval of John's character she never quite rejected him. In return he was always a dutiful son, though the only true recompense that he gave her was his death.

Henry, the first Earl, was born in 1612, the only surviving son of Charles, first Viscount Wilmot of Athlone. Henry was a professional soldier who had distinguished himself in battle during the second Scottish war in 1640, but was then injured, captured and taken prisoner. On his eventual release he became Member of Parliament for Tamworth. His career as a tribune of the people was more a sprint than a marathon. In June 1641 he was caught conspiring with the King to intimidate Parliament with the army, and was imprisoned for a spell in the Tower of London, with which his son became well acquainted after him. In December Henry was dismissed from the House of Commons. Undaunted, he returned to soldiering. When the raising of the royal standard at Nottingham on 22 August signalled the start of the Civil War, Henry was in charge of a troop of horse, and held the titles of commissary-general and muster-master. He led the cavalry at the battle of Edgehill in 1642. He was made lieutenant-general of horse in April 1643, and in June, at the age of thirty-one, was created first Baron Wilmot of Adderbury in Oxfordshire, the Wilmot family home. He was instrumental in securing the Royalist victories that followed at Roundway Down and, the next summer, at Cropredy Bridge in Oxfordshire, where he was wounded and taken prisoner. Despite his flawed character and ludicrous habits, his men adored him. They immediately rescued him.

He was now in a transcendent position and, just as his son was to do after him, instantly destroyed it. Charles I had never been fond of Henry, though he owed him a great debt of gratitude. Among other services, Henry had saved the Prince of Wales from capture at Edgehill, where the twelve-year-old Prince was trying to take on the entire Parliamentary force single-handed. The King was a thoughtful, serious man who found little to admire in the drunken, swaggering cavalier at his right hand who was keener on fighting with his own enemies than with the King's. The King did not trust him. He was proved right. In August 1644 Wilmot was caught plotting with the Earl of Essex, the Parliamentary commander, to put pressure on Charles to abdicate and set up the fourteen-year-old Prince of Wales in his place. Had the plan been carried out, it would have saved King Charles's head, but Henry received no thanks for that. He was arrested, deprived of his command and charged with conspiring with the enemy. The consequences would have been worse, had not his faithful men petitioned the King for mercy on his behalf. He was given permission to retire to Paris. However, instead of going, he seems to have kicked his heels in England from 1644 onwards, while the Royalists suffered ever more disastrous reverses. At Naseby in 1645 Cromwell's cavalry overwhelmed the Royalist army, and then took Bristol. In June 1646 the first Civil War ended with the capitulation of the Royalist headquarters, the City of Oxford.

Henry had first met Ann in September 1642 when he was quartered with Sir Francis Lee's mother, Lady Sussex, at St Albans. In the summer of 1645 he found her again. Her husband Sir Francis had died in 1639 after only two years of marriage, and she was left with two sons, Henry and Frank, aged four and six at the time of Henry's reappearance. The family was living at Ditchley Park, the Lees' seat in Oxfordshire, about ten miles from Wilmot's home at Adderbury, near Banbury in the same county. Ditchley was a low, ancient timber house, with a picturesque bowling green. It was hung with pictures of ancestors, a portrait of a pope and a head of Christ. There was a great gate and an old ditch, Grim's Ditch, running directly by the house, which was built on a hillside thick with ancient trees. The entrance led through the kitchen straight into the great hall, nine yards by nine yards. It was adorned with stags' horns, hung over poetic inscriptions on brass plates. It was a Puritan ancestral home. It was not luxurious, nor was it convivial.

While Henry had nothing better to do in Oxfordshire, he courted Ann, married her and in about August of 1646 sired a child upon her. One can only speculate about his motives. No one could have been less attractive to him as a character than his wife, though her appearance, later as forbidding as a cliff, was personable. It was quite pointless to contract a marriage when he was on his way to France for ever, least of all to a woman as deeply rooted as Ann. Perhaps, seeing the way things were going with the Royalists, it seemed no bad thing to accumulate a family of impeccable Puritan credentials. To complicate matters further, he also had been married before to Frances Morton and somewhere there was already an heir to his titles named Charles. The heir died between 1652 and 1657 while still a child, probably at Dunkirk, where his father was then living. Perhaps he was trying to link his first son to a family that had a strong chance of survival, as opposed to his own, which had not. The true answer, though, is probably money. At the beginning of the war, Henry had written to a friend greedily predicting the fat pickings that would accrue from the estates of Parliament men when the war was won. There was to be none of that now. The only alternative was a rich widow. Ann was by no means an heiress, but for Henry's purposes she was rich enough. The King was now back in exile, and Henry found himself in far greater danger from the Parliamentarians than he had ever been from Charles. At last it was time to go. He decamped to Paris, where he set about trying to gain favour with the Queen.

He remained in exile for the rest of his life. It is unlikely that he ever saw Ann again or that he ever saw his son John at all. Years later, when John was about seven, Ann made a determined effort to find Henry, and pursued him to France, taking John and his step-brothers Henry and Frank with her. She was there in 1653 and 1654, about the time of the heir's death, at the exiled Court of Charles II, of which she did not approve. Her cousin, Sir Edward Hyde, a prominent Royalist who later became the Earl of Clarendon, Lord Chancellor and the most powerful man in the land, tried to persuade Henry to meet his family, telling him that 'John was an excellent boy who deserved his father's fondness for him,' but Henry stayed in Germany raising money for the King. Hyde wrote again that Ann was refusing to go back to England until she had seen him, and that the family was unwell. A fortnight later Hyde repeated the message. Both times he was ignored. Finally, 1656 saw the family back at Ditchley. They had caught not a glimpse of Henry, and never did. All the boy ever saw of his father was a cloud of dust.

In the absence of her husband, Ann had been left with two houses, Ditchley, belonging to the Lee family, and Henry's Adderbury, a fine house with substantial land. She had her young sons by Sir Francis Lee and the baby by Henry to look after, and no money. She managed to bestride the differences between Parliamentarians and Royalists with considerable success. She and her first husband were descended from impeccable Parliamentarian roots, and this proved useful. What was not helpful was that she was now married to, and mother to the heir of, one of the most notorious of Royalists, now categorised as a 'malignant'. Cromwell had set up Committees of Expropriation to confiscate the lands and property of malignants. Ann's marriage to Henry was not her only involvement with the Royalists. She gave her cousin Hyde refuge during the war when he was on his way to join the King. She hid him in her home and the next day smuggled him away in her coach to the safety of another village. In 1642, at the beginning of the war, she had supplied the Royalists with arms. A fearless woman, she nevertheless had much to fear. For the time being such activities had to be anxiously concealed, but later they proved of great service to her.

She was an autocratic figure who during her lifetime managed to bully some of the most powerful men in England. She tyrannised politicians with the aim of getting seats in the new free Parliament for her long-standing adviser and friend Sir Ralph Verney, and her son Sir Harry Lee, and was enraged when money was demanded for the service. Many years later, in 1686, in a letter to Lord Lichfield she did the same for her thirteen-year-old great-grandson Lord Norreys. When Lichfield pointed out that he was, perhaps, a little young, she merely observed that Parliament was a good school for youth to be improved in. She had the type of hardness that enabled her to write years later to her grandson about a faithful friend, 'Poor Cary is so strangely afflicted by the death of his wife that I am very apprehensive of our losing him too. He takes on excessively for her; 'tis true he has lost a very good woman and an admirable housewife she was, but has been declining a long time and lived a *miracle* so long as she did.' The Commissioners of Expropriation had a fearsome opponent.

On Tuesday 30 January 1649, King Charles I had left the Palace of Whitehall to make his way to a scaffold and there lost his life to the headsman. He wore two shirts, so that shivering might not be mistaken for trembling. The last thing he said on handing the insignia of the Garter to Bishop Juxon, his chaplain, was the one word: 'Remember!' They would remember. The world had changed for ever. The news of the execution reached Charles in Holland on 5 February. He was nineteen years old, a king without a kingdom and a political and financial embarrassment to his hosts. There followed years of wandering from country to country, of plot and counter-plot, all supported and some devised by Wilmot. Despite his glaring faults Henry was a trusted emissary and was employed as a roving ambassador. He made a number of visits to England in disguise, spying for the King. In 1649 he became a gentleman of the bedchamber, and in 1650 a privy councillor. Though he was never bold enough to face his wife, he led a dangerous and exhilarating life.

Charles, in a plot hatched with his advisers, made an unholy bargain with the Scots; they would give him an army to invade England in return for his adoption of Presbyterianism. The King swore a great and solemn oath that he, Charles, King of Great Britain, France and Ireland, would impose Presbyterian government and worship upon his country, as approved by the general assembly of the Kirk and the Scottish Parliament. He promised that he would observe those laws in his own practice and family and that he would never make opposition to any of them nor endeavour any alteration therein. No doubt he had in mind the suggestion of his friend the Duke of Buckingham that once he had England he could forget about Scotland.

He went to live among his new Scots allies. Yet he loathed the country of his ancestors and detested the people. Nowhere could there have been a greater contrast to the enlightened cities of Europe that had fostered him and his little ragged Court in exile. The Scots were pious and squalid, and were scandalised by the loose and ungodly behaviour of Charles's attendants. The King was lectured and humiliated until he was in a state of sullen fury. He was heard to say in disgust of their endless graces before eating, 'At dinners, they lay as fiercely about 'em as in the pulpit.' On 3 September 1650, two months after swearing the Oath of the Covenant, the whole grisly episode reached its climax when he and his Scottish army were crushed by Cromwell at Dunbar. After that he was kept in Scotland a virtual prisoner, until a new uprising could be attempted; but the Scots were bickering among themselves and achieving nothing. In October he rode out of Perth and bolted for a distance of forty-two miles. He made his way past Dundee in the hope that some Highland Royalist force might join up with him. He was disappointed. He was eventually caught and taken back to Perth, where he was given another lecture.

In July of 1651 the Scots stopped dithering and Charles got what he had longed for. A force was mustered to march south into England. The banner was raised and on 5 August a straggling and forlorn band of demoralised warriors and squabbling officers crossed the border, hoping to gather support from the Royalist movement as they marched south. They had been misinformed. There were scattered bands of Royalists, but there was no Royalist movement. The English regarded the uncouth Scots as savages, and wanted nothing to do with them. In any case, the nation had been subdued by the harsh, authoritarian measures of the Cromwell government. Cromwell's spies had been thorough and any aspiring Royalist network had been firmly suppressed. Some two thousand sympathisers had been arrested and imprisoned. There was no hope of organised help. After three weeks, having lost most of its belongings including its shoes, the tatterdemalion army straggled into Worcester, a city which loyally supported the King.

They took up their positions in the town, and on 3 September, the anniversary of the rout at Dunbar, they marched into battle. At their head was the King in his celebrated uniform of buff coat, red sash and the 'George', the insignia of the Garter that had belonged to his father. It was a disaster. The Parliamentary forces were well armed, trained and provisioned, and outnumbered them by three to one. The King heroically led charge after charge. Henry Wilmot fought with great gallantry and was badly wounded, but the insurrectionists were slaughtered. Little thanks were due to the Scots cavalry, who refused to get involved and stayed watching from the sideline. Eventually they fled and allowed several hundred of their number to be captured by thirty Cromwellians, later explaining that because it was dark they had thought there might be more enemy than there were.

The twenty-one-year-old King and a little group of close companions set out to cross England and escape. If he had fallen into the hands of the enemy he would have become a disastrously powerful bargaining factor. He disguised himself as a woodsman, putting on a green jerkin, leather doublet, cloth breeches and a greasy hat over cropped hair. The embroidered tops were ripped from his socks. Soot was rubbed into his face, and his hands had to be stained with walnut leaves. His feet were enormous and the largest shoes that could be found were slashed to fit, but his skin was soon raw and bloody, and much of the journey was on foot. (For the rest of his life he maintained that the worst of his torments were the agonies he suffered from his feet.) He may not have looked much like a woodcutter but he did not look at all like a king. The only problem was his height. Charles was six foot two and as a result had a distinctive long loping gait. It nearly got him into serious trouble.

He dispensed with his entourage, which he thought would attract attention, and decided to head for London. He retained the services of Henry Wilmot, whose loyalty was beyond dispute. The same, alas, could not be said for his intellect. He was the type of military man who could not distinguish between action and activity. He took the name of Mr Barlow, but although he was about to accompany his sovereign, who was dressed as a servant, and a lady dressed as his mistress, he flatly refused to wear disguise. It ruined the overall effect, but he would not be shifted. He said that he would 'look frightfully' in his disguise and he insisted on keeping his batman with him. He finally compromised to the extent of wearing a hawk on his wrist, which he considered gave a suitably pastoral impression. What little this achieved was easily counteracted by his battered condition. He ignored his wounds bravely but he could not rely on others to do the same. He refused to walk, and would travel only on horseback. His progress throughout was slow and not in the least furtive. He always showed the greatest reluctance to leave a house where he had been well fed and watered. It may have been courage, but was more likely bone-headed stupidity, for when he did manage to identify a danger he was less than eager to confront it. Charles had to resort to sending him off on errands that would keep him out of sight. He later told Pepys, 'I took care not to keep him with me, but sent him a little before, or left to come after me.' The King and Wilmot made a secret arrangement to meet in London. The other peers begged not to be told the plan so that they could never be forced to confess it. It was a wise precaution. They were all quickly captured, except Buckingham, who made his way to France.

The King then changed his mind about London and elected to go to Wales instead. He made his way to Boscobel, where he received news of a gallant Royalist, Major Carlis, at present hiding in Boscobel Woods, which surrounded and protected the house. Charles went to look for him and found him in the legendary Boscobel Oak. They shared it for the day, the exhausted King fast asleep with his head on the Major's lap. From their hiding place they could see Cromwell's soldiers searching for them below. After spending the night in a priest hole in the old house, Charles set out for Moseley Old Hall about five miles away, where he was reunited with Henry. There was a narrow escape when soldiers came to search, then, after another visit to a priest hole that was too small to lie down in, the King headed for Bentley Hall, the home of a Colonel Lane, an old army comrade of Henry's. The Colonel's sister Jane was going to visit a friend who was about to have a baby at Abbots Leigh near Bristol.

Charles metamorphosed from an improbable woodsman into an equally improbable servant. He was now William Jackson and, dressed in an old grey hat, a worn green short coat and doublet, no less unmistakable. Thus the little party formed – Jane Lane, her servant and the gallant Henry, still equipped with his hawk. They relied on many loyal people on the way. There was a reward of £2,000 offered for the King, which must have been difficult for a poor family to overlook. They reached Lyme Regis, an ideal departure point for France, but a fair was being held there at which the proclamation of the reward would be made, so they headed instead for Chalmouth. Jane Lane's friend miscarried, so she had no further excuse for being on the road. She left after a fake letter was delivered to her saying that her father was ill. The precautions may seem excessive, but the households they visited were large. One contained twenty-six people, by no means all of whom could be relied on.

The group had to find a new cover. They took with them another young lady, Juliana Coningsby, who was a useful prop for their next masquerade as a young couple eloping. Henry was the bridegroom and Charles the servant. Henry secured a sea captain to take them over the Channel, but the man's wife guessed what her husband was up to. Determined that he should have nothing to do with fleeing Royalists, she locked him in the bedroom and refused to let him out, threatening to scream until the neighbours came if he tried to escape. The group was now without transport and also lost.

They stopped at the nearest inn, where they found a contingent of forty enemy soldiers in residence. Luckily the woman accompanying one of the military gave birth during the night, thereby diverting unwelcome attention. The King's party proceeded on their erratic course, day after day, lying low, covering their tracks, skulking, sidestepping. Everywhere there were notices saying, 'Wanted, a tall black man, six feet two inches high', offering a reward of £2,000 for information leading to his arrest. Finally, they arrived at Brighton, where they met a merchant who was prepared to let them on to his boat as illegal duellists. The only reward he wanted was enough ale to put him under the table. However, the master of the vessel recognised Charles, who had now promoted himself from servant to an inferior species of gentleman. Mercifully the man was loyal and kept quiet. They arranged a meeting for Shoreham the following day.

On Wednesday 15 October at four o'clock in the morning, six weeks to the day after Worcester, Charles finally left England's shores on the coal brig *Surprise* with the faithful Henry, who had so nearly ruined everything, just as Cromwell's troops were arriving to search the coast. Henry's masterstrokes of disorganisation on the mission had been many. He would fail to keep rendezvous purely because he had something better to do. With a gentlemanly lack of dissimulation, he repeatedly disclosed his true name and mission. He drew such attention to his presence in one house where he hid that he was forced to go to church the following Sunday to brazen it out as a lawful visitor. He caused a furore in Bridport, where his horse cast a shoe. When he had his horse shod the ostler observed that the three remaining shoes had all been put on in different counties, one of which was Worcestershire. The man went to the parson, John Wesley's great-grandfather, who was too busy with his prayers to entertain him. A justice was informed. He thought the matter of no significance. An army captain finally arrived with his men just after Charles had left the town. Henry's final triumph, resulting from a lapse of memory prompted by a drinking session, was to leave the whole of Charles's emergency gold reserve at a house near Chichester. Nevertheless, back in France he was appointed one of the committee of four whom Charles always consulted during his exile, and played a significant part in the King's planning. Naturally, he belonged to the hawks rather than the doves. It was characteristic of him to favour any action rather than none, a principle he unhesitatingly put into practice.

A year later, on 13 December 1652, Henry, Lord Wilmot was created Earl of Rochester. Legally the honour was meaningless: until the Restoration all titles granted by the King in exile were invalid by decree of Parliament. In February 1655 Rochester went to England to stir up insurrection, dodging Cromwell's troops around the country. He was twice stopped and questioned but wriggled out of the government's grasp. He travelled the kingdom trying to enlist support, approaching the task with his usual lack of finesse. In a coded letter purporting to be about the compounding of a debt, a fellow conspirator Daniel O'Neill ('Mr Bryan') wrote to 'Mr Jackson' (the King), saying, 'Mr. Rothall [Rochester] is gone to Yates [Yorkshire] to his own house. I must confess Mr. Rothall was the next best you could authorise to deal with your creditors [allies], but there were many that did not like him.' That day Henry arrived at Marston Moor expecting to see four thousand men prepared to fight in the King's cause, and found two hundred. There was a smattering of resistance around England and the uprising died a natural death. Henry only narrowly managed to flee the country in one piece, having abandoned his reservations about wearing disguise and posing as a Frenchman in a yellow periwig. He was captured at Aylesbury and detained by the magistrate for questioning but managed to escape by bribing the innkeeper who was to keep him locked up with the gift of a golden chain.

The battle for Rochester's property in England began in earnest in 1656. Cromwell's men gave orders that Henry send particulars of Ditchley Park for its division and disposal. Lady Rochester protested. After years of dogged resistance and the use of her own Puritan background and that of Sir Francis Lee she managed to hang on to the lands and property at Ditchley. She petitioned the Lord Protector on the ground that her husband had no interest in her jointure lands, and called upon him to 'stop all further proceedings touching or concerning the same and to discharge the petitioner from further trouble or attendance'. However, Henry was an enemy of the Puritan state. Cromwell's men failed to get their hands on any money because Henry had already found a better use for it, but the land at Adderbury was sequestrated. Only the house was left. The battle took many years of Ann's life.

In 1656 Charles was holding his Court in exile at Bruges. Henry was made colonel of one of the King's new regiments of guards, which later became the Grenadiers. But it was the end of his picaresque career. On 19 February 1657, at the age of forty-five, he died at Sluys. He was buried at Bruges. The King, who was famed for his generous appreciation of loyalty, promised Henry on his deathbed that he would look after his son John. Throughout his life he did his best to honour the promise, despite the constant obstacles placed in his way by an ungrateful beneficiary. The ten-year-old Viscount Wilmot of Athlone and Baron Wilmot of Adderbury was now the second unlawful Earl of Rochester. His half-brothers had left home and he grew up at Ditchley Hall as an only child. Through his mother and her faithful adviser Sir Ralph Verney he was nourished by the icy breast of Puritanism.

He had no company except for his tutor, one Francis Giffard, a young parson in his mid-twenties, who so doted on the boy that he slept with him to make sure he should come to no harm. Many years later Giffard was to claim that the boy learned little of Latin and nothing of Greek, but he was not a reliable witness. He was supplanted when the boy was sent away to school, and again when he went up to Oxford. Giffard's evidence is contradicted by Rochester's confessor, Gilbert Burnet; but one assertion which might be well founded was that sometimes the boy was constipated for three weeks or a month together. Later Rochester admitted to Burnet that he thought that the ailment was the source of 'that warmth and heat he always expressed, his brain being heated by the fumes and humours that ascended and evacuated themselves that way'. Unfortunately there are a number of other, more persuasive explanations for his disorderly life.

Giffard described a hopeful youth, 'very virtuous and good natured and willing and ready to follow good advice'. If at that time the boy was deficient in his knowledge of the classics, it could only be laid at Giffard's own door. In later years they comprised much of Rochester's reading, and his translations from Latin are among the finest ever written. Much of his best work is derived from Seneca, Lucretius,

Horace, Ovid and Petronius, and at least two of his own works are written in Latin. The tutor also claimed that before he died Rochester went to see him and they had a conversation in which the Earl sought to persuade him to visit more often. Giffard felt obliged to turn him down, 'he being a clergyman and his lordship being a very ill character of being a debauched man and an atheist and not fit looking company'. Rochester had replied, 'Mr Giffard, I may have been guilty of extravagancies but I will assure you I am no atheist.' This last was widely trumpeted by the Church after the Earl's death, but the whole account was blatant humbug. Giffard would never have rejected the approaches of an earl. It was loss of communion with that same Earl that had embittered his earlier years.

Lady Rochester decided to supplement her son's education by sending him to the free school across the Cotswolds at Burford, one of the top establishments of its day. The boy took lodgings in the town, presumably with suitable servants. He was tutored by the renowned master John Martin for a fourpenny entrance fee, and one penny every quarter. It was a hard regimen. The scholars had to attend school at six o'clock in the summer and seven in winter, stay till six o'clock in summer and four o'clock in winter, and go to church with the master. There were rules for the regular singing of psalms and reading of the Bible. On Sundays, they went to the master's house at eight o'clock in the morning to say prayers and to attend church with him. Four times a year the master ceremoniously exhorted them to give thanks to God. They recited the names of all the founders and benefactors, listed on a noticeboard in the School House, sang a psalm and then left. The school was an excellent one, and John was a diligent student, but the atmosphere was as oppressively pious as Ditchley's.

2

'Why should every creature drink but I?'
The Restoration

When he went to the University, the general joy which over-ran the whole nation upon his Majesty's Restoration but was not regulated with that sobriety and temperance that became a serious gratitude to God for so great a blessing, produced some of its ill effects on him: he began to love these disorders too much.

Gilbert Burnet, *Some Passages of the Life and Death of John Earl of Rochester*, 1680

On 23 January 1660 John Wilmot went up to Oxford University as a 'nobleman' or 'fellow commoner' of Wadham College, Oxford. He was twelve years old. His mother had put pressure on her cousin, the Earl of Clarendon, who was now Chancellor of the University, to admit him early. As the Rev. Robert Parsons, the family chaplain, proclaimed in his oration at the Earl's funeral, 'As for his education under the care of that wise and excellent governor Dr. Blandford, the late Right Reverend Bishop of Worcester, he laid a good foundation of learning and study, though he afterwards built upon that foundation hay and stubble.' As a nobleman he wore a different gown that set him apart from his less exalted brethren. He was a member of the Fellows' Common Room, and so mixed on equal terms with adults. His special gown was usually exchanged for a don's gown lent him by a louche fellow, Robert White-hall. All except dons were expected to be within their colleges by a respectable hour, and, if they were not, the proctors could arrest them. Whitehall's gown had the power of a cloak of darkness. Whitehall recalled it years later when he sent Rochester a portrait of himself:

> Not in vest, but in that gown
> Your Lordship daggled through this town,
> To keep up discipline and tell us
> Next morning where you found good fellows.

Whitehall's powers of versification had not flourished over the years. The don, whom Anthony Wood called 'a useless fellow of Merton College who clung onto that house for years', had a strong fancy for poetry and wine. His features were 'loined with sack [white wine] and laced with claret'. He had felt it his duty to lead the young Viscount astray, though quite how far is not known. There were contemporary suggestions that it included whoring and it has been suggested (improbably) that he contracted at that very young age the illness that so wretchedly destroyed him. Although he was only fourteen when he received his MA, he was quite old enough to have been sexually active, as indeed were most of his contemporaries. Life was short and passed very soon. People grew up and became old quickly, but Rochester did not display symptoms of the disease until he was twenty-two, almost certainly too late for him to have been infected at that early stage.

Rochester's career at Oxford began uneventfully and it seems that he was studious enough, if only for a matter of a few weeks. His tutor was a learned and good-natured young don, Phineas Bury. The College was the most recent foundation in the University, endowed by Dorothy Wadham in the reign of James I and given to advanced thinking. The last master of the College had been the free-thinking John Wilkins (surprisingly, brother-in-law of the pious Cromwell), who had already begun to turn it into a centre of scientific rationalism, a searching and open-minded society that accepted no religious dogma. After the end of the Civil Wars, Dr Wilkins's lodgings in Wadham College became a meeting place for scholars. Members of the University had begun to reason freely. The group was joined by gentlemen of a philosophical bent escaping the pitfalls of the real world and attracted by security and ease. They called themselves the Experimental Philosophical Club, and the King began to take an active interest. In 1660 it became known as the Royal Society, and was incorporated in 1682 and granted its charter with the King as its first president. It was widely thought that the excessive behaviour of Wadham undergraduates was the result of the innovative view of life taught them by their college. Even during the latter days of the Commonwealth the atmosphere in Oxford had been tolerant. Later, in honour of its relaxed principles, Wadham was nicknamed 'Sodom'.

While Rochester pursued his vestigial studies with his tutor and blossoming debauchery with Whitehall, much had been happening in the world outside. In September 1658, Oliver Cromwell had died and Richard Cromwell had taken the reins of state. It was not for long. He fell out with the army and resigned. There was friction throughout 1659 between Parliament and the army. In October Major-General Lambert and his troops took charge and imposed military government. Then Lambert's support melted away and Lawson, the Fleet Commander stationed in the Thames, announced his support for Parliament. General Monck, commander of the army in Scotland, issued a similar proclamation. On New Year's Day 1660 he crossed the border and marched south. He was greeted everywhere by crowds demanding a free Parliament. Lambert offered no resistance and there was a swell of excitement. In Oxford the undergraduates mocked the 'Rump Parliament' (what was left of Parliament after the expulsion of 121 Royalist members in 1648) by throwing rumps of beef into a great bonfire at the gate of Queen's College. One crashed through the window of the venerable Warden of All Souls, who was himself a member of the Rump. In February Monck went to Parliament and insisted that they readmit the 121 MPs. In London suddenly there were bonfires beyond number and the bells rang out from the churches for the first time in many years. Butchers were carving rumps in the street.

Parliament dissolved for a free election. There could only be one result. On 1 May a resolution was passed inviting Charles to return as king. May Day was celebrated anew. Cromwell had banned maypoles because of their pagan connotations and incitement to dancing. Oxford, one of the great supporting cities of the Royalist cause, was in a frenzy of excitement. There was a monumental maypole in Cornmarket Street and the taverns were packed. Bonfires roared and bells rang their changes. People fell on their knees to drink the King's health. 'The Puritans had made men eat religion with their bread until it had sickened them,' it was said. It was the dawn of a new age for England and for John, now truly the second Earl of Rochester.

On 25 May 1660 the King landed at Dover in the company of Pepys, a servant, a dog and a flotilla. He met up with Rochester's cousin, the twenty-year-old Barbara Villiers, now Mrs Palmer, who had been his mistress in exile. She was an outstandingly beautiful woman with deep-blue eyes and auburn hair, who had begun her career in bed with a notorious rakehell, the Earl of Chesterfield, at the age of sixteen. She stayed with the King for many years, until her promiscuity and filthy temper became too much even for Charles. Pepys wrote of the arrival at Dover:

I went, and Mr. Mansell and one of the King's footmen, with a dog that the King loved (which shit in the boat, which made us laugh and me think that a King and all that belonged to him are but just as others are) went in a boat by ourselfs; and so got on shore when the King did, who was received by General Monck, an infinite crowd of people and the gallantry of the horsemen, citizens and noblemen of all sorts. The mayor of the town came and gave him his white staff, the badge of his place which the King did give him again. The mayor also presented him from the town a very rich Bible, which he took and said it was the thing that he loved above all things in the world.

The King was prepared to say anything to regain his birthright. He had already sworn to impose the Scots religion, but mercifully that had been superseded by events. He had embraced the Bible at Dover. He gave Magna Carta one of its thirty-three confirmations and confirmed the Petition of Right of 1628. He spent the rest of his life trying to find a way round them. The vast exhilarated crowd cared as little about the Bible as Charles did. 'The shouting and joy expressed by all is past imagination,' exclaimed Pepys. The new monarch went to London on 29 May, his thirtieth birthday. The day before his coronation he went by state barge to the Tower of London. The next day in Westminster Abbey there was a great raised dais with a throne, all bedecked in red, where he was to be crowned. Pepys tells us how the officers, ecclesiastics and nobility entered with the Duke of York, the Earl of Sandwich and the King, all magnificently robed. Three times the King-at-Arms went to open spaces on the platform, and proclaimed that if anyone could show reason why Charles Stuart should not be king of England, he should speak. Then the ceremony of anointing and coronation was completed. Afterwards there was a banquet at Westminster Hall. The Knights of the Bath carried the first course in, and General Monck, now the Duke of Albemarle, solemnly tasted the food before it went to his Majesty. Lords Northumberland and Suffolk and the Duke of Ormonde remained on horseback throughout dinner, then ushered in Dymock, the King's Champion, also on horseback, in full armour with his lance and shield. The herald proclaimed three times that if any dare deny the right of Charles Stuart to be lawful king of England, here was a champion that would fight with him. The Champion then threw down the gauntlet. He rode to the King's table, where the King drank to him from a golden cup that he passed to the Champion to drain. The proceedings ended to the sound of twenty-four violins and a violent thunderstorm, which was agreed by all to be auspicious.

The Restoration rang in an abrupt end to Rochester's studies. 'The humour of that time', said Burnet, 'wrought so much on him, that he broke off the course of his studies; to which no means could ever effectually recall him.' Oxford was a carnival. The nation was celebrating. Drinking was a widespread diversion. For years alcohol had been grimly discouraged and there was a long, sombre thirst to be slaked. Burnet told later how 'with the restoration of the King, a spirit of extravagant joy spread over the nation, that brought on with it the throwing off of the very professions of virtue and piety. All ended in entertainments and drunkenness which over run the three kingdoms to such a degree, that it very much corrupted their morals. Under the colour of drinking the King's health, there were great disorders, and much riot everywhere.' In his 'Anacreontic on Drinking', the poet Abraham Cowley wrote:

> Nothing in nature's sober found,
> But an eternal health goes round.
> Fill up the bowl, then, fill it high,
> Fill all the glasses there – for why
> Should every creature drink but I?
> Why, man of morals, tell me why?

An anacreontic was a convivial or erotic poem in the style of Anacreon. As a poetic form it gained considerable currency during this period for reasons that do not need elaboration. Cowley was one of Rochester's favourite poets, and one of his exemplars.

Oxford University burgeoned from grove of academe to pagan forest. Anthony Wood, the antiquary and gossip, reported in pained tones, 'The entire student body seemed to have decided not to live as students ought to do, viz. temperate, abstemious and plain and grave in the apparel; but to live like gents, to keep dogs and horses, to turn their studios and coal holes into places to receive bottles, to swash it in grey coats with swords by their sides.' Pietro Aretino, an Italian poet of the previous century, had written a series of sonnets known as 'Aretino's Postures' to accompany a series of erotic engravings by the artist Giulio Romano. They made popular reading during the seventeenth century; their purpose is self-explanatory. Barbara Palmer, now Lady Castlemaine, was said to have become a virtuoso performer.

In 1660, a publication of University verses celebrating the Restoration contained a contribution in the name of Lord Rochester, 'To his Sacred Majesty'. He sent it to the King. It is lamentable poetry and is widely thought to have been written by or under the influence of Whitehall, whose subject was medicine.

> Virtue's triumphant shrine! Who do'st engage
> At once three Kingdoms in a pilgrimage;
> Which in ecstatic duty strive to come
> Out of themselves as well as from their home:
> Whilst England grows one camp, and London is
> Itself the nation, not metropolis;
> And loyal Kent renew her arts again,
> Fencing her ways with moving groves of men;
> Forgive this distant homage, which doth meet
> Your blessed approach on sedentary feet:
> And though my youth not patient yet to bear
> The weight of arms, denies me to appear
> In steel before you, yet, Great Sir, approve
> My manly wishes and more vigorous love;
> In whom a cold respect were treason to
> A father's ashes, greater then to you;
> Whose one ambition 'tis for to be known
> By daring loyalty
> > Your Wilmot's Son.
> Rochester
> Wadh. Coll.

Perhaps it was Whitehall's work. Perhaps it was the work of a thirteen-year-old boy who, under the teaching of Whitehall, could know no better. The style compares closely with other leaden efforts from the physician's hand. The offering was designed to remind the King of his loyal Earl's existence, but it failed.

Nothing daunted, in 1661 they tried again, this time with a dirge for the Queen Mother, mourning the death of her daughter the Princess of Orange. It was more sonorous nonsense in very much the same vein and may have embarrassed the young peer when he was older and a little wiser, but it did the trick. In February the King settled on him an annual pension of £500. It was a handsome sum, the sort of figure that would keep a knight and his household of twelve for a year, and it seemed a boon to the young Earl, who had little other income. His mother could give him a modest portion from her estates, his father had left nothing. The King, who owed a great debt of gratitude to Henry, was especially generous to Rochester all his life. He became truly fond of the boy and, despite the young wretch's casual ingratitude, settled more and more gifts and allowances and sinecures upon him. Sadly, though the King's heart was in the right place, the money was not: despite living in massive luxury, Charles was a pauper. His life was a continuous battle with Parliament to extract the funds he needed. He had some very greedy mistresses to support. Barbara Castlemaine alone cost as much to run as a small war. The diarist John Evelyn called her 'another lady of pleasure, and curse of our nation'. Later in 1672 Charles had to place a 'stop' on the Exchequer. He defaulted on his massive debts to his bankers and was once again destitute. It was like life in exile again. Charles's own indulgences continued as before, paid for by loans, bribes and imaginative taxation, or else not paid for at all. Few of Rochester's stipends were ever settled. Later in life there were embarrassing scenes as his creditors lobbied the First Lord of the Treasury, who was responsible for paying the King's debts. The £500 honorarium eventually faded into oblivion.

For the time being, however, he had enough pocket money to get drunk and stay drunk until his graduation. For eighteen months he studied for little but his downfall. On 9 September 1661, however, the University's Convocation awarded him the degree of Master of Arts. It goes without saying that no examination was required, which was fortunate because he had not opened a book for a long time. The Lord Chancellor, Lord Clarendon, Chancellor of the University, arrived in Oxford to be greeted by huge municipal and academic pomp. There were portentous speeches of welcome, and Clarendon graciously answered with a public denunciation of the Master of Magdalen for his 'factious and debauched scholars, and the lack of attention to the Book of Common Prayer in his hall' (according to Anthony Wood). The next day, after a further oration, he admitted the scarlet-robed Earl to the University together with Lord Lovelace and other noblemen, affectionately saluting his cousin Rochester with a kiss on the left cheek. Many years later Clarendon was rewarded for that salutation with another, firmly planted between the shoulderblades. The Earl presented Wadham College with a fitting souvenir, four beautifully engraved silver pint tankards which may be seen there today. His duty done, the fourteen-year-old Rochester left the great University, ready to embark on the turbulent seas of adulthood.

The King, doubtless with a view to the boy's need for improvement, sent him on a grand tour. This meant a slow journey through France and Italy looking at fine buildings and works of art and learning to eat and drink with discernment. The King selected for his companion a thirty-year-old physician and naturalist Sir Andrew Balfour, and the tour was to last three years. Dr Balfour was an ideal companion, a man of skill and distinction, who later became a famed physician in Scotland. It was he who lured the youth back into scholarship and sobriety. Later, Rochester acknowledged his lifelong affection and gratitude to his mentor. He told Burnet during their discussions that in his whole life he owed Balfour more than he owed anyone except his mother. He was especially touched by the way Balfour had by various schemes, like swapping free time for study time, manipulated him into a delight in books and reading, so that he could always take the opportunity to study in the intervals between his bouts of debauchery. If his choice of subjects was not always the most improving, the pleasure of reading and learning kept his mind alert. Even at the time of his greatest follies he was recognised as the most learned of his contemporaries at Court.

It is possible to infer what the tour entailed from *Letters to a Friend*, a book on travel in France and Italy that Balfour wrote years later. He did not say that it concerned this tour, and he had been on others, but it reveals his approach to touring. He advises his readers to leave Paris at about the beginning of June and then to go to Orléans, where they should stay with M. Ogilbie, 'sur l'Estape du Roy de la Grand Bretaigne'. A day or two was enough to see all that was of interest and visitors should include a trip to the 'Source' some two miles from the city, where there was a spring that became the River Loirette. They should go by boat to Blois, a short day's journey, taking notice on the way of St Dié, with the best claret in that country. Blois was famous for watchmaking, the sweetness of the air, the friendliness of the people and the purity of their language. Visitors should stay there for some days and go to Chambort, a very stately house belonging to the King.

Next they should go to Herbeau, the private house of a gentleman, which had very fine gardens, an orangery, fishponds, woods and meadows, and then to Beau Regard, another private house, where among other pretty things travellers could see a fine picture gallery. They should return to Blois at night, then go to Venice by water in an open boat, starting out along a canal near the side of the Po, and embarking on a larger vessel. If the wind were favourable, they could be there in ten or twelve hours. Arriving in Venice, they would need to lodge in the town, so they would do well to provide themselves with a recommendation to the English Consul. Once settled in their lodgings, visitors should explore the place for three or four weeks. The great town in the middle of the sea was spectacular, with all the houses edged by water and the nearest land four or five miles away. Although a traveller could never be sure of his timetable, it was best to be in Venice at carnival time for the operas and shows and extraordinary music. The great attraction in summer was to go along the Grand Canal in a gondola. Towards evening five or six hundred gondolas full of ladies and gentlemen could be seen touring up and down, many carrying singers and musicians. There were many curiosities due to the great numbers of foreigners, especially from the Levant. You could find medals, intaglios and cameos among the goldsmiths and there were pretty things made of glass. The booksellers' shops were worth visiting, for besides the rare books, particularly on botany, you would also find many that were prohibited in the rest of Italy.

Balfour and his charge crossed the Alps in the summer of 1664. This involved dismounting from their mules at the highest point of the pass, to be wheeled across in barrows by their guides. Eventually they reached Paris, where Rochester was presented to Henrietta, Duchesse d'Orléans. She was Charles's adored sister, and was in miserable circumstances at King Louis XIV's Court. She was known as 'Madame', though Charles called her 'Minette'. 'Monsieur', the Duc Philippe, was Louis' depraved brother who despite keeping a coterie of homosexuals, and dressing as a woman in public, was insanely jealous of his wife. He was vain and petty-minded, and had been known to burst into tears when his catamite, the Chevalier de Lorraine, refused to give him his new recipe for face-cream. In time of war he tended to baffle his enemies by charging at them wearing his make-up, his ribbons and his best jewellery (he refused to wear a hat, so as not to cover up his hairdo). He surprised them even more by the ferocity of his fighting.

The Duchesse gave the young Earl a letter to take back to the King. On Christmas Day 1664, it was a very self-possessed seventeen-year-old dressed in his most magnificent clothes who arrived at the English Court carrying the letter. As he made his practised flourish, one could almost hear the dull thud of Fate slamming the doors behind him.

He had left Oxford drunk, with contentious ideas about the governance of the realm fostered by Wadham College and the tradition of Dr Wilkins. He returned from the grand tour a learned young man, still with the same contentious ideas, but having acquired great poise and lost his appetite for liquor. Not long before he died, he assured Burnet, his confessor, that he would cheerfully have stayed sober from then on, but it was not to be. The King's Court was a seductive model of luxury and hedonism. Much later, John Evelyn wrote in his diary:

I can never forget the inexpressible luxury and profaneness, gaming and all dissoluteness, and as it were, total forgetfulness of God; the King sitting and toying with his concubines, a French boy singing love songs in that glorious gallery, whilst about twenty of the great courtiers and other dissolute persons were at Basset round a large table, a bank of at least 2000 in gold before them.

Charles had learned his dissipated habits while in exile, particularly in Paris. By 1652, when he was twenty-two, he was said to have taken up with his seventeenth mistress. At the time he wrote, 'We pass our lives as well as people can do that have no money, for we dance and play as if we had taken the Plate Fleet.' It was a way of life that was never to change.

3

'Here's a health to Kate'
The Court of Charles II

He had very early an inclination to intemperance, which he totally subdued in his travels; but when he became a courtier he unhappily addicted himself to dissolute and vicious company, by which his principles were corrupted and his manners depraved. He lost all sense of religious restraint; and finding it not convenient to admit the authority of laws which he was resolved not to obey, sheltered his wickedness behind infidelity.

Samuel Johnson, *Lives of the English Poets*, 1779

Something should be said about the world that lay in wait for the young Rochester. Dryden described the years after the Restoration as 'a very merry, dancing, drinking, laughing, quaffing, and unthinking time'. Thomas Shadwell, the playwright, demanded, 'Why dost thou abuse this age so? Methinks it's as pretty an honest, drinking, whoring age as a man could wish to live in.' There were over one hundred brothels in London, including a vessel on the Thames known as the *Showboat*. It was 1665 and Rochester's behaviour had been a model of decorum for four years. In their excitement, the King's courtiers on the other hand had been running completely out of control since 1660. As they were to become lifelong friends, there is no alternative but to meet them in all their naked horror.

There had been unforgettable escapades. In 1663 Sir Charles Sedley and Charles, Lord Buckhurst, later Earl of Dorset and Middlesex, appeared naked on the balcony of Oxford Kate's Tavern in Covent Garden. They proceeded to give an exhibition to the appalled crowd below, who expressed their opinion of the jape by stoning them. Sedley seems to have played the starring role. Pepys describes their antics with his usual fascinated disgust:

the trial of Sir Charles Sedley the other day before my Lord Chief Justice

Foster and the whole Bench, for his debauchery a little while since at Oxford Kate's; coming in *open day* into the balcony and showed his nakedness – acting all the postures of lust and buggery that could be imagined, and abusing of scripture and, as it were, from whence preaching a mountebank sermon from that pulpit, saying that there he hath to sell such a powder as should make all the cunts in town run after him. And that being done, he took a glass of wine and washed his prick in it and then drank it off; and then took another and drunk the king's health.

There was some doubt as to how much of it was mere acting. The two men narrowly escaped being lynched. When Sedley was brought up before the bench for his 'crimes', it was discovered that in law he had committed none. An incandescent Lord Chief Justice bellowed that it was for Sedley and such wicked wretches as he was 'that God's anger and judgements hung over us'. It was only God's judgement, however, because at the time there was no offence of public indecency. All that could be done was order that he be bound over to be of good behaviour in the sum of £5,000. This meant that it cost him nothing, unless he misbehaved again (which of course he did, though with impunity).

Sedley was a degenerate, but also a poet, dramatist, courtier and prominent member of the Court Wits. He was constantly in trouble, often in the company of Buckhurst. In later life he went into politics and was a Member of Parliament under William III. His plays were written between 1668 and 1687, but his finest works were his verse translations and lyrics, which were set exquisitely to music by Purcell. Like all his friends, he was a rakehell and a fanatical drinker. He was talented and strangely modest. Once, when one of his plays was being performed, the theatre roof fell in during the performance, injuring Sedley and a number of others. A friend tried to console him, saying that the play had been so full of fire it had blown up poet, theatre and audience. Sedley replied, 'Nonsense! It was so heavy it brought down the house and buried the poet in his own rubbish.' Years later Sedley and Buckhurst were still getting into trouble together. In October 1668 they were caught running up and down the streets all night with their behinds bare. They had a fight with the watch which they lost, and were thrown into gaol overnight. However, for reasons that remain obscure, the King was outraged not by their behaviour, but by their treatment. As a result the constable was summoned by Lord Chief Justice Keeling at the next sessions to explain himself, which he may have thought a little unfair. There was another discreditable incident when the great actor Kynaston unwisely played a role satirising Sedley. On the night of 31 January 1669 three men beat him up. Everyone knew who was responsible and the King was unamused, but with the usual manly forthrightness of the 'Merry Gang', as his friends were known, Sedley indignantly denied responsibility and escaped unpunished. Later in life, he turned against the Stuarts, outraged by James II's affair with his young daughter Catherine. He was instrumental in bringing about the revolution of 1688, and gave powerful support to William and Mary. He died in 1701.

His crony, Charles Sackville, Lord Buckhurst, was the son of the Earl of Dorset and a gentleman of the King's bedchamber. He was an early admirer of Nell Gwyn and for a time in 1667, when she was seventeen, persuaded her to leave the stage and retire with him to Epsom, where they ran a merry-house together. The affair ended and she went back to the stage. A notorious rake in his youth, Buckhurst later sobered up and distinguished himself in public service under Charles II. He was a generous, good-natured man, so shy that he scarcely ever spoke unless fuelled by alcohol. His character and his verse were light-hearted. He is best remembered for his ballad 'To all you ladies now on land'. Written at the beginning of the first Dutch war, it gained tremendous popularity. It contained the cheery salutation:

> Then if we write not by each post,
> Think not we are unkind;
> Nor yet conclude our ships are lost
> By Dutchmen or by wind:
> Our tears we'll send a speedier way,
> The tide shall bring them twice a day.

The ladies were enchanted.

After the peace of the Commonwealth, London was now an unnerving place to be. No one was holding the reins of state. It was wise, when going out at night, to hire the services of a linkboy to run ahead carrying a torch. Roundhead soldiers, who had been pardoned by the King, were only too happy to be alive and had mostly returned to their old trades. They gave little trouble. This resulted in less work for the Cavaliers. They, with nothing better to do, and no means of subsistence, roamed the streets heavily armed, robbing and thieving and committing mayhem. So, with less excuse, did the sprigs of the nobility. In 1662 Buckhurst distinguished himself together with his brother Edward Sackville and Sir Henry Belasyse by the robbery and murder near Waltham Cross of a tanner called 'Hoppy'. Buckhurst was imprisoned briefly, but he explained that it was all a mistake. He and the others had unfortunately mistaken Hoppy for a highwayman. They had set on him and made off with his money, thinking it was already stolen, and thus fair game. This was deemed reasonable, and he was released. Ruffians such as these were destined to become bosom cronies of the young Rochester.

King Charles was not a vengeful man. He had granted a general pardon to his opponents on his restoration to the throne, though he condemned the Regicides themselves. The men who had signed Charles I's death warrant were executed by hanging, drawing and quartering. Their heads were still adorning various city gates seven years later. Oliver Cromwell was already dead through natural causes in 1658, so he was dug up together with two others and hanged at Tyburn anyway. They were then decapitated and reburied under the scaffold, except for their heads, which were set up on poles above Westminster Hall. Cromwell would have understood. He himself had had a tendency to revenge and would ship his prisoners off to the West Indies as slaves. Charles is also said to have removed two thousand Presbyterian ministers from their churches in 1661 alone, which must have given him a little quiet satisfaction.

In 1662, Charles and Clarendon sold Dunkirk to France. It was an expensive garrison to run, and they managed to get £400,000 for it, which seemed a fair price. There was an extravagant Court to be accounted for and the money would prove useful. The public was outraged and never forgave the Lord Chancellor, whom they blamed for lining his own pockets with the proceeds. In 1663 Clarendon and the King's counsellors were forlornly trying to get the King to concentrate on affairs of state, but Charles was busy with more pressing matters. Abraham Cowley wrote:

> Fill the bowl with rosy wine,
> Around our temples roses twine

And let us cheerfully awhile
Like the wine and roses smile.
Today is ours; what do we fear?
Today is ours; we have it here.
Let's treat it kindly, that it may
Wish at least with us to stay.
Let's banish business, banish sorrow;
To the gods belong tomorrow.

Charles was of the same mind. He was not lazy but he had his own ideas about where to direct his energies. However vigorous the previous night's activity, he would be up at dawn each day for his game of tennis. He loved boats, especially yachting, which he and his brother the Duke of York had introduced from Holland. He played pell-mell, where the Mall now is, a type of galloping croquet which he had brought from France. He loved to go hawking with Rochester, who became keeper of the King's hawks. He was a keen fisherman. Rochester called him 'Flatfoot the Gudgeon-taker'. He was an excellent athlete and horseman. He made Newmarket the centre of British racing. It was there that he was given the nickname 'Old Rowley' by which he was known throughout the land, after a fabulously endowed stallion of that name. He took a modest pleasure in the distinction. According to legend, on overhearing a maid at Whitehall singing a popular ballad about 'Old Rowley the King', he wandered into the room. The girl asked him who he was. 'Old Rowley himself, madam,' he replied. It was no false flattery of a monarch by his humble subjects. The rumour was confirmed by Barbara Castlemaine. Her husband had been elevated to the peerage to give the royal bastards a proper name. Clarendon, who was disgusted with the whole business, flatly refused to sanction the instrument creating an English peerage, so it was necessary to procure an Irish peerage through the more flexible Lord Chancellor of Ireland. Pepys recorded in 1663 that Sir Thomas Carew had told him 'that the King doth mind nothing but pleasures and hates the very sight or thoughts of business; but my Lady Castlemaine rules him; who he says hath all the tricks of Aretine that are to be practised to give pleasure, in which he is too able, having a Large —'. Pepys complained that if a sober counsellor gave the King good advice and tried to get him to do something useful, the rival group, his 'counsellors of pleasure', would catch him in a happy mood when he was with Barbara and persuade him not to listen to the advice of 'dotards and advisers that had once been his enemies'.

In 1662 the King's long association with Barbara Castlemaine was momentarily interrupted. First, he married Catherine of Braganza. Portugal was so keen on the alliance that it presented him with a dowry consisting of Bombay, Tangier and £300,000. There had to be two ceremonies; the first was Roman Catholic and secret, to evade the outrage of the crowd. Next, the interruption was prolonged by the arrival of the fourteen-year-old Frances Stewart with her mother, who was to be maid of honour to the new Queen. Frances was exceptionally pretty and sweet-natured, but was no intellectual. The King was besotted with her and insisted on her modelling as Britannia on the other side of his coins. Brainless or not, she accomplished the rare feat of resisting the King's advances for five years until she finally ran off with the Duke of Richmond. Meanwhile, the King was so transported by lust that he took to writing poetry. One evening, during a heated debate about the legs of the Court ladies, he proclaimed that Frances's were the finest in England. She made the mistake of lifting her skirts well above the knee to prove the point, which drove the King to temporary insanity. It prompted an outpouring:

> I pass all my hours in a shady old grove,
> But I live not the day when I see not my love.
> I survey every walk now my Phyllis is gone
> And sigh when I think we were there all alone.
> Oh then 'tis I think there's no hell
> Like loving too well.

The King became so distracted that the Duke of Buckingham, Lord Arlington, Edward Montagu and friends, all members of the Merry Gang, took pity on him and founded a Committee for the Getting of Mistress Stewart for the King. In his campaign to procure her, the unspeakable Buckingham, the worst rake in England, spent endless hours playing card castles and other infants' games with the girl, while his cronies were gambling for vast sums at the other end of the room. She was so entranced that she began to feel lost without him, and he started to fall for her. He forgot about his Portuguese mistress and turned his affections towards Frances. She was deeply shocked and very firmly rejected him. It was an insufferable blow. Buckingham felt it deeply and retired hurt. Henry Bennett, Lord Arlington, who was Secretary of State and another notorious lecher, tried to take his place. However, Buckingham sabotaged him effectively. The Duke was a brilliant mimic, and he did a particularly good Arlington. Frances laughed so much that the Secretary of State also took offence and lost interest. Frances was left with a tearful monarch and the Court still in a fever of speculation about her romantic activities, something that continued for the rest of her life.

At this point Barbara Castlemaine decided to take a hand. She made a great show of adopting Frances as her favourite. Each time the King came to visit, Barbara invited Frances to supper. She kept her overnight in her bed, and when the King paid his regular morning visit to Barbara he would find them both huddled together. Precisely what message the *maîtresse en titre* wanted to convey can only be left to the imagination. It led, according to gossips, to a mock marriage between the two women, Stewart and Castlemaine. Pepys wrote:

Lady Castlemaine, a few days since, had Miss Stewart to an entertainment, and at night began a frolic that they two must be married; and married they were, with ring and all other ceremonies of church service, and ribbons with a sack posset in bed and flinging the stocking; but in the close, it is said that my Lady Castlemaine, who was the bridegroom, rose from the bed and the King got in and took her place.

In October 1663 it was rumoured that Frances was on the verge of capitulation, when the Queen suddenly became very ill. If the worst were to happen, it seemed possible that Frances might be chosen to replace her, so she held on to her ace and backed away from the game. However, the Queen recovered and they all went back to their original positions, the King sighing, Frances enticing and Castlemaine making love both to the King and to Henry Jermyn. Within six weeks of the King's marriage to Catherine, Barbara, who was pregnant with his child, demanded to move into Hampton Court Palace for her lying-in. As the new Queen did not yet know who Barbara was, she was forcibly dissuaded. Next, she had a fancy to become lady of the bedchamber to the new Queen, an unthinkable insult. She created a series of appalling scenes, as only she could, accusing the King of having ruined her. Her husband had left her, she was alone and she was pregnant. The whole affair became so overblown that historians call it 'The Royal Bedchamber Crisis'. Unable to face Barbara's screeching and sobbing, Charles gave in. Perhaps he hoped that his pious and innocent wife would not realise the truth. If so, he was due for a disappointment. The Queen remained in happy ignorance for a while then, when she found out, flew into a rage, sobbed, developed a nosebleed and collapsed in hysterics on the floor. Charles took the chivalrous course and sent the unfortunate Lord Chancellor to soothe her. Clarendon was unsuccessful. Charles's sister got to hear of it in Paris, and was disgusted. She wrote her brother a stern letter: 'It is said here that she is grieved beyond measure, and to speak frankly I think it is with reason.'

The hapless Clarendon had done his utmost to prevent the appointment. He was becoming ever more Barbara's anathema. Charles sent him the strongest letter he ever wrote: 'If you desire to have the continuance of my friendship meddle no more with this business.' Eventually, after a summer of competing jeremiads from the two women, it all calmed down. Charles sent almost all the Queen's stuffy Court ladies back to Portugal. The two women gradually learned to tolerate one another, and ended on friendly terms.

It was into this hothouse atmosphere that the seventeen-year-old Earl of Rochester was introduced. He was enchanted. Learning and sobriety were tossed aside. Life became an endless progression of desire and gratification. He was surrounded by a swarm of the most powerful young people in the land who had little to do but fornicate, divert themselves with the wives of others, gamble, get drunk, quarrel, duel and gossip. They lived hard, drank hard and were hard. The Earl of Clarendon wrote of them, 'the tenderness of the bowels, which is the quintessence of justice and compassion, the very mention of good nature was laughed at and looked upon as the mark and character of a fool; and a roughness of character or hard heartedness and cruelty was affected'. It was with this notorious group of talented and debauched men, the Court Wits or the Merry Gang, that the King had encompassed himself. They were to become Rochester's closest friends. From being their imitator he became their exemplar. Later, in 1668, they adopted the sobriquet of the 'Ballers' after a costume ball with Madam Bennet's girls where the costume was their skin. An awed Samuel Pepys recorded the event:

Over to Vauxhall and there fell into the company of Harry Killigrew, a rogue newly come back out of France but still in disgrace at our Court, and young Newport and others, as very rogues as any in the town, who were ready to take hold of every woman that came by them. And so to supper in an arbour; but Lord! Their mad talk did make my heart ache! And here I first understood by their talk the meaning of the company that lately were called Ballers: Harris telling how it was by a meeting of some young blades, where he was among them, and my Lady Bennett and her ladies; and their dancing naked, and all the roguish things in the world. But Lord! What loose, cursed company was this that I was in tonight, though full of wit and worth a man's being in for once, to know the nature of it and their manner of talk and lives.

The Henry Killigrew to whom Pepys referred also became a close friend of Rochester's. He was the son of Tom Killigrew, a theatre-owner and companion of the King. He was groom of the bedchamber to the Duke of York and, afterwards, to the King. He had wit, charm and no principles at all. Anthony Hamilton, who compiled another Court gossip, the Comte de Gramont's memoirs, described him as 'one of the most abominable and debauched scoundrels who ever disgraced the Court'. Among other exploits, Killigrew is supposed to have stamped one of his servants to death while under the influence of drink, and to have narrowly escaped hanging for drugging and raping a girl. In 1662 he married Lady Mary Savage, and when she died in 1677 he was not beset by grief. Henry Savile, Rochester's close friend, wrote, 'Harry Killigrew has been a widower these two days and laments his condition that fortune has made it possible for him to play the fool again, considering what use he is wont to make of the power of committing errors, besides human frailty in general.' He was a notorious gossip. When the King was on his deathbed and told not to talk, he joked that such a regimen would have killed Harry Killigrew. What came much closer to killing Harry was crossing the Duke of Buckingham.

The leader, the oldest (he was two years older than the King) and easily the most depraved of the Court Wits was George Villiers, second Duke of Buckingham. His biography reads like a novella. His father, Charles I's intimate friend, was assassinated in 1628. George was brought up by the royal family and became Charles II's closest companion. His career was hectic and disastrous. When he was refused permission to command the army at Worcester in 1651, he went on underwear strike, refusing to wash or change it until he got his own way. He acquired a bouquet, but not that of commander. After Worcester the King and he went their separate ways into exile. Buckingham returned to England in 1657, and was caught and imprisoned for two years. At the Restoration he became a gentleman of the bedchamber and a privy councillor. He was political and dangerous, and is thought to have been an agent for the King of France. He spent a great deal of time there, dazzling the French Court with his handsome looks and famed white satin suit. He captivated the Queen of France and had a liaison with her. Immediately after 1660 he started a faction to bring down Clarendon, the Lord Chancellor. In 1665 he met Rochester, who had recently come to Court, and the two became friends. Rochester then turned against his benefactor Clarendon. There was a brief intermission in Buckingham's war in 1667 when he was imprisoned for duelling, but he was released in time to help finish the Lord Chancellor off. He became a leader of the Cabal, the inner circle of ministers, but turned out to be an unsuitable adviser due to his unpredictable temper and his pre-occupation with debauchery. In 1674 Parliament had him dismissed from his post for alleged Catholic sympathies. For a while he sided with the opposition leader, Anthony Ashley Cooper, Earl of Shaftesbury, then found himself in prison again. In 1681, having frittered away a gigantic fortune, he withdrew to his Yorkshire estates. One of his least distinguished achievements was killing the Earl of Shrewsbury.

The duel arose because in 1667 Harry Killigrew and Anna Maria Brudenell, Countess of Shrewsbury, having 'nothing better to do' (as the gossip, the Comte de Gramont, puts it), decided to have an affair. Killigrew was proud of his conquest and could not understand why no one had tried to take her from him. He was a notorious braggart and, when drunk, repeatedly boasted of her more intimate beauties. It was unnecessary since they were already widely known, but not to Buckingham, who decided to find out for himself. When he had done so, a light-hearted affair began; but it ended in a duel and the death of Shrewsbury (of which more later). It turned out nonetheless to be one of the longest liaisons ever known at Court. Killigrew, out of pique, began to throw mud at her. His friends warned him, but he laughed and carried on. His travelling chair was run through by three sword-thrusts, one of which pierced his arm. The experience silenced him, and he retired forthwith to France. Buckingham was accused, but responded as he always did, with expressions of outraged innocence.

The King wrote to his sister, the Duchesse d'Orléans:

For Harry Killigrew, you may see him as you please, and though I cannot yet commend my Lady Shrewsbury's conduct in many things, yet Mr Killigrew's carriage towards her has been worse than I will repeat; and for his fight with My Lord Buckingham, he ought not to brag of it, for it was in all sorts most abominable. I am glad the poor wretch has got a means of subsistence, but have one caution of him, that you believe not one word that he says of us here for he is a most notorious liar and does not want wit to set forth his stories pleasantly enough.

He wrote to Minette again on 10 March 1668, saying that Buckingham was afraid that she considered him the cause of Harry Killigrew's failure to return to England (she had asked him to forgive the reprobate). Buckingham had nothing to do with the business, the King said, but Killigrew had offended so many of the Countess's relations that it would be unwise for him to show his face. For his own sake and the peace of everyone at Court, 'it will be of no inconvenience for him to have a little patience in other countries'.

Buckingham's debaucheries became so excessive that his debts climbed to £140,000 and his estates went to ruin. He was a ferocious drinker and lecher. As a result of a bout of plotting he was put on trial for heterosexual sodomy, a capital crime, but was acquitted. Many thought that the charge was trumped up. Many thought perhaps not. His most striking characteristic was a complete disregard for his own talents. He excelled at everything he tried his hand at, but invariably lost interest. Like everyone else, he wrote. His play *The Rehearsal*, a clever parody of Dryden's style of heroic drama, was excellently received, so he got bored with writing. In *Absalom and Achitophel* Dryden described Buckingham as:

> A man so various, that he seemed to be
> Not one, but all mankind's epitome:
> Stiff in opinions, always in the wrong;
> Was everything by starts and nothing long.

> But in the course of one revolving moon,
> Was chemist, fiddler, statesman and buffoon.

He was a lusty rogue with a magnificent constitution. He could spend a weekend with Rochester in the country, taking his dogs, the 'finest pack of hounds in England', for sport, leaving behind him a trail of drained bottles and women, and still be alert and ready for affairs of state at six on Monday morning.

Buckingham and Rochester were close friends and allies of Nelly, Mrs Eleanor Gwyn, the King's longest-serving mistress, who remained in service from 1669 until his death in 1685. Her father had died in a debtor's prison when she was a child, and her early years were spent working in her mother Old Madam Gwyn's alehouse and brothel, where she would serve the gentlemen with whatever they desired. In 1664 her sister Rose found her a job as orange girl at Drury Lane Theatre, and she graduated to actress with the King's Players at the age of fourteen. An excellent singer and dancer, she was soon very much in demand, creating a number of popular roles. She had a succession of lovers including Charles Hart, an actor, and Rochester's friend Charles, Lord Buckhurst. Later, having added the King to her list, she would refer to the three as 'Charles the First', 'Charles the Second' and 'Charles the Third'. She had a passionate affair with a playwright, later a protégé and rival of Rochester's, Thomas Otway, who always remained a good friend. Rochester, too, remained her friend until he died, and in later years he and Otway provided her with great practical assistance in managing her (slightly dubious) financial affairs. From 1666 to 1669, she was the leading comic actress in the King's Players, except for a brief absence in 1667 while she was Buckhurst's mistress and keeping the merry-house at Epsom with him.

In about 1668 Buckingham introduced her to the King, who was captivated by her charm and wit. He complimented her and her fellow actors on their performance at the theatre. 'Then, sir,' she replied, 'I hope that you will make them a handsome present.' The King explained that he did not carry any money, but that he might borrow a few guineas from one of his friends. 'Odd's fish,' she snorted, 'what kind of company have I got myself into?' She was seventeen.

They became lovers and by 1670 she was pregnant by him. She was not a great beauty. Physically she was tiny, rounded and dimpled with a pert expression. Her mouth was much desired. An admirer remarked that she had 'an outmouth that makes mine water at it'. It was said that she had 'the littlest foot in England' as well as perfect legs, for which his Majesty had a fatal weakness. The better to appreciate her talents he even paid for some of her theatrical costumes, in particular the 'rhinegraves', short divided skirts which flared seductively as the wearer danced. She was a pretty package. The King had her unwrapped and painted by Lely more than once. When the portrait was hung, it was ornamented by Rochester's addition of a few sensitive lines:

> She was so exquisite a whore
> That in the belly of her mother
> She placed her cunt so right before
> Her father fucked them both together.

Nelly was not offended. She was a sparkling woman with a sparkling wit, and an inexhaustible sense of humour.

Coarseness ran throughout Rochester's work; the pungency of his poems could not be appreciated without it – though, as always, it might be said that he went too far. He loathed all forms of affectation and found the customary euphemisms far more offensive than the actual obscenities. The result is not for the faint of heart, or the refined of sensibility, but as the anonymous author of one of the prologues to Rochester's play *Valentinian* put it, 'The sun on dunghills shining is as bright, As when his beams the fairest flowers invite, But all weak eyes are hurt by too much light.' His friend Robert Wolseley, after Rochester's death, pointed out a crucial fact about his poetry: it was intended solely for private consumption by a few intimates, and the outrage that it has attracted on behalf of 'the public' is inappropriate. They were never meant to see it. 'But though his obscene poetry cannot be directly justified in point of decency it may however be a little excused, and it may perhaps deserve pardon, if we consider not only when 'twas writ, but also to whom 'twas addressed,' Wolseley wrote. 'My Lord Rochester did not design those songs to be sung for anthems in the King's Chapel, any more than he did his other obscene writings for the cabinets of ladies, or the closets of divines, or for any public or common entertainment, but for the private diversion of those happy few whom he used to charm with his company and honour with his friendship.'

Nelly, though renowned for her 'eternal sweetness' and unmoved by Rochester's mud pies, revelled in spite against her competitors. She was said to have laced the actress Moll Davis's sweetmeats with laxative shortly before Moll was due to take dinner with the King. When Louise de Kerouaille, a rival for the King's affections and an incorrigible snob, went into mourning for some relative of great importance, Nell solemnly appeared in deepest mourning too, 'for the great Cham [Khan] of Tartary, a close relative of mine, you know'. At a dangerous time of unrest over the Church of Rome, she was mobbed in her carriage by crowds who had mistaken her for Louise de Kerouaille, shouting, 'Catholic whore! Catholic whore!' Nelly leaned out and yelled at them, 'Pray, good people, be civil; I am the *Protestant* whore!' She went on her way amid a roar of approval. For this sort of impudence she was known as the 'darling strumpet of the crowd'. Because of her humble beginnings and her comparative lack of ambition, she did not attain the rank of the other favourites, all of whom became duchesses. Nell never received a title and remained plain Mrs Eleanor Gwyn, though she was about to be made Countess of Greenwich when the King died. She was more concerned to acquire some title of respect for her son by the King, Charles Beauclerk. She brought her campaign into the open by addressing him in front of the King as 'You little bastard!' and demanding to know what else she should call the child, since he had no other name. It is said that matters came to a head in the early 1670s, when she threatened to drop the child out of the window into the river just as the King was passing, unless he gave him a title. Impressed by the argument, the King made the boy Baron Headington, then Earl of Burford, and ultimately, when he was fourteen, Duke of St Albans.

She clung to her bond with the King throughout her long career, and she was a good ally to her friends. Charles granted her some disputed lands in Ireland, probably unlawfully. Rochester was acting as her trustee in April 1677, writing on her behalf to the Earl of Essex, Lord Lieutenant of Ireland, to try to settle the disagreement in her favour. He used to advise her how to handle the King to maximum advantage: 'Take your measures just contrary to your rivals, live in peace with all the world, and easily with the King. Never be so ill-natured to stir up his anger against others, but let him forget the use of a passion which is never to do you good. Cherish his love wherever it inclines, and be assured you can't commit greater folly than pretending to be jealous; but on the contrary, with hand, body, heart, head and all the faculties you have, contribute to his pleasure all you can, and comply with his desires throughout; and for new intrigues, so you be at one end, 'tis no matter which: make sport when you can, at other times help it.'

She never made any pretence about what she was or where she had come from. Even the Court was shocked when she announced to the French Ambassador that the King would always rather sleep with her than with Louise and lifted her petticoats to show him how magnificent and how clean they were. By 1675, although not one of the great mercenaries, she had accumulated eight servants, a French coach and six, and an extravagant range of shoes. As well as 'darling strumpet of the crowd', she was known as 'Puddle Nell' and 'the hare-brained whore', neither of which upset her in the least. On his deathbed, Charles begged the Duke of York to look after the Duchess of Portsmouth (as Louise had become) and 'not let poor Nelly starve'. For her generosity, good temper, high spirits, wit and recklessness she was the only one of Charles's mistresses that the people loved. She never forgot her old friends and remained faithful to Charles from the beginning of their affair until his death. James II, in answer to his brother's plea, paid off her debts, gave her some cash and settled on her a pension of £1,500 a year. In March 1687, she suffered a stroke. She died eight months later, and was buried in the church of St Martin-in-the-Fields.

The King's Court was mainly peopled by the aristocracy, idle, dissolute and in an advanced state of decomposition. In 1728, Jonathan Swift wrote scathingly in *Gulliver's Travels*:

our young noblemen are bred from their childhood in idleness and luxury; but as soon as years will permit, they consume their vigour, and contract odious diseases among lewd females; and when their fortunes are almost ruined, they marry some woman of mean birth, disagreeable person, and unsound constitution, merely for the sake of money, whom they hate and despise.

For the productions of such marriages are generally scrofulous, rickety, or deformed children; by which means the family seldom continues above three generations unless the wife takes care to provide a healthy father among her neighbours or domestics, in order to improve and continue the breed ... The imperfections of his mind run parallel with those of his body, being a composition of spleen, dullness, ignorance, caprice, sensuality, and pride.

Swift was writing fifty years later, but nothing had changed. Precisely the same species had peopled Charles's Court. The Merry Gang, however, were more than mere drunks and hooligans. They had what were called 'parts'. They were able administrators, and poets and playwrights. They also had immense style, which unfortunately was calculated to attract the public eye more to their sins than to their achievements.

The young Earl was ecstatic. His wit and beauty made him instantly popular. His looks accorded with the seventeenth-century ideal: ascetic, tall, graceful and well built, though slender. Many thought him the handsomest man in the land, with an impudent air and a complexion that John Aubrey said was 'fair, clear, and rosy'. Burnet described his manner as 'polished, his conversation easy and agreeable. He carried himself with a natural modesty.' Indeed, when he was younger he was known to blush when he found himself the centre of attention. His wit was subtle and striking. He had a lively mind, expressed himself forcefully and had a rare power of imagery. He was highly educated and loved to argue about philosophy, but was said to have such charm that even those who disagreed with him nevertheless took pleasure in his disputation. When he first arrived at Court there was great excitement over a brilliant comet that had been visible for several nights. The King described it as 'no ordinary star'. He could have been referring to the newcomer. In Burnet's words, Rochester was 'very acceptable in a court'.

He had a happy knack of being able to compose verses extempore, mostly corrosive, which convulsed his peers and the King. From the monarch down, the great enemy of the Court was boredom, and the young wit was a welcome diversion. Because he was modest and rather shy, holding centre stage among a cast of such glamorous players was unnerving. He needed the reassurance of alcohol. His misfortune was that the more he drank the funnier he became. Wine served only to sharpen his wit, and his new friends kept him full to overflowing. Burnet lamented that 'The licentiousness of his temper with the briskness of his wit disposed him to love the conversation of those who divided their time between lewd actions and irregular mirth. And so he came to bend his wit, and direct his studies and endeavours to support and strengthen these ill principles both in himself and others.'

His glory shone ever more brightly. One night he was drinking with the King and the King's brother, the Duke of York, who was renowned for his lack of humour. Also present were the Duke of Monmouth, Charles's first illegitimate son by Lucy Walter, who was almost feeble-minded, the Duke of Lauderdale, who was so large and ugly that he was considered deformed, and Dr Alexander Frazier, the King's abortionist and pox-doctor, a mean and empty and ignorant man. The King 'being in a merry humour, upon the Earl of Rochester's coming in, says to him, "Rochester, they say you can make good verses extempore; prithee let's hear some of them now." "Upon what subject would your Majesty have them?" says Rochester. "Subject," says the King, looking about him, "let it be on all us that are here." "I beg your Majesty's pardon," replied Rochester, "I dare not do it." "Why so?" says the King. "For fear I should offend your Majesty," says he. "No, no," says the King. "You shan't offend me, say what you will, and therefore I command you to do it."' Rochester obeyed:

> Here's Monmouth the witty,
> And Lauderdale the pretty,
> And Frazier, that learned physician;
> But above all the rest,
> Here's the Duke for a jest,
> And the King for a grand politician.

'Oh my conscience!' cried the King. 'He has satirised upon us all! No wonder indeed that you begged my pardon, for you are resolved to stand in need of it!' The King was delighted, the others less so, particularly when a copy of the jibe was found mysteriously posted on Whitehall gate.

On another drunken occasion, according to a contemporary account, the King and his company were playing crambo, and no one could find a rhyme for 'Lisbon', the home of the Queen, Catherine of Braganza. The King said, 'Was Rochester but here, I'll engage he'd rhyme to it presently.' A gentleman-in-waiting was sent to fetch him. When Rochester sauntered in, the King said, 'My Lord, we're at crambo here, and none can rhyme to Lisbon.' Rochester replied, 'that's very strange, and 't please your Majesty.' 'Why, can you do it?' the King asked. 'Yes, Sir, in a stanza, if you'll pardon me.' 'You're thinking of some mischief now,' said the King. 'Well, I'll grant you pardon.' Rochester raised his glass and, in a startling piece of effrontery towards the Queen, Hyde (who was widely accused of procuring the King's marriage to a barren Queen, so as to keep the way clear for the accession of his own daughter, the Duchess of York) and the Bishop of London (who had solemnised the marriage), declaimed:

> Here's a health to Kate
> Our sovereign's mate
> Of the royal house of Lisbon.
> But the Devil take Hyde
> And the Bishop beside,
> Who made her bone his bone.

The King frowned and bid him be gone, then drained his glass and swiftly withdrew.

Perhaps the most famous quip of all came on another of those frolicsome evenings when the monarch and his friends were drinking together and in a sportive mood. Charles invited the company to compose verses impromptu and, since they were in private, to feel free to say anything they wanted. He would take nothing amiss. Rochester produced the famous quatrain, of which there are numerous versions:

> We have a pretty, witty king
>   Whose word no man relies on:
> He never said a foolish thing,
>   And never did a wise one.

The King's word for once could be relied on. Far from taking offence, he capped the joke with his reply that the matter was easily accounted for: his discourse was his own, but his actions were those of his ministers.

There were many more such morsels:

> A knight delights in deeds of arms,
> Perhaps a lady loves sweet music's charms,
> Rich men in store of wealth delighted be,
> Infants love dandling on their mother's knee.
> Coy maids love something which I'll not express.
> Keep the first letters of these lines and guess,

is attributed to him. From the lowly beginnings of satirical squibs, he began to experiment with genuine composition. Little of what now poured forth strayed above the waist and his reputation as a poet depended substantially on his skilful command of obscenity. Ironically, it was the same facility that disqualified his reputation as a poet after his death.

There was always an ulterior motive behind his compositions. It could be to seduce a girl or, more often, simply to tease his betters and his friends. It was fashionable at the time to write sentimental verse about a mistress's exquisite attractions, comparing them with the glories of nature, and proffering floral tributes. There was often a nymph or a shepherd involved and the style has been called the 'rococo pastoral'. Rochester inclined towards a more fundamental mode of expression.

Andrew Marvell, a friend and admirer of Rochester's, had written, 'The Picture of Little T.C. in a Prospect of Flowers'. It was an unfortunate title ('flowers' was also a common expression for menstruation) and a sitting target for the dirty minded. To Rochester it was an inspiration for awesome obscenity. What Marvell wrote was:

> See with what simplicity
> This nymph begins her golden days!
> In the green grass she loves to lie,
> And there with her fair aspect tames
> The wilder flowers, and gives them names...

The poem grows increasingly lyrical, almost anticipating Wordsworth. This type of work was altogether too much for the outspoken Rochester. He thought it should go more like this:

> By all love's soft, yet mighty powers,
>   It is a thing unfit
> That men should fuck in time of flowers

Or when the smock's beshit.

Fair nasty nymph, be clean and kind,
   And all my joys restore;
By using paper still behind
   And sponges for before.

It is easy to imagine his demure expression as he recited it amid the guffaws of the drunks and lechers at Whitehall. Marvell certainly took no offence, for he later told John Aubrey that Rochester was the best satirist in England and 'had the right vein'. Rochester built up such a reputation for scurrilous burlesque that he became a somewhat alarming figure. Gossip was the business of Court society, and the Earl its chief administrator. He disguised one of his footmen as a sentinel with a red coat and musket, and stationed him outside the bedrooms of ladies whom he suspected of scandalous behaviour. A sentry caused no alarm; there were soldiers posted all through the palace. They stood on duty silent and unmoving, dead as furniture. The spy would then report back. Sometimes, in the case of uninvited gentlemen visitors, Rochester knew of the latest romances before the ladies themselves.

Miss Henrietta Maria Price, maid of honour to the Queen and daughter of the Master of the Royal Household, was plaguing the Earl of Chesterfield. Her victim, hardened as he was, had begun to find her attentions a little overwhelming. Rochester found out that she had sent Chesterfield a pair of gloves and marked the occasion with an unpolished little offering, 'From Mistress Price, Maid of Honour to her Majesty, who sent me a pair of Italian Gloves':

My lord,
   These are the gloves that I did mention
Last night, and 'twas with the intention
That you should give me thanks and wear them,
For I most willingly can spare them.

When you this packet first do see
'Damn me,' cry you, 'she has writ to me!
I had better be at Bretby still
Than troubled with love against my will.

Besides this is not all my sorrow

She writ today, she'll come tomorrow.'
Then you consider the adventure
And think you never shall content her.

But when you do the inside see
You'll find things are as they should be,
And that 'tis neither love nor passion
But only for your recreation.

Bretby was Chesterfield's family seat. Together with the poem, Chesterfield received a pained little note from Miss Price, 'I had a mind that you should see these enclosed papers which were writ by the Lord Rochester, that hath occasioned you this trouble from your humble servant.' It was very low on the Rochester scale of incivility, but it shows the effectiveness of his intelligence network. In the end it mattered little. Miss Price went through a number of other gentlemen and Rochester tortured her with many satires. She eventually married one of Chesterfield's cousins, Alexander, with whom she was perfectly content.

Rochester was a born actor and went through life up to and including his dying breath striking one pose or another. His spirit survived within a series of brittle façades. He confessed to Burnet how he loved to go about in disguise. He would pretend to be a beggar or dress up as a porter to carry on a flirtation. He consorted with gypsies. He mastered the accents and argot of many disparate sections of society, and could make himself agreeable in any of them. He could alter his entire persona so that not even his intimates recognised him. He would change his name and become a City merchant, transforming himself from a beautiful young courtier into a dull and inconsequential figure, mimicking the talk and demeanour of his new City friends. He would stay with them for weeks at a time, go to their parties and live their lives, enjoy their pleasures and their women. In conversation he would fulminate against the disgraceful behaviour of the King and the Court. He would vilify the King's mistresses, comparing them unfavourably with the ladies present. A favourite theme was to speculate why fire had not descended from heaven on to Whitehall for tolerating wretches such as these, especially the disgraceful Earl of Rochester.

In later years he was to rue the speed with which his notoriety travelled the land, but he had only himself to blame. Why he did it one cannot tell. He was alone. He was not trying to impress anyone in particular. The simple explanation, though, is that he was easily bored. He would do anything to avoid what he called 'still life'. He was a natural actor and could not suppress his instincts. He tickled the Court with his one-man cabaret and his rude little ditties, flavoured with a subtle spice that was sometimes hard to discern. When Richard Lovelace, the great Cavalier poet, was going to the wars, he had written the famous lines to Lucasta:

> Tell me not, sweet, I am unkind,
> That from the nunnery
> Of thy chaste breast and quiet mind
> To war and arms I fly.
>
> ...
>
> I could not love thee, dear, so much
> Loved I not honour more.

Rochester was inspired to write the almost exact reverse of these sentiments in 'To a Lady in a Letter':

> Whilst I, my passion to pursue,
>   Whole nights am taking in
> The lusty juice of grapes, take you
>   The juice of lusty men.
>
> Upbraid me not that I design
>   Tricks to delude your charms
> When, running after mirth and wine,
>   I leave your longing arms.

Between moments of inspiration, he went happily about his business like a cockerel in a hencoop. Sooner or later there was bound to be trouble. The Comte de Gramont, the notorious gossip, thought Rochester one of the most handsome and attractive figures at Court, but also a fierce character who inspired terror because of his wit and skill with satire. If he was crossed he could be dangerous.

Sue Willis was a noted whore at Court, and notoriously greedy. She also may be the star of 'St James's Park'. She remained a whore all her life, and eventually became mistress of William III's favourite, the

Duke of Portland. She somehow offended Rochester, possibly by 'making him her slave' and then demanding payment for what he considered should have been a courtesy. 'On Mrs Willis' begins:

> Against the charms our bollocks have
>   How weak all human skill is!
> Since they can make a man a slave
>   To such a bitch as Willis.

And it ends:

> Bawdy in thoughts, precise in words,
>   Ill-natured, and a whore,
> Her belly is a bag of turds,
>   And her cunt's a common shore.

A 'shore' here is a sewer.

A new blast from Rochester gained rapid currency at Court. Gramont commented, 'Every person was eager to obtain the most insignificant trifle that came from the pen of Lord Rochester.' The unfortunate Miss Goditha Price crossed him. He had already written about her sister's gloves. Goditha's appearance was not seductive, but she was determined to have lovers and so was somewhat forward, even by contemporary standards. She was one of the Duchess of York's maids of honour and she interfered in a love affair Rochester was having with one of the other girls. She had quarrelled with the girl, then gossiped about the affair. Rochester was enraged. Any pursuit of a young lady thus made public would be halted abruptly by her guardians. No man ever wrote with more charm, more delicacy and more fluency, said Gramont, but in his satire Rochester's pen was merciless. Goditha's interference was followed by a flood of verses that made her life unbearable. Day in, day out, there would be a new crumb for the delectation of the courtiers. Goditha eventually withdrew, beaten.

Gramont tells us how Rochester turned his amorous attentions towards another of the Duchess of York's maids of honour, a pretty but vacuous girl called Ann Temple. She was dark and had a lovely shape, perfect teeth and soft eyes. Her complexion was like a flower and she carried herself with a deceptive air of intelligence and refinement. The Duchess asked a Miss Mary Hobart, one of the older maids of honour and daughter of a Norfolk baronet, to undertake the protection of Ann from Rochester. Unfortunately, this was an administrative slip. Miss Hobart was a lesbian and was after the girl too. Rochester was courting Ann with his customary flattery. He would read his poems to her as though no one but she could appreciate them. He would tell her that, if heaven had wished to captivate him by her beauty, he would have had no chance of escape, but thank the Lord he was interested only in her intellect, and so could enjoy a delightful friendship with her without untoward consequences. He followed this up by writing her poems praising her beauty and intelligence. This is the sort of thing:

> When innocence, beauty, and wit do conspire
> To betray, and engage, and inflame my desire,
> Why should I decline what I cannot avoid
> And let pleasing hope by base fear be destroyed?

Such bouquets easily turned the girl's head. However, so did sweets. Ann had a childish taste for confectionery and Miss Hobart pandered to it by letting her into the Duchess's closet, a small room where treasures were displayed. The Duchess's treasures consisted of all sorts of syrups and jams. One summer day, after a long ride, Ann went to Miss Hobart's room next to the Duchess's bathroom. She asked if she might take off her riding habit down to her chemise. Miss Hobart eagerly agreed. She inveigled the girl into the bathroom, where they could 'talk without being interrupted', and fed her with sweets. Then she proffered some advice. She warned her of the stupidity and dishonesty of the courtiers. They broke their promises and if necessary the law to have their way with the maids of honour. They treated the girls as toys provided for them personally, to stave off boredom. She attacked them bitterly, singling out Rochester for special mention. Indisputably he was the man with the most wit and the least honour in England. 'I would be prepared to bet', she told Ann, 'that you think he's honest and sincere. But, once he's made you fall for him, he'll have no idea what to do with you. You're the loveliest creature in the Court and all his experience is with the commonest trollops in town. He completely lost all judgement a long time ago.' She showed the girl a copy of one of Rochester's scurrilous poems about Goditha Price, but with Goditha's name replaced by Ann's. The girl burst into tears of fury and humiliation. Miss Hobart warned her never to speak to him again.

Whatever her motives Miss Hobart was undoubtedly right. Every depiction of Rochester emphasises his hypnotic attraction for women. In his friend Etherege's play *The Man of Mode*, the Rochester figure, Dorimant, has them falling over one another. Duke Nemours, the central character in Nathaniel Lee's *Princess of Cleves* and a rake also modelled on Rochester, is irresistible to every woman in the play, 'fatally attractive but vicious'. Aphra Behn demonstrates his technique as Willmore in her play *The Rover, Part I*:

FLORINDA: Heavens! What a filthy beast is this!

WILLMORE: I am so, and thou ought'st the sooner to lie with me for that reason; for look you, child, there will be no sin in't, because 'twas neither designed nor premeditated: 'tis pure accident on both sides, that's a certain thing now. Indeed, should I make love to you, and vow you fidelity, and swear and lie till you believed and yielded, that were to make it a *wilful* fornication, the crying sin of the nation. Thou art therefore, as thou art a good Christian, obliged in conscience to deny me nothing.

Miss Hobart did not know that the Earl had a friend in the household, Sarah, the niece of the mistress of the maids. When the others arrived, Sarah had been washing in one of the Duchess's baths, and had just had time to draw the curtains. She got into the bath, which was full of cold water and sat there listening and shivering. When it was safe to leave she ran straight to Rochester and it all came out. Rochester went to the Duchess's Court to see how the land lay. Ann was looking glorious, but she was in a peculiar mood. When he went over to greet her she turned her back on him. He smiled, walked insolently round her and stood in front of her again. 'Madam,' he said, 'how wonderful that you can sparkle after such a long day. First a three-hour ride and then Miss Hobart! It takes backbone to get through that.' The girl was so angry, she could only glare. Miss Hobart overheard and realised that Rochester knew. She pulled Ann away in alarm and they disappeared.

However, something else that Sarah had revealed was that Miss Hobart and Ann had hatched a girlish scheme to dress up in each other's clothes. They were going for a walk in the Mall that night at nine, the fashionable hour, wearing scarves and masks, each pretending to be the other. It was childish, but they were very young, and all the Court would indulge in any absurdity to ease the tedium. What followed could have been the plot of a baroque opera. Promptly at nine, Rochester and Harry Killigrew were waiting for them under the trees. Ann saw them and angrily insisted on dragging Miss Hobart up to them while she told Rochester what she thought of him. Hobart agreed to go across, but only if Ann promised not to speak. The men pretended to be fooled by the disguise. Rochester approached Miss Hobart as though she were Ann. Ann was left with Killigrew, who addressed her as 'Miss Hobart' and pretended to give her the disinterested advice of a friend. He rebuked her for blackening the character of the Earl who he said was one of the most honourable men at Court, and for the way that she had misused the lampoon. He also warned her against pursuing her designs on Ann. He suggested that she should try to make amends by reconciling Ann with Rochester, a man whose intentions were highly honourable and who would never have looked at the young lady if he had not meant to make her his wife. Ann listened, bewildered. There was nothing she could say.

When Miss Hobart and Rochester came over, Ann ran back to her room in Whitehall and began stripping off the other woman's clothes in fury. Miss Hobart followed her to find out what had happened. She came up behind the partially clothed girl and grabbed her. Ann shook her off and started to scream. Sarah and her aunt came running in. The aunt told Miss Hobart what she thought of her and ordered her out of the room. The story went round the Court with great speed, and Miss Hobart's reputation was badly shaken. But she survived; the Duchess of York supported her and scolded Ann for her credulity. The mistress of the maids and Sarah were dismissed. Rochester took them straight to the country to console them. Ann wanted to make it up to him, but the opportunity was gone. He was now banished. Some believe (probably wrongly) that he then trained Sarah for the stage, and that she became an actress in the King's company under the name of Sarah Cook. Sarah Cook was said to have been one of the prettiest and one of the worst actresses in the kingdom.

Ever since Rochester first came to Court, he had been banished without fail at least once a year, 'for whenever a word was on the tip of his tongue or at the end of his pen he let it fly, utterly regardless of the consequences,' said Gramont. The ministers, the mistresses and the master himself were the victims. If Charles had not been the best natured monarch in the world the first of these offences would have been the last. Rochester was not the only one to mock him. The Court Wits all did, though not always so blatantly. Rochester was always the one to be frankly impertinent, forcing the King to respond. However, Charles was not only soft-hearted, he was bored and discontented. The punishment would not be severe, since the King missed Rochester more than Rochester missed the Court. Much of the time the palace of Whitehall bounded Rochester's world. Even so he despised it as a cathedral consecrated to human folly. In his absences, while the King was pining for entertainment, Rochester was quite content in the country, recovering from the excesses of London and writing scurrilous verse. When he was back in favour he would set about ruffling even bigger and finer feathers. It was a happy way of life, ricocheting between rebellion and repose. The only dark cloud that loomed was the matter of his finances. Always modest, they were now rapidly dwindling.

In the spring of 1665, the merry-go-round was halted by the arrival at Court of a notoriously depraved old Cavalier from Somerset, Lord Hawley, with his pretty fourteen-year-old granddaughter, Elizabeth Malet. She was the daughter of Sir John Malet, of Enmore, who had died some years before. Her mother had married again, this time to Sir John Warre, Sheriff of Somerset and a Member of Parliament, a prominent and greedy man. Elizabeth was a beauty and heiress to a great fortune worth £2,500 per annum. She was witty, intelligent, wilful and determined and a number of suitors were already pursuing her. Among the front runners were Lord Herbert, heir to the Earl of Pembroke, Lord Hinchingbrooke, son of the Earl of Sandwich, Lord John Butler, son of the Duke of Ormonde, and Sir Francis Popham. Her stepfather and grandfather, who were charged with her care, wanted to sell her to the highest bidder and pocket the proceeds. The suitor who paid the biggest sweetener would get the heiress and the fortune.

The eighteen-year-old Rochester stood no chance. He had nothing to offer except the earldom, which was not enough. His cousin the Earl of Clarendon backed him. The King, who had been nobbled by Rochester's other cousin, Lady Castlemaine, had intervened more than once on Rochester's behalf. But even the monarch was unsuccessful. Rochester courted the young woman with flattery and poems, a combination calculated to have a lethal effect on unsuspecting young ladies. Elizabeth Malet, though by no means unsuspecting, was a romantic. She was shrewd and, as she was later to prove, had her own ideas. She was determined to marry a man of her own choosing. Banking on this, Rochester would proffer such tributes as,

> Insulting Beauty, you misspend
>   Those frowns upon your slave;
> Your scorn against such rebels bend,
> Who dare with confidence pretend
> That other eyes their hearts defend,
>   From all the charms you have.

Had he addressed his blandishments to her stepfather and her grandfather they would have been unmoved. But the girl was deeply emotional and she conceived a strong partiality towards the handsome young rogue. He had the same streak of mutiny as she. Then Rochester heard that Hinchingbrooke, the front runner, was on his way back from the continent. He panicked. His blood was hot, and so was his head. He decided, doubtless with Elizabeth's own complicity, to take matters into his own hands. On Friday 26 May 1665 Elizabeth had been to supper in Whitehall at the lodgings of Frances Stewart, beloved of the King. Late that night Lord Hawley fetched her in his coach. As they reached the gloomy depths of Charing Cross they were halted by a party of armed men, some mounted and some on foot. Elizabeth was grabbed and put into a coach and six, a powerful and fast conveyance. Two women were waiting to receive her and take her away. The whole affair was conducted with excellent taste. Rochester, who had been directing the proceedings, disappeared. He was tracked down and arrested at Uxbridge. One cannot be sure what he was doing there. It was on the road to his mother's house in Oxfordshire, but that was the last place he could have taken her. His father's family home was near his mother's. He may have been heading there. If he could have got her to Adderbury, it would not have been long before he was found, but it would have been too late. By then the girl would have been either married or unmarriageable. On the other hand, the distance from Uxbridge to Adderbury was fifty-eight miles. The Earl's equipage was fast but the roads were almost non-existent. Before a journey into the country the glass windows of a private coach had to be taken out and replaced by canvas screens, to stop them rattling to bits. The highways were dust in summer, and marsh in winter. The journey would have taken fourteen to sixteen hours. There would have been little chance of escaping a contingent of cavalry in pursuit. It was probably a case of an hereditary inability to think before acting.

The relatives appealed to the King, who was outraged. The next morning a proclamation was issued calling on 'all Sheriffs, Mayors, Officers of the Reave, and other his Majesty's men and loving subjects whom it may concern to search for all persons who shall appear guilty of the Misdemeanour, and having found, to apprehend and in safe custody to detain them until further order'. Even at the Court of Charles II such behaviour was considered uncouth, especially from one who had been given the King's own imprimatur. Rochester was flung in the Tower to cool off for an interminable three weeks. He wrote a poem, 'Sab Lost', whose meaning has always been a mystery. It must have had something to do with the abduction. It was found years later, written in his own hand. Down the left side of the page were a series of initials that seem to have denoted his servants. Whether it was because they were involved in the scheme or because he just happened to write the poem on a discarded piece of litter, nobody knows. Although there have been other instances of the word, 'Sab' must refer to the abduction of the Sabine women by Romulus (after which, it is said, they made excellent wives).

BLAC	
PAGE	
COACH	She yields, she yields, pale Envy said 'Amen',
WILL	The first of women to the last of men.
JA	Just so those frailer beings angels fell:
POST:	There's no midway (it seems) 'twixt heaven and hell.
GILL	Was it your end, in making her, to show
GARD:	Things must be raised high to fall so low?
BUT:	Since her nor angels their own worth secures,
UPHOLST:	Look to it gods! The next turn must be yours,
COOKE	You who in careless scorn laugh at the ways
DOLL	Of humble love and call 'em rude essays.

CK   Could you submit to let this heavy thing
I.B.   Artless and witless, no way meriting...?
FR:
SAR: A
H.M.
D.M.

'She yields, she yields ... the first of women to the last of men. Just so those frailer beings angels fell.' 'The first of women' must have been Elizabeth, 'the last of men' Rochester. How far 'yields' and 'the fall of angels' are meant to go is a matter for conjecture. History does not relate the girl's experiences. Her reputation remained intact and her admirers continued to court her as ardently as before. It is true that afterwards Elizabeth was extremely angry with the Earl, but in view of her subsequent behaviour it is likely that what irked her was not so much his attempt as his failure.

4

'Never marry!'

The Bachelor Husband

By a strange and melancholy paradox the finest lyrical poet of the Restoration was also its worst natured man. Infamous in a lax age for his debaucheries, the Earl of Rochester was unfaithful as a subject, shifting and treacherous as a friend, and untrustworthy as a man of honour. His habitual drunkenness may be taken perhaps as an excuse for the physical cowardice for which he was notorious, and his early decline in bodily strength as the cause of his extreme bitterness of tongue and savage malice. So sullen was his humour, so cruel his pursuit of sensual pleasure, that this figure seems to pass through the social history of his time, like that of a veritable Devil.

Sir Edmund Gosse, 1873

The regime in the Tower was in itself no great hardship. The prisoner, as befitted his rank, was well fed and watered. But there was an oppressive heatwave, and the cannon could be heard in London from Lowestoft as the second Dutch war began, a product of commercial rivalry between England and Holland. The plague of 1665 was beginning to take its murderous grip on the city, and there was little company except for the ravens that Charles had installed, and Robinson, the Lieutenant of the Tower, a corrupt and brutish man who fancied himself as a singer. Pepys, who knew him, called him 'a talking, bragging bufflehead, as very a coxcomb as I would have thought had been in the City', though as a singer he had 'a very good ear and strong voice, but no manner of skill'. Had it not been for the company, Rochester might have survived his captivity with greater fortitude. As it was, desperate measures were called for. He took the only course open to him; he grovelled to the King. He wrote an ingratiating petition:

To the King's Most Excellent Majesty

The Humble Peticion of ye Earle of Rochester.

Sheweth

That noe misfortune on earth could bee soe sensible to ye Petitioner as ye losse of yr Majesty's favour.

That Inadvertency, Ignorance in ye Law, and Passion were ye occasions of his offence.

That had hee reflected on ye fatall consequence of incurring yr Maties displeasure, he would rather have chosen death ten thousand times then have done it.

That ye Petitioner in all Humility & sence of his fault casts himself at yr Majesty's feet, beseeching you to pardon his first error, & not suffer one offence to bee his Ruine.

And hee most humbly prayes, that yr Ma^{ie} would bee pleased to restore him once more to yr favour, & that he may kisse your hand;

And he shall ever pray &C

It would have taken a hard-hearted prince indeed to ignore so noble an apology, however impudent, and Charles was not that prince. On 19 June the petition was answered. Lord Arlington, the Secretary of State, sent a warrant to the Lieutenant of the Tower to discharge the prisoner on securities to surrender to a Secretary of State on the first day of the Michaelmas term following.

In the meantime there was the problem of what to do with the miscreant. Doubtless Rochester had some good ideas, but the matter was taken out of his hands. At Charles's behest he became one of the 'King's men', a group of young aristocrats who would join up to fight the King's enemies in order to gain plunder and a reputation for courage. A name for gallantry was more precious than booty. Brave service for the King was the most admired characteristic of a gentleman. It could set him up in the world's estimation for the rest of his life. The Earl's father, whose courage was questioned by Clarendon, had nevertheless lived on the laurels of his heroic devotion to the King until he died. Although the gossips were crowing over the wreck of Rochester's chances with Elizabeth and the King was about to approve a match with Lord Hinchingbrooke, the culprit seemed unconcerned. There were plenty of hens in the palatial hencoop as yet untrod and he would pursue them sedulously. He summed up his ambitions in 'The Wish':

O that I could now by some chymic art,
To sperm convert my vitals and my heart,
That at one thrust I might my soul translate,
And in the womb regenerate:
There steeped in lust, nine months I would remain:
Then boldly fuck my passage out again.

However, money was now a more pressing need than the longer
term scheme of wedlock, that and atonement with the King. His only
possible hope of reinstating himself with the girl and her family was
to lay his hands on some plunder. His only way of soothing the
monarch was to do as he wished. Rochester also wanted, in accordance
with the custom, to acquire a reputation for courage in the King's
service. By virtue either of the irony of fate or of the King's sense of
humour, the commander of the fleet to which he became attached
was none other than the Earl of Sandwich, father of his principal rival
Lord Hinchingbrooke. On 6 July the King wrote to Sandwich:

The chief business of this letter is to recommend the bearer, my Lord
Rochester, to your care, who desires to go a volunteer with you; so I have
nothing more to say to you at this time, only to wish you good success, and
to assure you of my constant friendship and kindness,
    signed, C.R.

The recruit boarded ship on 15 July. On the 17th, Lord Sandwich
replied to the King, 'In obedience to your Majesty's commands by the
Earl of Rochester, I have accommodated him the best I can and shall
serve him in all things that I can.'

The aim of the expedition was to capture the Dutch East Indies
fleet, which was on its return voyage and laden with riches. The
English fleet blockaded the Dutch coast, expecting the enemy to seek
sanctuary in the neutral Norwegian port of Bergen. The English envoy,
Sir Gilbert Talbot, had negotiated a deal with the supposedly neutral
King Frederick III of Denmark and Norway whereby, in return for a
share of the proceeds, he would let the English fleet enter his harbour
and attack. The English Ambassador reported that Frederick had
approved the plan and had instructed the Governor of Bergen to
shoot only powder at the English. In his message to the Earl of
Sandwich he added: 'You are not to be surprised if he seem highly

displeased with your proceeding and that he make high complaint thereof against you, which nevertheless will be but in show to amuse the Hollanders and excuse himself outwardly to the world.'

The Dutch East India fleet sailed into port and Sandwich sent a detachment of twenty frigates under the charge of Sir Thomas Teddiman on the *Revenge*, the ship to which Rochester had been assigned. At the last moment it became apparent that the Governor of Bergen had gone back on the deal. The English had to kick their heels while negotiations with the Danes dragged on for thirty-four hours. It gave the Dutch ample time to prepare for the fight. Their warships drew up in front of their merchantmen to give them shelter, and their troops landed to set up gun batteries in the forts that surrounded the harbour.

During the night before the battle an odd incident occurred that was to colour Rochester's views of immortality and religion for the rest of his life. He and two other young officers, Edward Montagu and a Mr Wyndham, had premonitions of their approaching death. Rochester and Wyndham entered into a solemn agreement with religious oaths that, if either of them died, he should afterwards appear and tell the other what, if anything, lay beyond. Montagu refused to participate.

By dawn on 2 August Teddiman could wait no longer. At 5.00 a.m. he opened fire. The cannonade heralded disaster for the English. Teddiman had no room to manoeuvre his fleet and his vessels became stuck among the rocks. The wind was now coming off the land and prevented the use of the English fireships that were to carry combustible materials in among the enemy. A strong wind blew up, and the smoke of the guns was blown back into the faces of the English. Then the Dutch opened fire with catastrophic effect from their safe positions around the port. No English ships were lost, but four hundred men were killed including, as Rochester looked on, Montagu and Wyndham. It was a sight that he never forgot. Montagu had fought bravely and held to his place, which was one of the most dangerous. Wyndham had also kept his courage up till near the end of the action, when he suddenly began to tremble so badly that he could hardly stand. Montagu went to hold him up and, as they were in each other's arms, a cannonball killed Wyndham outright and took away Montagu's belly. He died within the hour. Rochester himself behaved with great courage and achieved at least one of his aims, a reputation for bravery in battle that resounded through London. There was of course no plunder. The one lasting thing that he gained was a deep mistrust of religion. Wyndham's ghost never appeared and from that he drew his own conclusions. They remained with him till the end of his life.

He wrote a long letter to his mother describing the way he had seen events unfold:

Madam,

I hope it will not be hard for your Ladyship to believe that it hath been want of opportunity, and no neglect in me, the not writing to your Ladyship all the while. I know nobody hath more reason to express their duty to you than I have. There have been many things past since I last wrote to your Ladyship.

He added that by the time the engagement began the English had 'already shared amongst us the rich lading of the East India merchants, some for diamonds, some for spices, others for rich silks and I for shirts and gold, which I had most need of; but reckoning without our host we were fain to reckon twice'. After describing the battle in sober terms he concluded:

We now lie off a little still expecting a wind that we may send in fire ships to make an end of the rest. Mr Mountague and Thomas Windham's brother were both killed with one shot just by me, but God almighty was pleased to preserve me from any kind of hurt. Madam, I have been tedious, but beg your ladyship's pardon, who am,

    your most obedient son

      Rochester

I have been as good a husband [saver] as I could, but in spite of my teeth have been fain to borrow money.

The detachment rejoined the main fleet on 18 August at Flamborough Head. Back on the flagship Rochester learned that Hinchingbrooke, his arch-rival and cause of the panic, had been back in England for only four days when he had been taken ill with smallpox, which had dramatically handicapped his pursuit of Elizabeth. The English fleet now badly needed a victory to atone for its feeble performance at Bergen. Its commanders chose simply to bide their time. Luck was on their side. When the Dutch East India fleet at length left Bergen, it was stricken by storms that scattered it and sent it running in small sections for the Dutch coast. Between 5 and 12 September the English fleet was able to pick off the dispersed Dutch, seize two East India ships full of valuables and a convoy of eighteen more Dutch ships, of which four were men of war. They also captured a thousand Dutch sailors. Sandwich gave to Rochester the happy task of taking the news back in a letter to the King. It listed the details of the victory and reported that the English had lost only one man. The Admiral generously referred the King for particulars to the bearer who, he said, had showed himself brave, industrious and of useful parts to his Majesty.

On Rochester's return the plague was at its height. What he had recently endured was far preferable to his fate had he remained. The Tower of London lay in the path of the disease and most of its garrison died. Only the dead, the dying and those too poor to leave now remained in London. Seven thousand had died in the course of the preceding week. The death toll was accelerating because, due to their lack of understanding of antiseptic procedures, most of the doctors were also dead. They dressed in a chilling uniform with a helmet that looked like a crow's head in an attempt to purify the air that they breathed. It was not enough. Very few remained to treat the sick. In July the Court had moved from Hampton Court to Oxford. It was there that Rochester caught up with the King. His peccadillo had been 'forgotten'. Charles was slow to forget a favour and quick to forget a slight. He rewarded Rochester with a gift of £750, for which the young hero had immediate and pressing need.

Despite the move, life at Court was little changed. The ladies were complaining about their Oxford lodgings and blaming Clarendon. A resentful populace had been ejected from their own homes to make room for arrogant courtiers who whiled away the hours sneering at the 'pedagogical' dons and befouling their houses. In November relations between the King and the Duke of York had become very tense and the Court was in uproar at their amours. The Duke, too, had fallen in love with Frances Stewart. The Duchess had fallen in love with Henry Sydney, her new Master of the Horse, and also with Rochester's friend, Harry Savile. 'God knows what will be the end of it,' cried Pepys. As the number of deaths from the plague approached

100,000 in London, the merriment in Oxford continued unabated. The King, deeply resentful of his brother, was panting for Frances Stewart more feverishly than ever despite the fact that his mistress, Castlemaine, was pregnant and confined to her lodgings at Merton College. The happy event occurred on 28 December, and a boy was born. Such was the elation of the citizenry that a £1,000 reward had to be offered for the identity of the writer of the message of 'congratulation' posted on her door. It was unclaimed.

Lord John Butler, the son of the Duke of Ormonde, was no longer in the running for Elizabeth's hand. Ormonde's agent Nicholls had tried to bring matters to a head. While the grandfather, Lord Hawley, was away he went down to Somerset to see Elizabeth herself. He showed Sir John Warre, the stepfather, a letter from Lord John Butler and proffered it to Elizabeth. Sir John was furious when he saw how eager the girl was to look at it, and warned Nicholls that no one was going to go above his head. Nicholls angrily accused him of being unfair. Elizabeth stood by, not daring to intervene on the visitor's behalf. Later she took it into her head to drink the Duke of Ormonde's health and Lord John's, in a very large glass half full of claret, which Nicholls considered most unladylike. However, Nicholls and Sir John Warre became good friends, Sir John assuring his visitor that they were all for Lord John. Nicholls privately noted that what they were all for was themselves. The next morning Elizabeth made sure she was among the company when the various interested parties gathered. Her mother tried to get rid of her but she refused to go. Nicholls chatted with the girl for an hour, loyally emphasising Lord John's good points and promising that her admirer would come to see her. Lady Warre intervened to say that her daughter would not receive him, so Nicholls asked the girl herself. She blushed and made no reply. Her mother reminded her that she had promised her grandfather to marry the family's choice. She repeated her promise but with a sullen, mutinous expression. Nicholls could see that they had 'cunningly inveigled' her into it, probably using the kidnapping as a weapon. (If Nicholls was right it seems more than ever likely that she was as much to blame as Rochester.)

The Court moved back to London in February 1666 as the plague finally petered out. Rochester had returned from the wars, beautiful and brave, with great honour but still no money. With a famous sea victory behind him, there ought to have been booty. If there was, it had disappeared without trace. There were none of the shirts and none of the gold that he had so greedily anticipated. Nevertheless, he determined to renew his attempts to marry his heiress. The girl was still baffling her guardians, agreeing to follow their advice while leaving no doubt that she intended to marry someone of her own choice. That month she appalled Hinchingbrooke by suggesting that they should elope and get married without consent. Hinchingbrooke was a staid, pious fellow and he told her father. Elizabeth was not pleased. When he went to see her in August at Tonbridge she told him that she had decided on someone else. He was deeply unimpressed by the 'vanity and liberty of her carriage'. That was the end of him for Elizabeth and of Elizabeth for Hinchingbrooke.

In September Sir George Carteret, Treasurer of the Navy, wrote to Lord Sandwich at sea that 'the lady of the west is at Court without any suitors, nor is likely to have any'. She was quite happy and no less determined. The new front runner was Lord Herbert, later Earl of Pembroke. While the lady shilly-shallied, Rochester was scheming. He was blowing hot and cold with her, one moment lovesick, the next indifferent. He was openly chasing other girls. It was an ancient and infallible technique. In a fit of amorousness he wrote 'A Song'. The first verse runs:

> Give me leave to rail at you,
> I ask nothing but my due;
> To call you false, and then to say
> You shall not keep my heart a day.
> But (alas) against my will
> I must be your captive still.
> Ah! be kinder then, for I
> Cannot change, and would not die.

And there still exists Elizabeth's reply, in her own handwriting, 'The Answer', which includes the lines:

> You grow constant through despair,
>   Love returned you would abuse.
> Though you still possess my heart,
>   Scorn and rigour I must feign.

73

> There remains no other art
> Your love, fond fugitive, to gain.

Suddenly at the end of May, for no apparent reason, Rochester disappeared back to sea. He had given no warning, even to his mother. At about this period he was in the course of promotion from the Court's chief purveyor of scandal to the chief subject of it. Apart from the general speculation about his prospects with Elizabeth (still generally rated as nil), his amours were becoming ever more notorious thanks to their scale and his catholicity of taste. The most plausible reason is that he had done something dreadful, but if so it is one of the few scandals that have not echoed down to us through time.

Although Rochester had not known it, the interview between Nicholls and Elizabeth had taken place three days before Bergen. He was also unaware, by the time he went to sea for the second time, that Butler had left the field. Lord Hawley's demands had proved too much. Lord John withdrew from the fray because his father, the Duke of Ormonde, one of the richest men in the land, was not prepared to pay the price demanded by the girl's family. On 30 May 1666 Sir George Carteret, Treasurer of the Navy until he was dismissed as a result of the war, wrote to Sandwich, who was on an embassy to Spain, 'My Lord Lieutenant having quitted all his pretensions to the lady of the west, Mr. Moore and I had divers meetings with her grandfather, who we found more addicted to his own interest than to anything else, and so unreasonable in his demands that we gave him over. The father-in-law was at all our meetings who agreed everything with the grandfather.'

On 31 May Rochester boarded ship with Sir Edward Spragge. The next day, his twentieth birthday, he took part in the Four Days' Battle, the most terrible of the war. In the crash of the cannon and the stinking clouds of smoke six thousand Englishmen lost their lives. Eight English ships were sunk, nine more captured. Almost every one of Rochester's fellow volunteers was killed. He was caught up in the fiercest action of the battle and emerged a hero. Sir Edward wanted to pass a message to the captain of another ship criticising his conduct and warning him to put his back into the fight. He called for volunteers and found none. Rochester undertook the task, which involved taking a rowing boat through the vicious wall of gunshot and cannon, delivering the message and then returning. It was an act of pointless heroism that was marvelled at by all who saw it. After the battle, he stayed with the fleet for July and was involved in a number of engagements in which the English were if anything the masters, but the whole campaign was drifting towards stalemate. There was nothing to gain by lingering. In October of 1666 he returned to London, this time to find that much of the city was no longer there. An area about one and a half miles by half a mile was rubble, smouldering from a fire that had begun on 2 September in Pudding Lane and raged for five days. Some thirteen thousand houses had gone, including shops and inns and all the public buildings. The old wood-framed houses had been like natural tinder. Pepys described it as:

A most horrid malicious, bloody flame, not like the flame of an ordinary fire. We stayed till, it being darkish, we saw the fire as only one entire arch of fire from this to the other side of the bridge, and in a bow up the hill, for an arch of almost a mile long. It made me weep to see it. The churches, houses, and all on fire and flaming at once, and a horrid noise the flames made, and the cracking of houses at their ruine.

Almost the whole of the city's 436 acres lay in ruins. Charles and the Duke of York had worked bravely during the fire to help rescue buildings and people. It was not enough to stop the mob later blaming the conflagration on divine wrath for the imperfections of the King and his Court.

Pepys saw Rochester at a ball on 15 November 1666:

Presently after the King was come in he took the Queen, and about fourteen more couple there was, and begun the Bransles [an old French dance]. As many of the men as I can remember presently, were: the King, Duke of York, Prince Rupert, Duke of Monmouth, Lord Douglas, Mr. Hamilton, Colonel Russell, Mr. Griffith, Lord Ossory, Lord Rochester. And of the ladies the Queen, Duchess of York, Mrs. Stuart, Duchess of Monmouth, Lady Essex Howard, Mrs. Temple, Swedish Ambassadress, Lady Arlington, Lord George Barclay's daughter. And many others I remember not. But all most excellently dressed, in rich petticoats and gowns and diamonds and pearls.

... the clothes and sight of the persons was indeed very pleasing, and worth my coming, being never likely to see more gallantry while I live, I should come some twenty times. About twelve at night it broke up, and I to hire a coach with much difficulty. So away home with my wife between displeased at the dull dancing, and satisfied that the clothes and persons, my Lady Castlemaine (without whom all is nothing) being there, very rich, though not dancing; and so after supper it being very cold, to bed.

Elizabeth was still playing ducks and drakes with her admirers. That same November Pepys recorded how the rich heiress Mrs Malet had said of her suitors that Lord Herbert would have had her; Lord Hinchingbrooke did not care whether he had her or not; Lord John Butler could not have her; Lord Rochester would have forced her; and Sir Francis Popham, who would kiss her backside to have her, nevertheless would probably get her. All the time Rochester was surreptitiously spinning his web round her, courting her with songs. In 'The Advice' he wrote:

> See gentle brooks, how quietly they glide,
> Kissing the rugged banks on either side,
> Whilst in their crystal streams at once they show
> And with them feed the flowers which they bestow.

> Though rudely thronged by a too near embrace,
> In gentle murmurs they keep on their pace
> To the loved sea, for even streams have desires;
> Cool as they are, they feel Love's powerful fires;

> And with such passion, that if any force
> Stop or molest 'em in their amorous course,
> They swell, break down with rage, and ravage o'er
> The banks they kissed, the flowers they fed before.

> Who would resist an empire so divine,
> Which universal Nature does enjoin?
> Submit then, Celia, ere you be reduced,
> For rebels vanquished once are vilely used.

It is surprising now to see the elaborate and drawn out masque of courtly love that couples enacted while the relatives haggled over the real business in the background. The charade of sighing lovers was a social prerequisite. Bows and curtseys, sly looks and shy smiles were exchanged. The 'servant', or hopeful swain, would pay traditional compliments and mouth formulae of desire; the lady would formally protest her modesty. Meanwhile each would be shrewdly assessing the other and deciding whether or not they could bear the thought of a lifetime together. In the case of Rochester and Elizabeth there were no formulae. Elizabeth was a romantic, and in love. Though Rochester was a lyrical liar, he loved her, after his fashion, and his to her is one of the few genuinely romantic poems that he wrote.

As Miss Hobart said of him – and she did not mean it as a compliment:

There is no doubt that Rochester is the most witty man in the kingdom; but then he is likewise the most unprincipled, and devoid even of the least tincture of honour. He is dangerous to our sex, and that to such a degree that there is not a woman who gives ear to him three times, but she irretrievably loses her reputation. He applauds your taste, submits to your sentiments, and whilst he himself does not believe a single word of what he is saying, he makes you believe it all.

In Elizabeth's eyes it was an approach that compared favourably with the stiff formalities of Hinchingbrooke and Butler. The speculation ended on 29 January 1667 when the couple eloped. The bride was seventeen, the groom twenty. Now that Elizabeth had her beautiful, dashing, drunken cavalier, what was she to do with him? The elopement had taken place with the full approval of the King, but the family still had plenty to say because no settlement had been reached over her property. Rochester's formidable mother, now the Dowager Countess, entered the fray and summoned her troops together. She wrote to Sir Ralph Verney, her son's former guardian, on the matter of:

my son Rochester's sudden marriage with Miss Malet contrary to all her friends' expectations. The King I thank God is very well satisfied with it, and they had his consent when they did it – but now we are in some care how to get the estate. They are come to desire two parties with friends, but I want a knowing friend in business, such a man as Sir Ralph Verney. Master Cool the lawyer and Cary [her agent] I have here. But I want one more of quality to help me.

Eventually, after prolonged infighting, the matter was settled. Elizabeth's property in law was now Rochester's. One of his rare virtues was that he took pains not to raid it, at least until last. It was useful to have a fortune to support his home and family, but for himself, when possible, he relied on his pay from the Crown. Sadly, it was not often possible. The King's debts were seldom paid.

He had influence, however, and his fortunes improved in March 1667 when the King appointed him a gentleman of the bedchamber. Elizabeth became groom of the stole to the Duchess of York. The appointment as gentleman was no sinecure. It carried a yearly fee of £1,000 for life, though inevitably the 'docquet' authorising the first payment failed to pass the Treasury until eight months later. His duties were to spend a week of every quarter in the King's bedroom, and to lie by the King in a pallet bed all night. If the groom of the stole were absent, he had to dress the King, and he had to wait on him when he ate in private. The duties were onerous only because the principal occupant of the King's bedchamber was Charles II, who was entranced by clocks. He had no fewer than six in his room that chimed at different times throughout the night. He made a practice of keeping at least six of his beloved spaniels about him in his chamber, indeed in his bed, where they constantly befouled the sheets and, from time to time, whelped. There were other fauna passing through on a more or less regular basis, though they tended to whelp elsewhere. Their offspring became dukes. Sleep was practical only when drunk, as the King and his gentlemen usually were.

The appointment involved great intimacy with the monarch. The gentlemen were the King's closest friends and advisers. No one was selected unless already highly favoured and wholly trusted. Most had similar tastes to the King, and viewed his failings with amusement. Charles was a good and sweet-tempered man, though subject to occasional rages. He was generous and kind. His great fault was moral degeneracy. He believed that wickedness and plotting mischief were the only things God hated. Merely to gratify his appetites was permissible, provided that they did no harm to anyone. He used to say, 'All appetites are free and God will never damn a man for allowing himself a little pleasure.' This, according to canonical thinking, was heresy, and if a citizen had said it to a parson he would have been corrected on the point, but Charles was king, and one who had been Hobbes's pupil. He cared little for metaphysical thought. He adored women, to the extent of putting up with the most monstrous treatment from them. He had the knack of remaining good friends with them after the affairs were over, helped by the distribution of dukedoms, pensions and jewellery. Barbara Castlemaine alone, described as 'enormously vicious and ravenous', was one of the heaviest burdens the taxpayer had to bear.

For a while the happy Rochesters were to be seen together in London. Presumably Elizabeth had her duties to perform as groom of the stole to the Duchess of York, as her husband had his to the King. Rochester seems to have loved his wife very much and after they were married there was a period of intense affection. His letters to her during this period show a devoted and affectionate husband. It was not part of a courtship ritual. He wrote her letters that were genuinely heartfelt and touching.

Madam if it were worth anything to be beloved by me you were the richest woman in the world. Since my love is of so little value, chide your own eyes making such poor conquests. This I write to assure your Ladyship 'tis not through vanity that I affect the title of your servant, but I feel a truth within my heart which my mouth rather does *confess* than boast of, – that there is left for me no pleasure but in your smiles, no life but in your favour, no heaven but in your life, when I deserve so ill that if you would torment, kill and damn me, Madam you need but hate me.

Later, perhaps after the arguments started, he wrote,

I kiss my dear wife a thousand times. Think upon me as long as it is pleasant and convenient to you to do so and afterwards forget me, for though I would fain make you the author and foundation of my happiness, yet would I not be the cause of your disturbance, for I love not myself so much as I do you, neither do I value my own satisfaction equally as I do yours,

farewell,

Rochester

That spring he went to Newmarket. It was the practice of the Court to go there every year in the autumn and sometimes also in the spring. By now Elizabeth was back in Oxfordshire, where she remained. What happened to her duties at the Palace is unknown, but there had not yet been any perceptible rift between the two. From Newmarket he wrote: 'I'll hold you six to four I love you with all my heart. If I would bet with other people I am sure I could get two to one, but because my passion is not so expensive to reach to everybody, I am not in pain to satisfy many. It will content me if you believe me and love me...'

The letters show how much time the two were apart. They were seen together by Pepys in February at a performance of *Heraclius* at the Duke's Theatre. The house was packed with the fashionable, and Frances Stewart looked very fine, like several other great ladies with her hair done up with 'puffs'.

I saw my Lord Rochester and his lady, Mrs. Malet, who hath after all this ado married him; and as I hear some say in the Pit, it is a great act of charity, for he hath no estate. But it was pleasant to see how everybody rose up when my Lord John Butler, the Duke of Ormonde's son came into the Pit towards the end of the play, who was a servant to Mrs. Malet, – and now smiled upon her, and she upon him.

That, sadly, is the last record of the two being seen together in London. Of course Rochester had £1,000 a year to earn and duties which kept him chained to the carousel. One of his principal tasks was to provide company for the King when he needed it. He missed his wife while he was at Court and she was chatelaine of Adderbury. She was unhappy about their situation and concerned about what was inevitably happening in her absence. Her husband took little trouble to disguise it, not through cruelty but because in contemporary terms he was doing nothing unusual or wrong. He was handsome, bored and lonely; and beautiful and willing women thronged about him. He wrote 'A Song':

> Absent from thee I languish still,
>> Then ask me not when I return.
> The straying fool 'twill plainly kill,
>> To wish all day, all night to mourn.

> . . .

> When wearied with a world of woe,
>> To thy safe bosom I retire,
> Where love and peace and truth does flow.
>> May I contented there expire.

Though a Protestant, not long after his marriage he induced his wife to convert to Catholicism, for reasons unknown. It was meant to be secret but eventually became known because one Trooper College from his troop of horse in Prince Rupert's regiment gossiped about being told to fetch the priest who inducted her. The details emerged in 1678, the time of the Popish Plot. The Rev. Titus Oates, who was an inveterate liar, had made accusations against a number of people, including prominent clergy, of a fictitious plot to assassinate the King and re-establish the Roman Church. The Privy Council accepted his evidence, and the fire was fanned by the murder of a well-known magistrate. It was the beginning of a reign of terror for Catholics. Within a few months, eight clergymen had been executed, and five more died in prison. Oates was tried and acquitted on a trumped-up charge of buggery, and London was seething with plots and counter-plots. Rochester was briefly drawn into the affair, but the problem passed him by, for by that time he was dead. The truth was, he had even less regard for Rome than for other persuasions:

> If Rome can pardon sin, as Romans hold,
> And if those pardons can be bought and sold,
> It were no sin t' adore, and worship gold.

And he added:

> At this rate they are happiest that have most,
> They'll purchase heaven at their own proper cost.
> Alas, the poor! All that are so are lost.

Elizabeth's apostasy was extraordinary at a time when there was so much tension between Protestants and Catholics. At the end of his life her husband prevailed upon her to revert to Protestantism. It may be that earlier he was reflecting on the fact that the King, who was Protestant, had no legitimate son. The heir to the Crown was his ardently Catholic brother, the Duke of York, who became James II. Perhaps Rochester had the foresight to realise that the Catholics would one day be the masters and was making provision accordingly. He himself did not subscribe to any Church, and no one would have believed him had he pretended to.

Rochester soon lost interest in Elizabeth. The novelty of marriage had worn off.

> To all young men that love to woo,

> To kiss and dance, and tumble too;
> Draw near and counsel take of me,
> Your faithful pilot I will be;
> Kiss who you please, Joan, Kate or Mary,
> But still this counsel with you carry,
> Never marry!

His wife was in the country. She seldom came to London now, and he did not encourage her. He was in a demi-paradise of spectacular and wicked women and witty and disgraceful friends, surrounded by a sea of fine wine that would have taken an iron character to resist. Rochester's character was not made of iron. Though capable of great courage and perseverance, he was essentially weak. Confronted by a powerful influence like lust, thirst, hellfire or the Duke of Buckingham, he would ultimately bow his head. Now he had everything. It was from this moment that Rochester, at the summit, an admired and favourite courtier whose beauty was desired, even envied by women, a gentleman of the bedchamber and friend of the King, married to a wealthy wife, with money in his pocket, began his remorseless and accelerating descent. Ten years later, he was to look back and see a 'gay, glittering fool, with all his noise, his tawdry clothes and loves'. He got drunk and stayed drunk for five years.

That noisy, happy bachelor life in London was sketched in some lines written for the stage:

DAINTY: I shall never sleep again – and 'twere no matter, if it did not make me look *thin*; for I hate to be so long absent from myself those seven dull hours, – and yet methinks *not* to sleep till the sun rise is an odd effect of my disease, and makes the night tedious, – without a woman. Reading would relieve me, but books treat of other men's affairs, and to me that's tiresome. Besides I seldom have a candle, but I am resolved to write some love passages of my own life. They will make a pretty novel. When I go to bed, I [will] divert myself with reading my *own* story, which will be pleasant enough. Boy!

BOY: Sir!

DAINTY: Who knocked at the door just now? Was it some woman?

BOY: Mrs Mannours's maid, sir, with a posset for you.

DAINTY: And you never brought her up, you rascal? How can you be so ill bred and belong to me? See who knocks there ... Some other woman!

This Mrs Mannours's fondness of me is very useful, for besides the good things she always sends me and money I borrow of her sometimes, I have a further prospect, Sir Lionel's daughters, which are in her charge. Both like me, but the youngest I pitch upon, and because I can't marry 'em both, Mr Squabb shall have the other sister, but I'll bubble [cheat] him afterwards. Thus I'll raise my fortune, which is all I want, for I am an agreeable man and *everybody* likes me.

BOY: 'Tis Mr Squabb, sir.

DAINTY: Call him up, but comb your periwig first. Let me comb it — you are the laziest sloven!

This fragment foreshadows the bumptious frivolity of Wilde, as did Rochester, who wrote it. It is taken from a play he never completed which was going to be called *Mr. Dainty's Chamber* and was a satire on himself. He does not seem to have got beyond page one. What he did write shows an affected, vain and unprincipled young man with Rochester's famed talent for abusing his servants and tolerating their backchat. He did not hesitate to pillory his own failings along with those of others. It was part of an easy charm that was irresistible to both sexes. His friend Robert Wolseley said of him after his death:

As he was the both the delight and the wonder of men, the love and the dotage of women, so he was a continual curb to impertinence and the public censor of folly. Never did man stay in his company unentertained or leave it uninstructed; never was his understanding biased, or his pleasantness forced; never did he laugh in the wrong place, or prostitute his sense to serve his luxury; never did he stab into the wounds of fallen virtue with a base and cowardly insult, or smooth the face of prosperous villainy with the paint and washes of a mercenary wit; never did he spare a fop for being rich, or flatter a knave for being great. Never was his talk thought too much or his visit too long; enjoyment did but increase his appetite, and the more men had of his company, the less willing they were to part with it.

Rochester became a close friend of George Etherege, the easygoing 'Gentle George', who was responsible for the creation of the Restoration comedy of manners, a witty and detached satire on contemporary manners and affectations. It was long imitated by Etherege's successors, Wycherley, Vanbrugh, Congreve and Farquhar, and lasted into modern times, with Wilde, Coward and Maugham. His first comedy, *The Comical Revenge, or Love in a Tub* was put on at Lincoln's Inn Fields Theatre in 1664 and was an instant success, though his second, *She Would If She Could,* was rendered a failure by atrocious acting. In his last comedy, *The Man of Mode, or Sir Fopling Flutter,* the central character, Dorimant, was an immortal portrayal of a Restoration rake, based on his friend Rochester (he was also a soulmate of Sedley and Buckhurst). It is still acted to the delight of audiences today.

Etherege was a skilful poet who wrote some of the most lyrical poetry of his time. He was also responsible for some of the least:

> The life of Nelly truly shown,
> From coal-yard and cellar to the throne,
> Till into the grave she tumbled down.
> To Buckhurst thus resigned in friendly wise,
> Our glaring lass begins to rise,
> Distributing her favours very thick,
> And sometimes witty Wilmot had a lick.

Clearly he, at least, believed that his two friends had consummated their long friendship at some time in the past. No offence was intended, and none was taken. The three, Rochester, Etherege and Nell, remained on the best of terms all their lives, even though Etherege at some stage had an affair with Elizabeth Barry, an actress with whom Rochester had been wildly in love. (So, for that matter, did Buckhurst.)

The Man of Mode was first performed in March 1676, an affectionate satire on a loved friend who was by then very ill. As usual in Restoration drama the plot is one of Byzantine complexity, but it centres round the activities of Mr Dorimant, a man of wit with somewhat patchy scruples, and Sir Fopling Flutter, a fop. The first act opens by telling us something that the whole audience already knew, that Dorimant is Rochester. After the first performance the critic John Dennis declared that on the strength of this act alone everyone loved the Dorimant character, seeing in him many of the Earl's qualities – his wit, his spirit, his amorous inclinations, the attraction he held for the fair sex, his falsehood and his inconstancy, his amiable way of chiding his servants and his habit of repeating the verses of Edmund Waller.

As he enters, Dorimant is murmuring poetry to himself, one of eleven passages by Waller that appear in the play. Rochester had written of his hero, 'Waller by nature for the bays designed, With spirit force and fancy unconfined, In panegyric is above mankind' ('bays' denotes the laureateship). Everyone in the theatre will have known of his admiration of the older poet, and there would have been a gale of laughter when the words were spoken. From that moment the audience will have settled in their seats, relishing what was to come. Dorimant calls for a footman and then exclaims, 'Dogs! Will they ever lie snoring abed till noon?', which prompts the retort, ' 'Tis all one, sir: if they're up, you indulge 'em so, they're ever poaching after whores all the morning.' As his friend Wolseley recorded, Rochester was admired for his ability to deal with his servants on intimate terms without losing their respect. His household was one where the master was first among equals. The servants were not mere employees but friends whose failings he tolerated in the same good spirit as he tolerated his own. In the play Dorimant is consistently rude to the lowlier species and they are equally impertinent to him. There is never a suggestion of the grandee pulling rank, though there is never any doubt about who is master. Rochester was ready to deal with anyone as an equal; he spoke the language of the loftiest aristocrat and of the lowest brothel keeper. He mixed with both equally happily, and with equal regularity. In this he was perfectly sincere. He loathed all forms of pretension and practised none himself.

His *bêtes noires* were the self-satisfied bourgeoisie whom he loved to shock, and portentous dignitaries whose bubble he longed to prick with the barb of his satire. He would go to the country often and spend months absorbed by his studies or his poetry, which he gradually came to devote to lampoonery. There were some people who could not be kept in order, he said, or admonished except in this way. He considered that a man 'could not write with life unless he were heated by revenge; for to make a satire without resentments, upon the cold notions of philosophy, was as if a man would in cold blood cut men's throats who had never offended him'. Though engagingly frank, he was not always truthful. He considered a narrow-minded adherence to the truth to be a bourgeois virtue, which he despised accordingly. He admitted that he often put lies in his 'libels' as ornaments, which 'could not be spared without spoiling the beauty of the poems'. He would get carried away by his loathing of the pompous, the pretentious and the smug. He would stop at nothing in his lust for their blood.

After his death, it was said of him in an oration in the theatre delivered as a preface to his play *Valentinian*:

> As sharply could he wound, as sweetly engage,
> As soft his love, and as divine his rage.
> He charmed the tenderest virgins to delight
> And with his style did fiercest blockheads fright.
> Some beauties here I see –
> Though now demure, have felt his powerful charms,
> And languished in the circle of his arms.
> But for ye fops, his satire reached ye all,
> Under his lash your whole vast herd did fall.

His most singular characteristic, of course, was his fascination with and for women. He was cruel to them, both during and after their intrigues. Somehow, though, his charm continued to bind them to him as admirers and friends. In Nathaniel Lee's *Princess of Cleves* the lead character, Duke Nemours, in his 'fury of wine and fury of women' was confidently believed to represent Rochester, Lee's patron. He seduces a lady, Tournon.

TOURNON: Undone, undone! Will your sinful grace never give over? Will you never leave ruining of bodies and damning of souls? What have you done?

NEMOURS: No harm, pretty rogue, no harm. Nay, prithee leave blubbering.

TOURNON: 'Tis 'blubbering' now, plain blubbering; but before you had your will 'twas another tone, – 'Why, madam, do you waste those precious tears? Each falling drop shines like an orient pearl and sets a gaiety on the face of sorrow.'

Nemours cares little, 'for never was a woman mine once, but was mine always'.

Etherege's play is about Dorimant's use and abuse of women, which in the end is neatly countered by the women, leaving him helpless in the arms of the heroine. In the first act, we witness his casual cruelty when he declares, 'Next to the coming to a good understanding with a new mistress, I love a quarrel with an old one. But the Devil's in't, there has been such a calm in my affairs of late, I have not had the pleasure of making a woman so much as break her fan, to be sullen, or forswear herself, these three days.' Rochester could never cope with close relationships, least of all marriage. All his attachments collapsed under their own weight. 'The cloy of all pleasure, the luggage of life, Is the best that can be said for a very good wife!' He was walking in the street in London once when a dog bit him. He rounded on the animal and snapped, 'I wish you were married and living in the country!' In the play Dorimant encourages his young friend Bellair to marry his beloved, with the sole intention of seducing her afterwards himself.

DORIMANT: She's a discreet maid, and I believe nothing can corrupt her but a husband.

MEDLEY: A husband?

DORIMANT: Yes, a husband. I have known many women make a difficulty of losing a maidenhead, who have afterwards made none of making a cuckold.

Rochester's egalitarian attitudes embraced his women as enthusiastically as he did. Though exhilarated by his amours with some of the grandest ladies in the land he was as happy, if not happier, courting the lowest. In the play Dorimant receives a letter. Medley looks at it and sneers, 'The very scrawl and spelling of a true-bred whore,' to which Dorimant replies with satisfaction, 'I know the hand. The style is admirable, I assure you.' As Miss Hobart had said, 'All his experience is with the commonest trollops in town. He completely lost all judgement long ago.' But he never possessed any judgement. It had not occurred to him that there was very much scope for differentiation. His only criteria were a beguiling appearance and an entertaining character. He made no secret of his dalliance with strumpets. At least they were uncomplicated and it was a common pastime among the nobility; even the King had no qualms about tossing a few coins to an obliging young lady, and almost any young lady would oblige. Rochester's preference was for the least socially distinguished.

In *The Rover, Part II* Aphra Behn's Willmore, the Rochester character, falls in love with La Nuche, a famed whore who may represent Elizabeth Barry. Certainly, she played the part in the opening performance shortly after Rochester's death. Beaumond tells Willmore of 'a beauty here in town' but declines to give her name, explaining, 'it is a name too cheaply known And she that owns it may be as cheaply purchased'.

WILLMORE: Hah! Cheaply purchased too. I languish for her.
BEAUMOND: Aye, there's the devil on't. She is — a whore —
WILLMORE: Ah, what a charming sound that mighty word bears.
BEAUMOND: Damn her, she'll be thine or anybody's.
WILLMORE: I die for her —
BEAUMOND: Then for her qualities —
WILLMORE: No more — ye gods, I ask no more.
           Be she fair and much a whore, — come let's to her.

To Rochester the fact that everyone knew of his proclivities was a matter of the greatest indifference. He never spared his reputation; indeed, he seems to have relished smearing it. He was driven compulsively to cock snooks at all accepted forms of behaviour, and at those who accepted them. He was convinced that everyone had the same faults as he. He scorned the hypocrisy of those too timid to do as they pleased, or who did as they pleased with the craven pretence that they did not. His reputation accordingly was dreadful. Much of it was unjustified, but he took no steps to correct the record. Etherege's Dorimant also gives off a faint reek of sulphur. He is told that one woman 'thinks you an arrant *Devil*: should she see you, on my conscience she would look if you had not a cloven foot!' Rochester revelled in his disrepute. He wrote 'Régime de Vivre' about himself. It has been suggested that someone else wrote it about him, and also that Rochester wrote it about someone else, but the preponderance of opinion is that it was shameless self-mockery. Damning himself was a favourite occupation.

> I rise at eleven, I dine about two,
> I get drunk before seven, and the next thing I do,
> I send for my whore, when for fear of a clap,
> I spend in her hand, and I spew in her lap;
> Then we quarrel and scold, till I fall fast asleep,
> When the bitch growing bold, to my pocket does creep.
> Then slyly she leaves me, and to revenge the affront,
> At once she bereaves me of money and cunt.
> If by chance then I wake, hot headed and drunk,
> What a coil do I make for the loss of my punk!
> I storm, and I roar, and I fall in a rage.
> And missing my whore, I bugger my page.

Then crop-sick all morning I rail at my men,
And in bed I lie yawning till eleven again.

Rochester disdained common ideals of decency and good behaviour as sheer pretence. He was a moral anarchist who would not stoop to petty sham, hence the painful clarity of some of his verse. The French philosopher Pierre Bayle called him 'One of those atheists who live according to their principles, for he submersed himself in the most frightening excesses of drunkenness and lewdness'. In *The Princess of Cleves* Duke Nemours insists that what sets a gentleman apart from the crowd is his lack of dissimulation. When 'two or three well-bred fops' find fault with his obscenity he replies, 'Why, 'tis the way of ye all. Only you sneak with it under your cloaks like tailors and barbers; and I, as a gentleman should do, walk with it in my hand.' Rochester always walked with it in his hand.

5

'Whether the boy fucked you, or I the boy'
Sex

That Rochester should write a satire on man, I am not surprised: it is the business of the libertine to degrade his species, and debase the dignity of human nature, and thereby destroy the most efficacious incitements to lovely and laudable actions.

Joseph Wharton, 'An Essay on the Writings of Pope', 1782

Much of Rochester's satire was devoted to the folly of fops, men of high social and low intellectual pretensions, who made themselves absurd in outlandish clothing that they thought chic. Being groomed did not make a man a fool. Dorimant says in Act I of Etherege's *The Man of Mode*, 'I love to be well dressed, sir, and think it no scandal to my understanding.' Sir Fopling Flutter, the man of mode himself, was a fool, with gloves up to his elbows, a periwig 'more exactly curled than a ladies head newly dressed for a ball' and an affected lisp. Rochester despised them for their folly. 'That a man's excellency should lie in neatly tying of a ribbon or a cravat!' Dorimant snorts. Rochester was outraged by the way so many young women preferred the attention of fops to that of wits. Irritatingly, fops tended to be rich and successful with women, and they wormed their way into positions of influence at Court. He admired 'wits', who were not merely amusing but sensitive and intelligent. They were 'clever', a word which had not yet taken on its present pejorative meaning in England. Like many clever men Rochester had a weakness for a pretty halfwit, and was bitterly disappointed when she preferred her male counterpart. There are many hints in his work of his resentment of the common female prejudice in favour of men who could boast of what was between their legs rather than of what was between their ears. It was with a sense of personal outrage that he wrote 'A Familiar Dialogue betwixt Strephon and Sylvia'. 'Sylvia, ne'er despise my love For Colin's

mightier dart,' implores Strephon. 'To *fools* such *monsters* Nature sends
For want of brains, – a dull amends.' But Sylvia taunts him with an
unwelcome compromise ('swive' means fuck):

> you methinks, sweet sir, should know,
> 'Tis *substance* that prevails below.
> To each then his just dole I'll give,
> With you I'll talk, with him I'll swive.
> Your wit shall raise my strong desires,
> And he shall quench my raging fires.
> Thus both your merits I'll unite,
> You shall my ear, he please my appetite.

Strephon can only splutter:

> This said, with speed the cursed bitch retired,
> And left me with just indignation fired;
> But taught in women's prostituted schools
> That men of wit but pimp for well-hung fools.

Harry Killigrew once wrote to Rochester in the country:

In the meantime your Lordship has been extremely wanting here, to make
friends at the Customs House where has been lately, unfortunately, seized a
box of those leather instruments [dildos] your Lordship carried down one
of. But these barbarian farmers [that is, customs officers – to whom the
right to collect excise duties was farmed out], prompted by the villainous
instigation of their wives, voted them prohibited goods so that they were
burnt without mercy – notwithstanding Sedley and I made *two* journeys into
the city in their defence. By this, my Lord you will see what things are done
in your absence, and then pray consider whether it is fit for you to be
blowing of coals in the country when there is a revenge due to the ashes of
these martyrs. Your Lordship is chosen general in this war between the
Ballers and the farmers; nor shall peace ever be made till they grant us our
wine and our dildos *custom free*.

There were two types of leather dildo in use at the time. They were
made in France and were tastefully decorated with pink or red tips.
One was solid, the other hollow and used as a penis extension. We
are not told which sort Harry meant, but Samuel Butler, mourning the

same event, seems to have thought it was the latter. In his offering, 'Dildoides' he wrote:

> Such a sad tale prepare to hear,
> As claims from either sex a tear.
> Twelve dildoes (means for the support
> Of aged lechers of the Court)
> Were lately burnt by impious hand...

Whichever it was, if Rochester *did* take one of them home to Adderbury, how was he going to use it, with whom, and why?

The question is not simply prurient. A substantial part of the poet's work is devoted to impotence and sexual inadequacy. Apart from a general air of confusion over sex, he was by no means satisfied with his sexual endowment, whether its size or its efficiency. In 'The Fall' he begged: 'Be not you so severe to say You love me for a frailer part.' He was clearly in a spiteful mood over the question of physical adequacy when he wrote (in the song that begins 'Oh what a damned age we do live in'):

> Besides, the damned tailors of France
> To Great Britain's defamation
> Have made better pintles by chance
> Than the gods of the English nation.
>
> But now there's nothing will do,
> Their cunts are grown so wide,
> Except with a French leather dildo
> They get on each other and ride.

In 'Tunbridge Wells' he is said to have written a damning indictment of women for whom the normal male endowment was not enough, blaming it on their own bulk in that area that made it impossible to penetrate:

> Thrice blessed be he who dildo did invent,
> To ram the neighbouring hole to fundament:
> Which may be lengthened, thickened in its measure,
> And used as lecherous trulls' pleasure:
> For ne'er was bulk or stomach given to tarses,
> Either to fill or swell such foggy arses.

Restoration poets used 'arse' for vagina when they wanted a rhyme for 'tarse' (penis).

Sex confused Rochester. One particular lament, 'The Imperfect Enjoyment', is clearly the product of personal experience, despite its derivation from Ovid. It was the misfortune of being so overcome by rapture that he was unable to do service to his lady.

> Naked, she lay clasped in my longing arms,
> I, filled with love and she all over charms,
> Both equally inspired with eager fire,
> Melting through kindness, flaming in desire:
> With arms, legs, lips, close clinging to embrace,
> She clips me to her breast, and sucks me to her face.
>
> The nimble tongue (love's lesser lightning) played
> Within my mouth, and to my thoughts conveyed
> Swift orders, that I should prepare to throw
> The all-dissolving thunderbolt below.
> My fluttering soul, sprung with the pointed kiss
> Hangs hovering o'er her balmy brinks of bliss.
>
> But whilst her busy hand would guide that part
> Which should convey my soul up to her heart,
> In liquid raptures I *dissolve* all o'er,
> Melt into sperm, and spend at every pore;
> A touch from any part of her had done't,
> Her hand, her foot, her very look's a cunt.
>
> Smiling, she chides in a kind murmuring noise
> And from her body wipes the clammy joys;
> When with a thousand kisses wand'ring o'er
> My panting bosom, and – 'Is there then no more?'
> She cries. 'All this to love and rapture's due;
> Must we not pay a debt to pleasure too?'

This particular embarrassment was caused by overexcitement due to love as opposed to mere lust. It helps to explain his preference for women who conducted their affairs in a businesslike fashion. And he was to suffer impotence in his last years.

There was unmistakably something of Don Juan about him. Perhaps those who say the Don Juan character is trying to prove his own sexual adequacy are right. Rochester needed to conquer and, having conquered, to lay waste. In Lee's *Princess of Cleves*, Nemours exclaims, 'Willing! That willingness spoils all, my dear, my honey, my jewel. It palls the appetite like sack at meals. Give me the smart, disdainful she that, like brisk champagne or sprightly burgundy, makes me smack my lips after she's down and long for t'other glass'. When the virginal heroine falls for him, Nemours exults, 'She loves, she loves, and I'm the happy man,' but he is already beginning to lose interest and her attempts to keep him become a cloying irritation. Rochester wrote a verse that was originally called 'The Expostulation', which later appeared in his play *Valentinian*. A nymph cries:

> Injurious charmer of my vanquished heart,
> Canst thou feel love, and yet no pity know?
> Since of myself from thee I cannot part
> Invent some gentle way to let me go.
> > For what with joy thou did'st obtain,
> > And I with more did give,
> > In time will make thee false and vain,
> > And me unfit to live.

Deep inside he was fascinated and not a little mystified by the anatomy of romance. Despite his wide experience, he could never quite believe what was happening. He wrote quizzically:

> Strange how it looks; methinks it smells like ling.
> It has a beard so sad. The mouth's all raw;
> The strangest creature that I ever saw —
> Are these the beasts that keep men in such awe?

As time passed and Rochester became disenchanted with the world, he became disenchanted with women. Syphilis and the treatment for it probably coloured his judgement, but as he grew older his interest in romance began to dwindle. It never completely left him, but there appeared in him a deep ambivalence. The dominant theme of his work changed from sex to malice, with satires on his enemies, friends, society, himself and, ultimately, all mankind. He may have become a misanthropist, but he was by nature no misogynist. He had loved women, all of them impartially, though he deplored their mercenary streak. As Willmore announces in *The Rover, Part II*: 'a pox on't, you women have all a certain jargon, or gibberish, peculiar to yourselves; of value, rate, present, interest, settlement, advantage, price, maintenance, and the devil and all of fopperies, which in plain terms signify ready money, by way of fine before entrance, so that an honest well-meaning merchant of love finds no credit amongst ye, without his bill of lading'.

Rochester was never keen to restrict his affections to any particular woman, but many were lifelong friends and he had high respect for their judgment. In a fragment of verse he assumes the voice of a woman to protest against the way her sex were condescended to by men:

> What vain unnecessary things are men,
> How well we do without 'em. Tell me then
> Whence comes that mean submissiveness we find
> This ill-bred age has wrought on womankind...
>
> At the appearance of an unknown face
> Up steps the arrogant pretending ass,
> Pulling by the elbow his companion Huff,
> Cries, 'Lookee, by God that wench is well enough,
> Fair and well-shaped, good lips and teeth – 'twill do:
> She shall be tawdry for a month or two
> At my expense; be rude and take upon her,
> Show her contempt of quality and honour,
> And with the general fate of errant woman,
> Be very proud awhile, then very common.'
>
> Ere bear this scorn, I'd be shut up at home,
> Content with humouring myself alone...
>
> Then after all you find, whate'er we say,
> Things must go on in their lewd natural way.
> Besides the beastly men we daily see
> Can please themselves alone as well as we.

In his early days of braggadocio he had thought that he understood the opposite sex. In *The Princess of Cleves* Nemours announces, 'I know the souls of women better than themselves. I know the ingredients that make 'em up, all to loose grains, the subtlest volatile atoms, with the whole mish-mash of their composition.' In later years Rochester was no longer under any such illusion. He had seen what formidable opponents they were. Inevitably he was to meet his own Nemesis. So long as a girl had loved him more than he loved the girl he was impervious, and Rochester really loved no one. Then the unthinkable happened. He met Elizabeth Barry, an actress for whom he fell utterly, whom he loved as much as or more than she loved him. In his usual way he was persistently unfaithful, and was shocked and incredulous when she retaliated in kind. His fatal flaw was a yearning to be challenged. His eventual reward for past mischief was the agonising end to the only relationship in his life that ever mattered.

His was a complex make-up. He was notoriously vain, but knew it and turned it into a joke against himself. At the same time he was capable of great humility. Like many actors his vanity was based perhaps less on self-satisfaction than on self-dissatisfaction. Etherege made a joke of it. When Bellair tells him, 'I am confident she loves no man but you', Dorimant answers, 'The good fortune were enough to make me vain, but that I am in my nature modest.' Surprisingly, Rochester *was* by nature a modest man. Many times in his work and in his letters to Harry Savile and to his wife he castigated his own folly. He confessed his own inadequacies as lover, statesman and poet but still delighted in his camp charade of self-adoration, not realising, or not caring, that those about him were completely taken in by it.

His effeminate appearance and style were not mere affectation, however. He had a strong female streak in him. Much of his work was written from a woman's viewpoint, such as 'The Platonic Lady':

> I love a youth will give me leave
> His body in my arms to wreath;
> To press him gently and to kiss,
> To sigh and look with eyes that wish.

His insight into the heart of a woman in this poem is so deep that many have attributed it to Rochester's passion for another man, although it is quite clearly written in a woman's voice. In view of his background, with an absent father and fiercely strong mother, it is perhaps unsurprising that he was bisexual. There was no stigma. Recreational homosexuality was a popular pastime at Court. Sodomy

96

was punishable by death, but no one took the slightest notice. It was a camp epoch. Young men at Court postured effetely and with abandon. In *The Man of Mode* when Medley enters, a scene takes place that would still startle an unsuspecting audience:

MEDLEY: Dorimant, my life, my joy, my *darling* sin! How do'st thou? (*Embraces him*)

ORANGE-WOMAN: Lord, what a filthy trick these men have got of kissing one another! (*She spits*)

Gentlemen had taken to embracing one another openly and with evident enthusiasm, much to the disgust of the lower orders. It was not merely a fashionable pretence. Buggery was rife in London, especially at Court. Pepys wrote, 'Sir J. Mennes and Mr. Batten both say that buggery is now almost grown as common among our gallants as in Italy, and that the very pages of the town begin to complain of their masters for it. But blessed be God, I do not to this day know what is the meaning of this sin, nor which is the agent nor which the patient.' In *The Princess of Cleves* Nemours oozes desire for the flesh of either sex. He caresses a male character Poltrot on stage so intimately that Poltrot is left wriggling to control his erection. Nemours warns another man, 'Be gone and no more of this provoking discourse, lest ravishing should follow thee at the heels and spoil my sober design.' He is not making a camp joke. He means it.

Rochester, naturally, made it clear that he had no scruples about homosexual sodomy as an adjunct to his sexual arsenal:

> Then give me health, wealth, mirth, and wine,
>   And if busy love entrenches,
> There's a sweet soft page of mine
>   Does the trick worth forty wenches.

Nor about incorporating sodomy into troilism:

> Nor shall our love-fits, Chloris, be forgot,
> When each the well-looked linkboy strove t'enjoy,
> And the best kiss was the deciding lot
> Whether the boy fucked you, or I the boy.

And we have already this confession:

97

> I storm, and I roar, and I fall in a rage.
> And missing my whore, I bugger my page.

In 'The Imperfect Enjoyment', on the occasion of a drooping member, he referred in his fury to:

> This dart of love, who's piercing point oft tried,
> With virgin blood *ten thousand* maids has dyed;
> Stiffly resolved, 'twould carelessly invade
> Woman or man, nor aught its fury stayed.

He composed a charming poem based upon a work by the French poet Ronsard in the style of Anacreon, the libertine poet of the sixth century BC:

> Vulcan, contrive me such a cup
> As Nestor used of old;
> Show all thy skill to trim it up,
> Damask it round with gold.
>
> . . .
>
> But carve thereon a spreading vine
> Then add two lovely boys;
> Their limbs in amorous fold entwine,
> The type of future joys.
>
> Cupid and Bacchus my saints are,
> May drink and love still reign;
> With wine I wash away my cares,
> And then to cunt again.

The only departures from the more solemn original are his ultimate destination announced in the last line and the call for two lovely boys. One of Rochester's later works, his play *Valentinian*, was based closely on a drama originally written by the Jacobean playwright John Fletcher. Rochester's version follows the original in that Valentinian loves Lucina, who is raped and commits suicide. Rochester then departs completely from the blueprint, making Valentinian fall in love with a boy, Lycias the eunuch. Act V, scene 5 opens with Valentinian, on a couch with the youth, declaiming: 'Oh let me press these balmy lips all day, And bathe my love-scorched soul in thy moist kisses,' only to declare that he does so 'To the dear memory of my Lucina'.

In the last years of his life Rochester had a long relationship with his valet, one Jean Baptiste de Belle-Fasse, who seems to have been his catamite, and whom he delighted in calling 'Mr Baptist' as a passing insult to the Church. The valet was also a singer. (The similarities between Rochester and Byron became uncannily consistent.) In November 1679 he sent Mr Baptist as a present to his friend Henry Savile in Paris, introducing him in a letter:

The news I have to send, and the sort alone which could be so to you, are things which I dare not trust to this pretty fool the bearer, whom I heartily recommend to your favour and protection and whose qualities will recommend him more. And truly if it might suit with your character at your times of leisure to make Mr Baptist's acquaintance, the happy consequence would be singing, and in which your excellence might have a share not unworthy the greatest ambassadors, nor to be despised even by a cardinal-legate. The greatest and gravest of this Court of both sexes have tasted his beauties, and I'll assure you Rome gains upon us here in this point mainly, and there is no part of the Plot carried with so much secrecy and vigour as this.

What Mr Baptist was sent to France to provide, and what both sexes had tasted at Court, was not his singing. Singing seems to have been used in a coded sense, to indicate a less ethereal activity. If this is correct, it is interesting in view of Rochester's usual frankness that he felt obliged to use code. But buggery was unlawful, and the information could be disastrous if it fell into the wrong hands. The 'Plot' that he referred to was the Popish Plot in which allegations of sodomy had been made, and the Jesuits and the Italian nobles were widely believed to commit habitual buggery. It is always possible that Rochester was simply being frivolous *pour épater les bourgeois*, but the theme of homosexuality is so consistent that it seems to be genuine. In any case, if others were doing it with apparent enjoyment he would have felt it his duty to join in.

Henry Savile, to whom he sent the boy singer, was Rochester's closest friend. They were either together or corresponding until almost the moment of Rochester's death. Clarendon called Savile 'a young man of wit and incredible confidence and presumption. He was hard drinking, attractive and irresponsible.' He and Rochester met at Court in 1665 when Savile, then twenty-three, became a groom of the bedchamber to the Duke of York. He came from a prominent Royalist family in Yorkshire and was the younger brother of George Savile, Marquess of Halifax. Although somewhat stout, he was a gallant lover and duellist. In December 1674, Savile, naming Rochester as his second, challenged the detested Lord Mulgrave to a duel. The King's men frustrated it. He was also locked up in the Tower for carrying a challenge from the Duke of Buckingham to Sir William Coventry. In November 1665, while the Court was at Oxford avoiding the plague, he had a *grande affaire* with the Duchess of York – though the grandeur was diminished by having to share her with her new Master of the Horse.

In July of 1679, not long after a visit to Madam Fourcard's establishment for curing the pox, Savile was sent to France on a delicate mission for the King. It was an attempt to smooth over a row between the Duchess of Cleveland and Ann, Countess of Sussex, her daughter by the King. He acquitted himself well and thereafter enjoyed a distinguished career as a diplomat. Despite insulting the Duke of York so often in 1675–6 that he was dismissed from Court, in 1679 he was finally sent to replace Montagu, the disgraced Ambassador in Paris. From then on he saw little of his friend Rochester. He died in 1687 at the age of forty-five after an operation, having been ill with syphilis for at least ten years.

The correspondence between Harry and Rochester is revealing and discloses Rochester's true character more completely than any other evidence. All the rest is disguised or disfigured by spite, affection, rumour and, principally, his own posing. He never posed for Harry, and it is through Harry's eyes that we can see the sad, ill, spiteful but kindly and philosophical man that Rochester really was.

6

'I would send for my good Lord Rochester'
Courtship and Courtier

The fact is that the muse of Rochester resembles nothing so much
as a beautiful child which has wantonly rolled itself in the mud, and
which has grown so dirty that the ordinary wayfarer would rather
pass it hurriedly by, than do justice to its native charms.

Sir Edmund Gosse, 1873

In April 1667, while Elizabeth stayed in the country, Rochester went
back to the bacchanals. But he had little time to enjoy his bachelordom,
his longing to be 'constantly tried', for he suddenly found himself
absorbed in picking up the pieces of a grief-stricken King. Frances
Stewart had suddenly eloped with the Duke of Richmond. She had
abandoned all hopes of the throne and was tired of the constant
pressure on her virtue from the King and all the others. Many thought
she had surrendered long before. As early as 1666 Pepys wrote, 'Mr
Pierce able to tell me of all the business of the Court – the amours
and the mad doings that are there – how for certain, Mrs Stewart doth
do everything now with the King that a mistress should do.' Like
many of Pepys's reports, however, its accuracy is suspect.

The King was first of all horrified at the elopement, then bitterly
upset. Usually his attachment to his mistresses was not profound, but
Frances was different. He had been paying court to her for five years,
and now had abjectly failed. She returned all the jewellery that he had
given her, which was ladylike and bitterly hurtful. Charles needed to
be cheated to believe in a woman's love. He voiced his indignation to
his sister. 'You may think me ill natured, but if you consider how hard
a thing 'tis to swallow an injury done by a person I had so much
tenderness for, you will be in some degree understanding the resentment I use towards her.' The next year Frances caught smallpox. The
King tried not to gloat. Happily, despite some damage to one eye, she

was left unmarked, and he eventually confided to his sister that the girl's illness had made him forget all that had gone before. 'I cannot hinder myself from wishing her very well,' he confessed. The Duke of Richmond was sent to Denmark as ambassador, and Frances went with him. Richmond died young and his widow never remarried. She lived alone with cats and cards, her sex life remaining the subject of wild speculation until she too died.

Rochester helped look after the grieving monarch until he cheered up and found something else to amuse him. The Earl was once again free to roam the Court, directing his amorous energies quite impartially at those who passed his way. He stalked the maids of honour with indefatigable charm. He hid a poem in one victim's prayer book, composed after Malherbe:

Fling this useless book away,
And presume no more to pray:
Heaven is just, and can bestow
Mercy on none but those that mercy show.

Phyllis, to calm the angry powers,
And save my soul as well as yours,
Relieve poor mortals from despair,
And justify the gods that made you fair:
And in those bright and charming eyes
Let pity first appear, then love;
That we by easy steps may rise
Through all the joys on earth to those above.

There were few chaste girls at Court; those that were seldom remained so for long. With a man of Rochester's looks they were in danger, but with a man of Rochester's talent for poetry they were doomed. He would write them little lyrics of reproach, some of them very sly. He would mock chastity and play on every girl's terror, the swift passage of time.

Phyllis be gentler, I advise,
Make up for time misspent,
When beauty on its death-bed lies,
'Tis high time to repent.

Such is the malice of your fate,
   That makes you old so soon,
Your pleasure ever comes too late,
   How early e'er begun.

Think what a wretched thing is she
   Whose stars contrive in spite
The morning of her love should be
   Her fading beauty's night.

Then if to make your ruin more
   You'll peevishly be coy,
Die with the scandal of a whore,
   And never know the joy.

Now that he was back he could frolic unrestrained with his friends, with the exception of the Duke of Buckingham, who was imprisoned in the Tower of London for duelling. The King loathed the activity and was determined to stamp it out. Anyone who became involved in an encounter, even in the role of second or challenge-bearer, would find himself in the Tower. Etherege, Savile and Rochester all got into trouble for fighting, as did most of their contemporaries. But Buckingham had been much more than second or challenge-bearer – as we have seen, in 1667 he had killed the Earl of Shrewsbury.

The Duke and Lady Shrewsbury had had a long affair. That alone surprised everyone, since both lovers' history of dependability was patchy. The romance would have trickled on happily undisturbed, but Lord Shrewsbury, who had overlooked his wife's behaviour many times in the past, decided at last that he should do something. He called the Duke of Buckingham out, and Buckingham killed him. Duelling, though popular with all but the King, was not often seriously meant. To vindicate himself a party needed only to draw the smallest amount of blood, or even merely strike. Killing one's opponent, unless there was a very deep grudge, was thought to be a little excessive, but Buckingham was always excessive. The object of their affections was present at the scene disguised as a pageboy, watching and holding Buckingham's horse as her lover slaughtered her husband. After the fight the victor took his mistress home. He was confronted by a seething Duchess, who informed him that she would not tolerate the presence of 'that woman' under her roof. The Duke agreed that she was quite right. That was why he had ordered a carriage to take the Duchess to her mother's. After a suitable interval he was pardoned by the King, whereon he caused even greater offence by having his and Lady Shrewsbury's bastard son christened in Westminster Abbey and bestowing a spurious title on him. This was considered by the decorous to strike a jarring note.

Rochester was a bosom companion of Buckingham's and was involved in a number of duels himself, more or less half-heartedly. He did his best to emulate the grotesque excesses of his mentor – and his senior by nearly twenty years – but he could not compete with him in lust and homicide, only in poetry and thirst, and there the competition was very close run.

Rochester's drinking was spiralling into a new dimension, as he announced in another anacreontic (here 'first' means thirsty):

> The heavens carouse each day a cup,
> No wonder Atlas holds them up.
> The trees suck up the earth and ground,
> And in their brown bowls drink around.
> The sea too, whom the salt makes dry,
> His greedy thirst to satisfy
> Ten thousand rivers drinks, and then
> Grows drunk, and spews 'em up again.
> The sun (and who so right as he)
> Sits up all night to drink the sea.
> The moon quaffs up the sun, her brother,
> And wishes she could tope another.
> Everything fuddles: then that I,
> Is't any reason, should be dry?
> Well, I'll be content to thirst,
> But too much drink shall make me first.

His prodigious thirst had not been slaked by the summer of 1667. He was seen drinking startling quantities in the company of Sedley at the merry-house at Epsom run by his friends Lord Buckhurst and Nell Gwyn. It was, of course, the ubiquitous and disapproving Pepys who wrote, 'to the town, to the King's Head; and hear that my Lord Buckhurst and Nelly are lodged at the next house, and Sir Charles

Sedley with them; and keep a merry house. Poor girl! I pity her; but more the loss of her at the King's House [theatre].'

On 5 October 1667 Lords Rochester and Mulgrave took their seats in the House of Lords. They were both twenty and there was a serious constitutional argument as to whether or not they were entitled to sit. There were fierce objections from the peers, but it was a mark of the distinction of both men that the King was prepared to overrule in their favour the minimum age of twenty-one. He quashed the peers' objections and ordered that the two should be appointed to their places. Mulgrave was the only one of the Court Wits who was younger than Rochester and there was great bitterness between them. Rochester only ever made scant use of his right to sit in Parliament, whereas Mulgrave went on to become a prominent statesman and was rewarded with the dukedom, ironically, of Buckingham, after the death of George Villiers.

John Sheffield, third Earl of Mulgrave, was a statesman and, later, patron of Dryden, he himself writing bombastic poetry in heroic couplets. He served under the King and remained in great favour until 1682, when he incurred Charles's displeasure by courting his niece Princess Anne, and was banished from Court. He was notoriously arrogant, his face contorted by a fixed sneer, and earned himself the nickname King John, or 'Bajazet', after the haughty Turkish Sultan who was captured in 1402 and depicted in Marlowe's *Tamburlaine the Great, 1590*. In 1675 Rochester's friend George Etherege used the name publicly in his spiteful 'Letter from Ephelia to Bajazet'. Rochester wrote an equally spiteful supposed reply, 'A Very Heroical Epistle in Answer to Ephelia'. After that Mulgrave was known as Bajazet for many years. He considered himself to be an outstanding poet, lover and soldier and was thoroughly unpopular with the Court Wits. Rochester too, in his later years, when he was ill and tired of his wayward life, began to think seriously about politics and was toying with the idea of applying for a state appointment, but he lacked the necessary determination and ingratiating manners. He could never have brought himself to fawn on dignitaries whom he despised. He attended the House of Lords no more than sporadically.

In 1667 the King and Clarendon, the Lord Chancellor, fell out. Clarendon had been with Charles ever since he was a boy in exile and still treated him as a child, which perhaps was not inappropriate. He would rebuke the King publicly for his loose living and neglect of duty. What was infinitely worse was that Charles had heard that Clarendon had been instrumental in persuading Frances Stewart to run off with the Duke of Richmond. The Chancellor may well have done this in an effort to get the monarch to concentrate on matters of state. He did his best for Charles, with the result that there was a great deal of acrimony against him throughout the Court circle. The courtiers objected to his encouraging the King to fritter away his time on his duty to his country, when he should have been making merry and doing his duty to them. Clarendon in turn never bothered to conceal his contempt for the feckless aristocracy who lolled about Whitehall getting in the way of proper governance.

The King had now had time to think the situation through. He had conceived his own ideas on government, which did not coincide with Clarendon's. His principal grievance was that Clarendon was failing to control Parliament sufficiently to produce money for the King's coffers. The Lord Chancellor was generally unpopular with the nation for marrying his daughter to the Duke of York. It was seen as a motive for Clarendon's securing the King's marriage to a barren Queen, thus putting his daughter closer to succession to the crown. He also had to face a powerful group of opponents in Yorkshire, led as always by the Duke of Buckingham. Furthermore, Barbara Castlemaine and Clarendon loathed each other and, though Charles was never greatly moved by his mistresses' opinions, she did her determined best to pour poison into the ear of the man who had long been Clarendon's only support.

Sir William Coventry, a commissioner of the Treasury, opened the public attack on the Lord Chancellor. He was supported by the Earl of Arlington, Secretary of State from 1662 to 1674, who always wore an unnecessary plaster over the bridge of his nose to draw attention to a minuscule wound he had suffered for the King in the Civil War. Clarendon's windows in Piccadilly were broken by the mob. The debate was invigorated by Buckingham's wicked impersonation of Clarendon's peculiar walk, using a pair of tongs to demonstrate. Parliament was determined to ruin him. Articles of impeachment were drawn up against him in the Commons, which the Lords refused to ratify on the ground that there had been no treason. The true reason was that the Lords mistrusted the Lower House more than they mistrusted the Lord Chancellor. A protest against the Lords' refusal to ratify the impeachment was signed by a number of peers including Rochester.

It is disquieting that Rochester was so readily prepared to stab his kinsman in the back, the man who had looked after him at Oxford and backed his marriage to Elizabeth. On the face of it he had every reason to help him. However, Clarendon had been heard to make highly derogatory remarks about Rochester's father. References to Henry's haughty and ambitious nature, stupidity, cowardice, broken promises and lack of honour or integrity were not forgotten. Clarendon had grown too used to speaking his mind, and Rochester had not forgiven him. Although he never knew the father who had abandoned him as a child, he was proud of his daredevil reputation and its contribution to the family's prestige. On this subject his cynicism failed him.

The King halted the proceedings for impeachment by suggesting to Clarendon the compromise of leaving the country and living in exile. As the Lord Chancellor passed beneath Barbara Castlemaine's window he saw her in her dressing-gown, gloating over him, together with Arlington, her great friend and protégé. He looked up, fixed her with an adamantine stare and said, 'Pray remember that if you live, you will grow *old*.' It was a satisfying irony that not long afterwards Barbara's own tenure in office was coming to an end, and it was under the same window that the King had a slightly unnecessary ballad sung to her, beginning with the words, 'Alinda's growing old ...' One wonders who composed it.

Rochester celebrated Clarendon's exit with:

> Pride, lust, ambition and the people's hate,
> The Kingdom's broker, ruin of the State,
> Dunkirk's sad loss, divider of the fleet,
> Tangier's compounder for a barren sheet:
> This shrub of gentry married to the Crown,
> His daughter to the heir, is tumbled down.
> The grand despiser of the nobles lies
> Grovelling in dust, a just sacrifice.

The Lord Chancellor's fall prompted intemperate joy at Court. The air of disapproval given off by the *éminence grise* as he tried to sober their leader and reproved them for their indolence and dissipation was not missed. Life at Court grew if possible more disorderly. No one was left to chide the King out of his self-indulgent torpor. One who tried was Tom Killigrew, father of Harry, and a venerable actor and playhouse proprietor who had been intimate with the monarch all his life. Tom, who had been in exile with Charles, was responsible for building the original Theatre Royal in Drury Lane, and was a privileged friend. In 1663 he became Master of the Revels. He was the Court jester, and by virtue of that office one of the few who were allowed to tell the King what he really thought. He would nag the King, telling him that there was an honest, able man at Court, at present out of employment, who could mend all things, and his name was Charles Stuart, but the honest, able man was busy with other interests. He gained no satisfaction from the exercise of power and simply found it irksome. On one occasion, Charles was with Rochester and other nobles who had been drinking the best part of the night. Tom Killigrew came in. 'Now,' said the King, 'we shall hear of our faults.' 'No, faith,' Killigrew rebuked him, 'I don't care to trouble my head with that which all the town talks of.' Indeed, the town did. So did Andrew Marvell, who wrote:

> He spends all his days
> In running to plays
> When in his shop he should be poring;
> And wastes all his nights
> In his constant delights
> Of revelling, drinking and whoring.

The town was talking so much that Charles tried to have the coffee houses closed. He was dissuaded.

As a result of Clarendon's departure, Buckingham won rapid advancement. He, Clifford, Arlington, Ashby and Lauderdale formed a powerful group round the King, known by the acronym of their names as the 'Cabal'. Buckingham remained a member for some years until once again he disgraced himself. His first manoeuvre was to try to persuade the King to divorce the Queen, marry again and beget an heir, but Charles would have nothing to do with such a dishonourable scheme.

For Rochester life went on the same, most commonly drunk and enfolded in the arms of a woman, nevertheless generally maintaining good terms with his wife. His letters to her took on a sort of jovial good fellowship that was occasionally touched by asperity. In May of 1668 he wrote a friendly gossiping letter which would have been of great interest to her, containing as it did a tit-bit about her disgraceful grandfather Lord Hawley.

You know not how much I am pleased when I hear from you; if you did you would be so obliging to write oftener to me. I do seriously with all my heart wish myself with you, and am endeavouring every day to get away from this place which I am so weary of, that I may be said rather to languish than live in it. There is no news, but that the Duchess of Richmond will lose an eye, the Duchess of Monmouth has put out her thigh, my Lord Hawley is to be married to my Lady Munnings. He drinks puppy dog water to make himself handsome, but she, they say, having heard he had a clap, has refused to enter into conjugal bonds till she be better assured of his soundness.

Puppy-dog water was applied externally to improve the complexion. The substance is commonly understood to have been puppies' urine, but in 1690 Mary Evelyn in her publication *Mundus Muliebris* described it as a mixture of wine and roast puppy-dog – almost as unattractive as the cat-dung and vinegar that was used as a depilatory.

It may be that Rochester was telling the truth when he claimed that he could not escape from the Palace. Although he loved his dissolute life in London, after an extended period he had to get away. Between bouts of conviviality he needed large draughts of rural peace to help him recover. Once restored, his appetite for depravity would be newly refreshed. He admitted that at Brentford on the road back to London, however good his intentions, a devil would enter him, not to leave him until he once again returned home. He often complained how imperious were the constant demands on his time at Court. Doubtless sometimes it was a mere excuse, but not always. As a gentleman of the bedchamber he was expected to be available for any service that the King might require including humouring him, amusing him, plotting with him, procuring women, pacifying women, and being a loyal member of the team. There is an account of a typical meeting between them which was recorded verbatim by the poet Edmund Waller. The occasion was dinner at Rochester's lodgings. Rochester was comparatively sober, said Waller, who noted with approval that he did not try to shine or dominate the company but was simply a most agreeable dinner companion. Late in the evening the King was heard arriving. Rochester told his guests, 'Something has vexed him. He never does me this honour but when he is in an ill-humour.'

THE KING: How the Devil have I got here? The knaves have sold every cloak in the wardrobe.

ROCHESTER: Those knaves are fools. That is a part of dress, which, for their own sakes, your Majesty ought never to be without.

THE KING: Pshaw! I'm vexed.

ROCHESTER: I hate still life – I'm glad of it. Your Majesty is never as entertaining as when...

THE KING: Ridiculous! I believe the English are the most intractable people on earth.

ROCHESTER: I most humbly beg your Majesty's pardon if I presume in that respect...

THE KING: You would find them so if you were in my place and obliged to govern.

ROCHESTER: Were I in your Majesty's place I would not govern at all.

THE KING: How then?

ROCHESTER: I would send for my good Lord Rochester and command him to govern.

THE KING: But the singular modesty of that nobleman!

ROCHESTER: He would certainly conform himself to your Majesty's bright example. How gloriously would the two grand social virtues flourish under his auspices.

THE KING: *O prisca fides!* What can these be?

ROCHESTER: The love of wine and women.

THE KING: God bless your Majesty!

ROCHESTER: These attachments keep the world in good humour and therefore I say they are social virtues. Let the Bishop of Salisbury deny it if he can...

THE KING: He died last night; have you a mind to succeed *him*?

ROCHESTER: On condition that I shall neither be called upon to preach on the thirtieth of January, nor on the twenty-ninth of May [the dates of the execution of King Charles I and the restoration of Charles II].

THE KING: Those conditions are curious ... you object to the first, I suppose because it would be a melancholy subject, but the other...

ROCHESTER: Would be a melancholy subject too.

THE KING: That is too much...

ROCHESTER: Nay, I only mean that the business would be a little too grave for the day. Nothing but the indulgence of the two grand social virtues could be a proper testimony of my joy upon that occasion.

THE KING: Thou art the happiest fellow in my dominions! Let me perish if I do not envy thee thy impudence!

This was his Lordship's business at Court. It is fascinating to watch as he teases the monarch to the very brink and just succeeds in stepping back at the last moment, but it works. He starts with a gloomy, angry king and turns him back with a sorcerer's touch into his usual cheerful self. If he could do that whenever the King was feeling low (and the King often suffered from depression), he more than made up for all his impudence and misbehaviour. However, while he was at Court humouring his monarch he was not at home humouring his wife, and she would grow restless. She was well aware what he was getting up to in London, for the details were helpfully supplied by her mother and her mother's friends. Once, when a period of silence had lasted longer than usual, she sent a letter with a servant to try to extract a reply. He answered with an impromptu poem of great charm, written on her own note, and sent the messenger back with it, 'To his More than Meritorious Wife':

> I am by fate slave to your will,
> And I will be obedient still;
> To show my love I will compose ye,
> For your fair finger's ring, a poesy,
> In which shall be expressed my duty
> And how I'll be forever true t'ye,
> With low-made legs and sugared speeches,
> Yielding to your fair bum the breeches,
> And show myself in all I can
> Your very humble servant, John.

'Low-made legs' are deep bows.

In February of 1668 Dryden was appointed Poet Laureate. Rochester, who was beginning to interest himself in literary affairs, helped to procure the office for him from the King. Until they quarrelled in 1675 he remained a friend of Dryden's, despite his low opinion of the Laureate as a man. He admired his talent, though he criticised him sharply. Dryden's sympathisers accuse Rochester of having bullied him because he resented a commoner showing greater skill than his own. He did indeed write about Dryden's efforts in acid terms, but up to the time of Rochester's death Dryden had written very little that was memorable. At this stage of his career he had published none of the great works for which he was later lionised. What Rochester disapproved of was Dryden's writing to please the public, whom he felt should be ignored. He overlooked the fact that Dryden had to make his living through writing, and the public was his master. The result is that admirers of Dryden have castigated Rochester for being an envious snob and poetaster. It is an unjust criticism. Rochester was never envious and never a snob, and his work could sometimes outshine even the Laureate's.

Matthew Prior, a protégé of the Earl of Dorset, wrote, a little unkindly:

> Sedley indeed and Rochester might write
> For their own credit and their friends' delight,
> Showing how far they could the rest outdo,
> As in their fortunes, so their writings too;
> But should drudge Dryden this example take,
> And Absaloms for empty glory make,
> He'd soon perceive his income scarce enough
> To feed his nostrils with inspiring snuff,
> Starving for meat, nor surfeiting on praise,
> He'd find his brain as barren as his bays.

Rochester was also unimpressed by the oil that Dryden poured over him in return for his help. It was customary to thank a patron in overblown terms, but Dryden's efforts would have left his benefactor feeling a little unwell, or wondering if he was the victim of sarcasm, for there were a number of perceptible barbs, which Rochester would not have missed.

In July 1678 Dryden wrote, 'I find it is not for me to contend in any way with your Lordship, who can write better on the meanest subject than I can on the best.' This has two meanings: the apparent one, and Rochester's tendency to write filth. The letter continued:

My only relief is that what I have written is public [that is, Rochester had no such restraint upon him] and I am so much my own friend as to conceal your Lordship's letter. For that which would have given vanity to any other poet has only given me confusion. You see my Lord how far you have pushed me; I dare not own the honour you have done me, for fear of showing it to my own disadvantage. You are above any incense I can give you [I can't make your work smell better], and have all the happiness of an idle life, joined with the good nature of an active [you are a mere amateur].

There was much more in the same vein.

Rochester's own work had now begun to take a gentler, more lyrical form and some of his verses from this period are among the most exquisite that he wrote. With very few exceptions, however, his poems are not romantic. They all have an ulterior motive or a sudden twist – almost all his love poetry is a barb or a lament. He wrote many of his verses simply for their own beauty, adopting various personae just as he did when sporting a disguise, and acknowledged only a handful of them. Some of the rest achieved wide currency by word of mouth or dissemination in more or less divergent copy-texts, starting at Court and spreading eventually throughout the country. Many were destroyed, some were not discovered for centuries. It is known however that his approach to seduction was through poetry, and it is equally known that there were a great many seductions, so statistically there is a high degree of probability that most of these works were directed at flesh-and-blood human beings.

'The Platonic Lady' is spoken through the mouth of a young lady who prefers cuddling to actual sex. A number of other contemporaries had written 'platonic' verses, but they were always dictated by considerations of honour and virtue. Rochester's version is a mockery of these. It expresses no elevated emotion whatsoever, declaring only that foreplay is the enjoyable part of sex and the culmination a disappointment because it puts an end to desire. It may be relevant that in the seventeenth century men believed that orgasms (called 'enjoyment' in the poem) would cause pregnancy, and took care to ensure that women did not have them. A further complication was that the female orgasm was regarded as the source of women's carnality, and Aphra Behn was repeating a commonplace when she suggested in 1682 that the demands of young wives for multiple orgasms were often responsible for the sexual exhaustion of their husbands. So greedy were women for sexual arousal, it was thought, that a married man had to strike a delicate balance between leaving his wife frustrated and over-stimulating her – afflictions equally likely to lure her into a lover's bed. Furthermore, society and the Church had warned the husband against over-passionate lovemaking with his wife, for it was impure to love her like an adulteress. Having children was intended to secure his lineage, and cuckoldry threatened the proper descent of his estate. In 'The Platonic Lady' Rochester wrote:

> I could love thee till I die,
> Would'st thou love me modestly,
> And ne'er press, whilst I live,
> For more than willingly I would give;
>> Which should sufficient be to prove
>> I'd understand the art of love.
>
> I hate the thing is called enjoyment,
> Besides it is a dull employment.
> It cuts off all that's life and fire,
> From that which may be termed desire.
>> Just like the bee whose sting is gone,
>> Converts the owner to a drone.
>
> I love a youth will give me leave
> His body in my arms to wreath;
> To press him gently and to kiss,
> To sigh and look with eyes that wish.
>> For what if I could once obtain,
>> I would neglect with flat disdain.
>
> I'd give him liberty to toy
> And play with me, and count it joy.
> Our freedom should be full complete,
> And nothing wanting but the feat:
>> Let's practise them, and we shall prove,
>> These are the only sweets of love.

The song 'As Cloris Full of Harmless Thought' is perhaps a little less lyrical than the last, carrying as it does the faint whiff of rape. Men in those days were not reconstructed and both sexes anticipated a certain level of vigorous persuasion. Many males laboured under the horrifying illusion that women were voracious for sex and that they merely required the social niceties to be observed. The Earl of Rochester, it has to be said, was a 'bodice-ripper'. His exceptional beauty, however, seems to have mitigated the crime in the eyes of his victims.

> As Cloris full of harmless thought
> Beneath the willows lay,
> Kind love a comely shepherd brought
> To pass the time away.
>
> She blushed to be encountered so,
> And chid the amorous swain;
> But as she strove to rise and go
> He pulled her down again.
>
> A sudden passion seized her heart
> In spite of her disdain,
> She found a pulse in every part
> And love in every vein:
>
> 'Ah youth,' quoth she, 'what charms are these
> That conquer and surprise?
> Ah let me, for unless you please,
> I have no power to rise.'
>
> She faintly spoke, and trembling lay,
> For fear he should comply,
> But virgins' eyes their hearts betray
> And give their tongues the lie;
>
> Thus she who princes had denied,
> With all their pompous train,
> Was in the lucky minute tried
> And yielded to a swain.

He was incapable of sustaining a serious mood for long. His love lyrics were just as likely to descend into frivolity as his most scurrilous satires. In the next 'Song', he chooses to depict the fair Cloris not, as his contemporaries might have thought appropriate, in a field of flowers or a secluded bower, but in a pigsty. Only Rochester could have dreamed of such a variation on the common theme.

> Fair Cloris in a pigsty lay,
>   Her tender herd lay by her.
> She slept; in murmuring gruntlings they,
> Complaining of the scorching day,
>   Her slumbers thus inspire.
>
> She dreamed while she with careful pains
>   Her snowy arms employed
> In ivory pails to fill out grains,
> One of her love-convicted swains
>   Thus hasting to her, cried:
>
> 'Fly nymph, oh fly, ere 'tis too late
>   A dear-loved life to save,
> Rescue your bosom pig from Fate
> Who now expires, hung in the gate
>   That leads to Flora's cave.
>
> 'Myself had tried to set him free
>   Rather than brought the news,
> But I am so abhorred by thee
> That even thy darling's life from me
>   I know thou would'st refuse.'
>
> Struck with the news, as quick she flies
>   As blushes to her face,
> Not the bright lightning from the skies,
> Nor love shot from her brighter eyes
>   Move half so swift a pace.
>
> This plot it seems the lustful slave
>   Had laid against her honour,
> Which not one god took care to save,
> For he pursues her to the cave
>   And throws himself upon her.

Now piercèd is her virgin zone –
   She feels a foe within it,
She hears a broken amorous groan,
The panting lover's fainting moan,
   Just in the happy minute.

Frighted she wakes, and waking frigs.
   Nature thus kindly eased
In dreams raised by her murmuring pigs
And by her own thumb between her legs,
   She's innocent and pleased.

Flora was the goddess of spring; 'frigs' means masturbates.

While Rochester was pouring out his desires to the Court ladies, his attentions to his wife were waning and her complaints were becoming more bitter and more frequent. In 1669 he wrote indignantly:

I am sorry, Madam, to hear that you are not well and as much troubled that you should believe I have not writ to you all this while. I who am not used to flatter, do assure you that if two letters from me came not to your hands this last week and that before, they have miscarried. Nothing is so much my business now as to make haste to wait on you. I think in that, I comply with your commands, as I do with the hearty inclination of
   your humble servant,
     Rochester

The letter lost in the post is a time-honoured excuse, but at the time there was only a primitive and erratic postal service. It was not helped by the King's use of its profits to fund a pension for Barbara Castlemaine. It was impossible, therefore, to treat Rochester's claims as lies, noted liar though he was. Indeed, her Ladyship used the same excuse for two missing letters herself, and was rewarded with blunt disbelief from her husband. Nothing much worked under the new regime, least of all the King, the nobility and Parliament.

The Restoration had not turned out to be the joyous salvation that the nation had anticipated. The King's control of the country's affairs was lamentably weak, partially due to Parliament's refusal to give him the funds to rule as he wished. Rochester was not being gratuitously spiteful in the savage poems that he occasionally wrote about him. He was criticising a man of whom he was deeply fond, who he knew was abusing his position and failing to honour his contract with the country. Rochester was an adherent of Hobbes. Despite his scathing attacks on philosophy, much of his work, including 'A Satyr against Reason and Mankind' and 'Upon Nothing', was profoundly influenced by the philosopher, as was his own life. In *The Leviathan*, Hobbes's thesis was that the social contract obliged the people to obey the king, and the king to rule the people in return, in order to prevent anarchy. On the whole, the people played their part, except perhaps for the recalcitrance of Parliament. The King, however, did not play his. The result was, Rochester considered, the venality and uselessness of the placemen entrusted with governing the country. It was they whom he made the favourite targets of his satires.

The country constantly complained of Charles's dogged pacifism, though without money he could not make war. His apparent abrogation of responsibility was one of the few things that merited reproof, and Rochester duly reproved him. In an exceptionally clever piece of Latin punning, 'Ad Regem Carolum II', he wrote:

> Bella fugis, Bellas sequeris, Belloque repugnas,
>   Et Bellatori sunt tibi Bella Tori.
>   Imbelles imbellis amas; audaxque videris
> Mars ad opus Veneris, Martis ad arma Venus.

'You run away from war (Bella), you chase after beautiful women (Bellas), you fight against fighting (Bello), and your battlefields (Bellatori) are the beds of lovely women (Bella Tori). You are a pacifist (imbellis) and love those that don't put up any resistance (imbelles); and Mars to you is bold in the work of Venus, and Venus bold in the arms of Mars.'

There were others who thought the same. 'The History of the Insipids' was blamed on Rochester, doubtless to his great gratification, since it was one of the best satires of its generation. It is now thought to have been written by John Freke or Andrew Marvell.

> Chaste, pious, prudent Charles the Second,
>   The miracle of thy restoration
> May like to that of quails be reckoned
>   Rained on the Israelitic nation:

The wished for blessing from heaven sent
Became their curse and punishment.

Charles was as ever magnanimous. It took a generous-hearted ruler
to pardon someone like Captain Blood, who stole his Crown Jewels,
to which he was greatly attached. Despite all his insolence he made
Rochester keeper of the King's game in Oxford. In April the Earl was
petitioning the King for a grant of the offices of four bailiwicks in
Whittlewood Forest. These sinecures were intended by both parties to
bring money, but from the King's purse none was forthcoming. Britain
was well on the way to bankruptcy.

By the end of 1668, Charles had negotiated a triple alliance with
Holland and Sweden (the second Dutch war had been concluded the
year before by the Treaty of Breda). France, in panic, entered into a
treaty with Spain. Charles's financial position was described as 'desperate but not serious'. Buckingham, who was in the pay of France
and liked trouble for the sake of it, fostered the chaos in government.
He began to attack his allies on an apparently random basis. Meanwhile,
in an attempt to outmanoeuvre Parliament, Charles began to negotiate
secretly with France.

At Court Nell Gwyn had entered the picture. At the time she was
a successful actress at the King's Theatre, Drury Lane. The King had
finally tired of Barbara's dreadful temper and habits, and the matter
was brought to a head in 1667, when Barbara was caught out in her
long affair with Henry Jermyn, a notorious gambler and rake. The
King was deeply pained. It is difficult to understand why. He must
have known her outrageous reputation as well as everyone else in
England. Perhaps it was just the final straw at time when his affection
for her was already exhausted. Jermyn was forced to leave the Court
for six months. Barbara, with her genius for self-preservation, remained
maîtresse en titre for a while. Scurrilous poems were circulated about
her, though they tended to concentrate on her recent conversion to
Catholicism, which was of far greater significance to the mob than her
many other lapses. Finally, she was asked to leave her apartments in
Whitehall. As a retirement present the King created her Duchess of
Cleveland, in addition to Countess of Southampton and Baroness
Nonsuch, and awarded her a vast pension from the Secret Service
fund. He finally bade her farewell with the words, 'Madam, all that I

ask of you for your own sake is, live so for the future as to make the least noise you can, and I care not who you love.'

With the superannuation of Cleveland, Nelly stepped in and her old friend Rochester received a further boost to his standing. Buckingham had introduced her to the King some time before January 1668. She was on good terms with the Duke and had been visiting him in the Tower during one of his sojourns there. By 1670, she had become pregnant by the monarch and given birth to a son. She was set up in a little house at the east end of Pall Mall and reigned supreme through 1670 and most of 1671. She had a sharp natural wit, something that the King particularly relished. She was pert to him and he revelled in it. She was once heard telling him how to mend his finances. 'Send the French into France again,' she proposed, 'set me on the stage again, and lock up your cod piece!' Pepys called her 'Mrs. Nelly, the impudent comedian'.

She was close to Rochester. She was said to have had an affair with him before she met the King, though there is no evidence of it. But he was a friend long before she was elevated to the royal bed, so in view of her occupation and his inclination a sexual alliance was highly likely. Certainly they were friends until the end, and in later life he was her trustee. She proved a useful ally. She had the ear of the monarch and, though others later superseded her, she always remained on intimate terms with him. She never failed to make herself available as a 'supply' mistress. She had no other man for the rest of her days. Thus, like the others, she was a powerful figure; but the others had their day and went. Nelly never went. Her usefulness was still in evidence nearly ten years later when, in an unholy alliance with Rochester and the Merry Gang, she rescued Buckingham from yet another period of imprisonment in the tower.

Rochester's position at Court was flourishing but his constitution was not. His behaviour became ever more destructive. Naturally intemperate, he was now wholly absorbed by his excesses. He was indifferent to any diversion that was not wholly outrageous. A generous and good-natured man when sober, he would get carried away when he was drunk and there was mischief to be done. However, though his diary was full, the Treasury was empty. His source of earnings had dried up with the Privy Purse and his finances were under severe strain. Although he was married to a great heiress he tried to preserve his wife's funds intact. He was by no means always successful, but he was not bound to preserve them at all. Her property was now, subject to a few restrictions, his by law. At one impoverished time he wrote to her complaining that he had had the revenues from Somerset for some time, and had told her to send for the amount she wanted, but she hadn't, so now he had spent half of it. However, he added grudgingly, if she wanted it, she must have it. On another occasion when she was complaining about his constant absences and his failure to provide some goods that she wanted, he remarked piteously that he had a poor living to get so that he might be less burdensome to her. If she had sent her own money to buy the goods she could have had them by now, but the pittance he got in London was hardly enough to keep him alone. He explained in answer to another complaint that though it had been a long time since he had been home he was more in demand at Court than ever. He had spent all his money and hers too, and he had had to stay on to find some funds. He had got them now, and he would be at Adderbury soon. Later he queried a complaint that she needed five pounds to pay the servants. All her money had so far as possible been used to support her and her dependents, he protested, and he would provide her with full accounts to prove it. 'If I prove an ill steward at least you never had a better, which is some kind of satisfaction to your humble servant', he added, hinting darkly at the raids on her trusts by her family before marriage.

On 2 December 1668, Pepys was at Court when he heard the King telling a tale about Rochester. It was still less than two years after the marriage, and Elizabeth was now pregnant with their first child. 'The play done, we to Whitehall; where my wife stayed, while I up to the Duchess's and Queen's side, to speak with the Duke of York; and here saw all the ladies, and heard the silly discourse of the King with his people about him, telling a story of my Lord Rochester's having of his clothes stole, while he was with a wench; and his gold all gone, but his clothes found afterwards stuffed into a feather bed by the wench that stole them.'

On 7 February 1669 an event took place that was trivial on the face of it, but was to have an indelible effect on Rochester's life. Pepys recorded:

The King dining yesterday at the Dutch Ambassador's, after dinner they drank, and were pretty merry; and among the rest of the King's company, there was that worthy fellow my Lord of Rochester and Tom Killigrew, whose mirth and raillery offended the former so much that he did give Tom Killigrew a box on the ear in the King's presence which do give much offence to the people here at Court, to see how cheap the King makes himself and the more, for that the King hath not only passed by the thing, and pardoned it to Rochester already, but this very morning the King did publicly walk up and down, and Rochester I saw with him as free as ever; to the King's everlasting shame, to have so idle a rogue as his companion. How Tom Killigrew takes it, I do not hear...

Rochester had taken exception to a jibe from old Killigrew about his 'keeping his wife in the country', and had smacked the older man's face. London was scandalised, as was Pepys, but then Pepys was not one of Rochester's admirers. Had he ever heard of him, Rochester would not have admired the diarist. He was a prime specimen of the sort of citizen whom the Earl most despised, who led a disgraceful life in secret and put on a public show of virtue. It would not have weighed in his favour that he had to account to a hot-blooded French wife, of whom he was terrified. Lady Sunderland wrote a letter in which she said of the Killigrew affair that Rochester 'was in a case not to know what he did', that is, he had been very drunk indeed. The King was unmoved by the incident. He had a more light-hearted view of his own dignity than did his courtiers. Perhaps, since Killigrew was even more insolent than Rochester, he was secretly delighted. On this occasion he did not banish the miscreant. However, because of public disapproval of Rochester's open disrespect, he had to be seen to take action. He suggested that the young man's interest would best be served by a holiday in France. Of course when he was sober Rochester apologised to Tom's son, the scoundrel Harry. *In loco parentis*, Harry generously accepted the gesture. The King, far from consigning the culprit to genuine disgrace, handed him a letter to his sister, the Duchesse d'Orléans, in Paris. It stated that Rochester 'had a mind to take a little journey to Paris, and would not kiss your hands without a letter from me; pray use him as one I have a very good opinion of. You will find him not to want wit, and did behave himself in all the Dutch war as well as anybody, as a volunteer.'

Needless to say, having been told to go to France, Rochester stayed in England. It was a haunting echo of his father before him. He went on a trip to Newmarket with the King, who was obviously not troubled by his continued attendance. Although Newmarket races had existed before King Charles adopted them, it was he who built them into an institution. He would go there with his entire Court as often as three times a year. He rode his own horses and won. He did not expect the jockeys to hold back and they did not. He rode the winner in 1671, leading among others his son the Duke of Monmouth, and was still taking part and winning when he was in his forties. His mounts lived in luxury. They were fed with new-laid eggs and Spanish wine. He had restored the stables at ruinous expense in 1661 with wainscoting and carvings like a drawing room. He kept four jockeys in ordinary. The Court lived in tents and pavilions, but the King would stay at Audley End House with the Earl of Suffolk. He eventually found Audley End so convenient for racing that in 1669 he bought it for £50,000. Inevitably, he had insufficient funds. He never actually paid the full price, though he managed to spend £10,000 on it straight away for 'essential improvements'. He would get so excited by the races that he watched them from his horse, riding parallel with the runners as they came up to the finishing line. In the evenings, he would join in the revelry with his friends at an inn. He would call on his fiddlers to sing their repertoire of obscene ditties that necessarily included a number of works by Rochester. There was a song to the tune of 'Chevy Chase', a sixteenth-century ballad and favourite of Henry VIII, that Rochester adapted for community singing. One verse ran:

> The mayor of London town
> Is flogged by his own sheriffs;
> The bishops bugger up and down
> And all beshit their sleeves.

They watched Lord Digby walk five miles in an hour over the heath stark naked and barefoot for a bet. Theophilus Cibber records a tale of one of Rochester's pranks at Newmarket, when the Earl and one of Charles's mistresses, presumably Nell Gwyn, hatched a scheme to punish him for his nightly excursions. The King agreed to go out one night with Rochester to a celebrated bawdy house where he was assured that the finest women in England were to be found. He unhesitatingly donned his usual disguise and joined him. While he was engaged with a lady who had been tipped off by Rochester, she picked his pocket of all his money and his watch. No one in the bawdy house, least of all the girl, had the least suspicion of the identity of their visitor. When the interlude was over the King called for Rochester but was told that he had gone.

He searched his pockets to pay his bill and found his money gone. He was reduced to begging for credit till the next day as the gentleman who had come with him was to have paid for both of them. He was abused and mocked. The old madame told him that she had been stung before. She refused to let him move until the bill was paid and called one of her brutes to take care of him. After much argument the King took a ring off his finger and offered it as a pledge. She refused because she was not convinced of its value. The King suggested that she call a jeweller to value it, but was told that it was impossible, as it was late and no one would be up. After a lengthy argument he got them to wake the jeweller and show him the item. When the man saw it he was aghast. He demanded to know who they had got in their house and was told, 'A black looking, ugly son of a whore, who had no money in his pocket and was obliged to pawn his ring.' The jeweller said there was only one man in the kingdom who could afford that ring and that was the King himself. On entering the house the jeweller knelt and humbly presented the ring to his Majesty. The onlookers were awestruck. They fell to their knees and begged the King's pardon. He forgave them in the best-natured way, and asked 'whether the ring would not bear another bottle'. The King was delighted by the prank. Until the end of his days he never tired of repeating the story, weeping with laughter.

Another discreditable tale told of life at Newmarket involved Buckingham and Rochester, who happened to be in disgrace at Court at the same time. They disguised themselves and became landlords of the Green Mare Inn at Six Mile Bottom, on the Newmarket Road. They set out to seduce every woman in the area, and 'considered not whether they were maids, wives nor widows'. They were so lavish with their hospitality that every man in the area went to their inn and took his wife with him. While the husbands got drunk Rochester and Buckingham made inroads on the women. One old man who had a young and beautiful wife used to arrive every evening alone, leaving the girl at home in the care of his sister. Rochester's interest was piqued. One night while Buckingham plied the old man with drink Rochester went to the man's house dressed convincingly in women's clothes. The sister opened the door and Rochester drew from his skirts a bottle of 'cordial', which he pretended her brother had sent to her from the inn. He gave her some, it was opium, and she fell asleep. As Rochester chatted to the wife she began to complain that her husband was too old to pleasure her and shut her up in the house to stop her amusing herself elsewhere. Rochester, still in women's clothing, saw that there could be no danger in unmasking and one thing led to another. When they had sated themselves, he suggested she open her husband's boxes and take his savings. They got back to the inn and Buckingham took his turn with her. When they were bored they advised her to find another husband and sent her off to London. The husband found his wife and his savings gone and humorously hanged himself from a beam. Soon afterwards Charles and the Court arrived at the inn on the way to Newmarket. Buckingham and Rochester took off their disguises and told the King their tale. He was so delighted that he forgave them their transgressions and restored them to his favour. Then they found him 'a pretty whore' and things were back to normal.

But in 1669 life for the gilded courtier, the Earl of Rochester, took a turn for the worse.

7

'Reputation is nice'
The Duel

Thus in a course of drunken gaiety and gross sensuality, with intervals
of study perhaps yet more criminal, with an avowed contempt of all
decency and order, a total disregard to every moral, and a resolute
denial of every religious obligation, he lived worthless and useless,
and blazed out his youth and his health in lavish voluptuousness,
till, at the age of one and thirty, he had exhausted the fund of life,
and reduced himself to a state of weakness and decay. As he cannot
be supposed to have found leisure for any course of continued study,
his pieces are commonly short, such as one fit of resolution would
produce. In all his works there is sprightliness and vigour, and
everywhere is to be found tokens of a mind which study might have
carried to excellence. What more can be expected from a life spent
in ostentatious contempt of regularity, and ended before the abilities
of many other men began to be displayed?

Samuel Johnson, *Lives of the English Poets*, 1779

After a prolonged visit to Newmarket, Rochester finally dragged
himself off to France in March 1669. He did so via London, where he
risked even more trouble by getting involved in another duel. On this
occasion he agreed to act as second in an affair of honour between
the Duke of Richmond and Mr James Hamilton, but it was prevented
at the last minute. It was an unwise moment for duelling. The King
had just put Rochester's friend Henry Savile in the Tower for carrying
a challenge from the Duke of Buckingham to Sir William Coventry
after they had had an argument at the dinner table. Finally the Earl
left England. In France his conduct was unexceptionable, but even
when trying to behave he was a lightning conductor for trouble. His
visit to Paris got off to an inauspicious start when Louis XIV, a cousin
of King Charles and ally of all monarchs everywhere, took exception

on behalf of his breed to the way Rochester had treated his own sovereign. He refused to receive him at Court. It meant that Rochester was unable to present himself and the letter to Minette, which caused a certain degree of embarrassment between the two rulers. The problem was quickly overcome, probably as a result of pressure from Minette. Louis was fonder of his sister-in-law than was thought entirely appropriate.

A few weeks after Rochester's arrival he attended a ceremony of great guns in a field outside Paris, where the King wanted to show off his troops and artillery with a massive exhibition of firepower. On his way home he was stopped in his sedan chair crossing the Pont Rouge, and robbed of his periwig and some twenty-two pistols. The mystery is why he was carrying twenty-two pistols in the first place. He was a servant of the King, who had sent him there. Unreliable as he was, his position and his recklessness might have involved him in almost any adventure. He was still in a bad mood when he wrote his next letter home to Elizabeth a fortnight before she was due to give birth to their first child Ann: 'I should be infinitely pleased (Madam) with the news of your health. Hitherto, I have not been so fortunate to hear any of you, but assure yourself my wishes are of your side as much as is possible. Pray only that they may be effectual, and you will not want for happiness.'

Although his tone was not placatory, his concern was genuine. In July he was in trouble, once again through no fault of his own. He went to the opera with the Earl of Cavendish, later Duke of Devonshire, to see a performance of *Scaramouche*. A group of Frenchmen took exception to the presence of Englishmen, and insulted Cavendish, who retaliated with a blow to the face. There was a pitched battle and the French came off worst. Cavendish killed two of them but in the process was wounded seven times and nearly died. He was saved by the intervention of a servant of Montagu, the English Ambassador, who threw him into the pit out of harm's way. History does not relate the part that Rochester played. Offering violence to the Englishmen was politically unacceptable and Louis XIV was enraged. As a gesture, which he may well not have meant, he threatened to hang the surviving Frenchmen. Even had they not been hanged, they would have been imprisoned and ruined, but Cavendish and Rochester intervened through the British Ambassador. They assured Louis that they did not wish the Frenchmen to suffer further punishment, and insisted that they had received all the satisfaction that they could possibly have demanded. Louis was thus obliged to pardon his people.

Paris had been amusing, and it was soon to become painfully apparent how much Rochester had amused himself. But he began to fret. Elizabeth was about to have the baby, and he was mystifyingly anxious to be back in time for the baptism. On 15 July 1669 he applied for permission to return to England. Montagu, the English Ambassador, supported his request in a letter of recommendation to Lord Arlington, the Secretary of State. He believed that there was 'nothing the Earl was more desirous of than Arlington's favour and countenance; and if thereafter he continued to live as discreetly as he had done ever since he had been in Paris, he had other good qualities enough to deserve it, and to make himself acceptable wherever he went'. Rochester was thereby given the official seal of good conduct between one monstrous rake, Montagu, and Arlington, another. Luckily, no mention was made of the one poetic offering that he had composed in France. It had been scrawled up on a public monument and caused some commotion. At the time there was a popular Latin couplet current at the French Court boasting of Louis' conquests; the English translation would have been, 'Lorraine a day, a week Burgundy; Flanders a month; what would a year have done?' Rochester wrote the Latin question:

> Una dies Lothero, Burgundos hebdomas una,
> Una domat Batavos luna; quid annus aget?

and underneath it the English answer:

> Lorraine you stole; by fraud you got Burgundy:
> Flanders you bought; by God you shall pay for it one day.

Fortunately his artistic reputation was not as widely known in France as in England, because the style is unmistakable.

Eventually he was allowed to return to England and, although he was still away when his daughter Ann was born, he was back home for the baptism on 30 August. She grew into a beauty and a poetess. 'In her conduct we see fairly writ, Her mother's heavenly modesty, her father's powerful wit,' said the poet Robert Gould. She was married twice during her life, the first time to a Wiltshire gentleman, Henry

Baynton, and then to Francis Greville, son of Lord Brooke. Her father adored his children, and, little as he saw of them, he always remembered them affectionately in his better-tempered letters. He sent them presents when he could afford it, such as a portrait by William Wissing of his son Charles sitting with a King Charles spaniel on his knee, or, for Ann, a doll in the form of Louise de la Vallière, mistress to King Louis.

Less than two months after his return home Rochester was in serious trouble. Possibly dating from a previous time, but almost certainly from his visit to Paris, he was clearly infected with the pox. In September, at the age of twenty-two, the gorgeous young courtier found himself a guest at Madam Fourcard's bathhouse in Leather Lane, off Hatton Garden. The establishment had once been a public bathhouse. In the fifteenth century the bathhouse was very popular. Paris had so many that Parisians are said to have washed more frequently then than they do now. There was little segregation of the sexes and a great deal of frolicking, which led inevitably to infection. When this fertile source of disease was identified, bathhouses began to close and by the end of the sixteenth century they had almost disappeared. In their stead, Europe embraced filth. Bath owners were barber–surgeons as well. They adapted their establishments to the treatment of disease rather than its dissemination. Genuine physicians were more than happy to leave it to the 'quacksalvers'. ('Quacksalver' was a composite of 'quack' and 'quicksilver', their stock in trade.) Physicians wanted nothing to do with an illness 'that began in one of the most degrading and ignoble places of the body'. In any case, skin diseases had historically been within the province of surgeons since the early Renaissance. Mercury was the treatment of choice, for the sole reason that it had long been used to treat skin diseases, and syphilis made its first appearance on the skin. The mercury was rubbed into open sores as an ointment mixed with fat, butter, vinegar, myrrh, turpentine, incense, lead and sulphur, then the patient was saturated in a fumigating chamber. Patients would be swathed in towels and kept in a tub in a stiflingly hot closed room, where they would be anointed several times a day for months, breathing as much mercury as air. Hence:

Rub-a-dub-dub,

Three men in a tub,
And how do you think they got there?
The butcher, the baker,
The candlestick-maker,
They all jumped out of a rotten potato,
'Twas enough to make a man stare.

Mercury poisoning makes the sufferer drool, and medical orthodoxy dictated that salivating and sweating were needed to expel the 'excrements of evil' from the body. Some quacks insisted on the loss of four pints of saliva on the first day. Half the patients died of dehydration, heart failure, suffocation or straightforward poisoning. It was common for patients under treatment to lose their red blood cells, become emotionally disturbed and unable to keep food down, then succumb to kidney and liver failure. A number killed themselves rather than suffer the treatment. After such an experience sex tended to lose much of its charm. Men became suspicious of women, and women of men. (Schopenhauer, for example, is said to have become a total misogynist as a result of the illness and treatment.)

Patients were also dosed with purgatives, mercury enemas, sudorifics and tonics. They were bombarded with mercury both from outside and from within. The surgeons took a high moral tone, announcing that syphilis could not be cured 'except under the influence of a medication which imposes on the body a chastisement of its impurity and on the soul, a punishment of its errors'. The treatment was utterly pointless. It did no good whatsoever. However, it coincided sooner or later with the natural remission of the secondary symptoms, and so survived for centuries without discredit. No one realised how poisonous mercury was. It is now understood to be one of the most toxic substances known to man.

Acute mercury poisoning causes the absorbed mercury to be concentrated in the kidneys, where it poisons the blood-filtering structures. As a result there is first a decrease and then a complete cessation in urine output, causing the accumulation of toxic substances in the blood (uraemia) and death. *Chronic* mercury poisoning usually results from the inhalation of mercury vapours. For example, in the nineteenth century, vapour from the hot mercuric nitrate used in making felt hats injured the hatters' kidneys and affected their nervous systems. They became tremulous and emotionally unstable (hence 'mad as a hatter'). Mercury poisoning leads to loss of weight and appetite, pain, numbness and tremor in the extremities, together with mental and personality changes. There is significant impairment of sexual performance, intellectual functioning and short-term memory. Central nervous system toxicity usually improves gradually after the removal of the mercury, but this must be prompt and accompanied by proper medical treatment. Once the central nervous system disorder and the behavioural changes have become deep rooted, the damage is irreversible, despite cessation of exposure. It was said that 'five minutes with Venus meant a lifetime with Mercury'.

Sufferers say that the mental effects are the most distressing part of the illness. The psychopathological effects, polyneuritis, include abnormal irritability, amnesia, excitability, fearfulness, restlessness, insomnia, depression, timidity, fatigue, weakness, drowsiness and photophobia. The poisoning affects the peripheral part of the nerve branches and manifests itself through degeneration of the sheaths of the fine nerve bundles. Toxins get into the bloodstream and are deposited in various tissues and organs, causing disease throughout the system.

Mercury may cause poisoning through mere inhalation; the most common modern cause is through mercury leaking from dental amalgam fillings. There have been reports of people detained for insanity because they have become violent after ingestion of mercury that has leaked from their fillings. Dentists have been afflicted by feelings of depression and futility after using amalgam. There have been complaints from crematorium workers about the toxic effects of breathing mercurous gas from the deceased's fillings. A single filling contains approximately a gram of mercury, which is infinitesimal compared to the amounts that were used in treatment for the pox. There have been suggestions that pregnant mothers should have their amalgam fillings removed, because the toxicity can cross the placenta into the unborn child. All these effects are of recent discovery. As late as the 1940s and 1950s mercury was commonly administered as Calomel (mercurous chloride), a very strong laxative, and it was still in use in 1955 as a laxative, de-wormer and teething paste.

During his treatment at Madam Fourcard's, Rochester wrote frankly to his wife in a wry letter styled as a spoof on legal documents:

From our tub at Mrs Fourcard's this 18th of October
Wife,

Our gut has already been griped [his kidneys had been felt for a stone by squeezing between finger and thumb] and we are now in bed, so that we are not in a condition of writing either according to thy merit or our desert; we therefore do command thy benign acceptance of these our letters in what way so ever by us inscribed or directed, willing thee therewithal to assure our sole daughter and heir issue female, the Lady Ann, part of our best respects; this with your care and diligence in the erection of our furnaces is at present the utmost of our will and pleasure.

'Tis not an easy thing to be entirely happy, but to be kind is very easy, and that is the greatest measure of happiness. I say not this to you in mind of being kind to me; you have practised that so long that I have a joyful confidence you will never forget it; but to shew that I myself have a sense of what the methods of my life seem so utterly to contradict. I must not be too wise about my own follies, else this letter had been a book dedicated to you and published to the world.

It will be more pertinent to tell you that very shortly the King goes to Newmarket, and then I shall wait on you at Adderbury: In the meantime think of anything you would have me do, and I shall thank you for the occasion of pleasing you...

There is a theory that the physician who treated him was Monsieur Florence Foucade, one of the King's doctors. It is more likely that the establishment in Leather Lane was given the nickname of Fourcard ironically, as a pun on the royal doctor's name. The letter was written from Rochester's 'tub', and what patients were treated for in a tub was the pox.

By the time of his first illness he had drawn far enough back from Hobbism to accept the possibility that the soul was a substance distinct from matter. When he seemed close to dying and thought that he had only an hour to live, he accepted that death was not the ending of the soul but only the separation of it from matter. As always with Rochester, it is impossible to tell whether his new belief that soul was separate from body was influenced by the belief that his body was about to die. He suffered great remorse for his past life but it was a general, dark horror rather than any consciousness of sinning against God. He was sorry that he had destroyed his health so quickly and brought so bad a name upon himself. He allowed priests to be sent for, though this meant nothing. It was only to humour his friends. It was 'but a piece of his breeding to desire them to pray by him, in which he joined little himself', he later told Burnet. Having spent the month of October in Madame Fourcard's establishment Rochester left it in a pitiable state of infirmity with acute mercury poisoning, probably chronic mercury poisoning, and hardly able to stand up. He was suffering from polyneuritis. His muscles were atrophied, he was suffering from total fatigue, and from physical and mental debility.

His lifelong enemy Mulgrave chose this moment to challenge him to a duel. The reasons are oblique, even according to Mulgrave's version of events. The pretext for it was that Rochester had slandered Mulgrave. Mulgrave wrote an account of the matter a safe period after Rochester's death. It is a masterpiece of humbug:

During this time and heat of temper, I had the good fortune not to be engaged in more than one quarrel; but that had somewhat in it singular enough to be related. I was informed that the Earl of Rochester had said something of me which, according to his custom was very malicious; I therefore sent Colonel Aston, a very mettled friend of mine to call him to account for it. He denied the words, and indeed I was soon convinced that he had never said them; but the mere report, though I found it to be false, obliged me (as I then foolishly thought) to go on with the quarrel; and the next day was appointed for us to fight on horseback, a way in England a little unusual, but it was his part to choose.

Mulgrave relates that he and his second 'lay the night before at Knightsbridge privately, to avoid being secured at London upon any suspicion'. In the morning they met Rochester at the appointed place, only to find that, instead of the agreed second, he had brought 'an errant lifeguardsman whom nobody knew'. Aston objected, 'especially considering how extremely well [the lifeguardsman] was mounted, whereas we had only a couple of pads'. The upshot was that they all agreed to fight on foot. Mulgrave's account continues: 'But as my Lord Rochester and I were riding into the next field in order to it, he told me that he had at first chosen to fight on horseback because he was so weak with a certain distemper that he found himself unfit to fight at all any way, much less afoot.' Mulgrave expressed his surprise and 'took the liberty of representing what a ridiculous story it would make if we returned without fighting'. He therefore advised Rochester 'for both our sakes, especially for his own, to consider better of it; since I must be obliged in my own defence to lay the fault on him by telling the truth of the matter'. Rochester replied that:

he submitted to it and hoped that I would not desire the advantage of having to do with any man in so weak a condition. I replied that by such an argument he had sufficiently tied my hands, upon condition I might call our seconds to be witnesses of the whole business; which he consented to, and so we parted. When we returned to London, we found it full of this quarrel, upon our being absent so long; and therefore Mr Aston thought himself obliged to write down every word and circumstance of the whole matter, in order to spread everywhere the true reason of our returning without having fought; which, being never in the least either contradicted or resented by the Lord Rochester, entirely ruined his reputation as to courage (of which I was really sorry to be the occasion) though nobody had still a greater as to wit; which supported him pretty well in the world, notwithstanding some more accidents of the same kind that never fail to succeed one another when once people know a man's weakness.

Oddly, Mulgrave omits the fact that, according to the records of the House of Lords, the King had been warned that the duel would be fought on the morning of 23 November 1669, and sent an officer of the guard to prevent it. Mulgrave could not be found. He was in Knightsbridge with Colonel Aston lying up before the fight, as he said. Rochester was discovered at his lodgings. He promised the officer that he would not try to escape, made an excuse to leave the room and ran off. He appears then to have presented himself for the combat, which does not seem to suggest a great degree of reluctance.

The House of Lords ordered that both men be arrested and brought before the House. Mulgrave was caught on 24 November, held in custody in Suffolk Street and taken before the Lords. He was told to issue no further challenges to Rochester and to report to the House any that he received from him. He gave his promise 'on his honour'. On the 25th Black Rod informed the Lords that Rochester was in custody. He too was brought to the House the following day, and given the same warning as Mulgrave. He promised, 'My Lords, I shall ever be ready to give obedience to your Lordships' commands, and am sure I shall easily do it in this particular. I have never been angry with the Earl of Mulgrave, and I have no reason to believe he was so with me; for his Lordship hath always carried himself so gently and civilly towards me that I am confident there will no occasion of any difference between us.'

When the parties met, the challenged party was entitled by convention to specify the manner of fighting. Rochester had chosen to do so on horseback because he found it difficult to stand. But his second was bigger than the man that he had named, and the second's horse a massive cavalry beast. (The soldier seems to have been a trooper in Colonel Aston's own regiment.) Mulgrave's objections were that the seconds were unequal, and that their mounts were also unequal. The seconds were liable to become involved in the duel, taking the fight over from the principals. When Mulgrave complained that the terms were unfair and asked for the duel to be fought on foot, Rochester had the prerogative to insist, but did not.

It is difficult to understand why Rochester should have agreed to fight on foot when he knew that he could not. He may have been drunk. It was during his five years of constant insobriety and he had probably needed recourse to the bottle during his treatment. He had given his explanation and expressed the hope that Mulgrave would not take unfair advantage of the situation when they returned to the Court. Colonel Aston did it for him. Rochester had made enemies at Court. He had never quite realised how deeply his barbs pierced. He meant to puncture the inflated egos of the self-satisfied. He forgot that those were the people who would wait longest for revenge. The story was a gift to them. His reputation for bravery was dead.

It was a crisis in the poet's life. The agony caused by merriment and women and the shock of seeing his reputation for courage slip away distressed him deeply. It is likely that he was now suffering from chronic mercury poisoning, and it may have affected his mind for the rest of his life. From this time onwards, at the age of twenty-two, his moods, his writings and his poetry became darker and more desperate. He seems to have done nothing to refute Colonel Aston. Perhaps he scorned explanation. His reputation among the Court idlers may no longer have been of concern to him. Perhaps he was putting into practice his own philosophy, 'for all men would be cowards if they durst'.

He was disenchanted with men and repelled by women:

Love a woman! Y'are an ass!
　'Tis a most insipid passion
To choose out for your happiness
　The idlest part of God's creation.

. . .

Farewell woman, I intend,
　Henceforth every night to sit,
With my lewd well-natured friend,
　Drinking to engender wit.

He was still denouncing women for spreading the pox three years later. He chose for special attention ladies from Ireland, such as the daughters of Charles Coote, Earl of Mountrath (one blonde, one dark), the Countess of Clanbrazil whom the Irish interest in spring 1671 were trying to put forward as mistress for the King, and 'Fox', who was probably Mrs Jean Fox, an Irish adventuress. The position of mistress was clearly becoming vacant: in March 1669, there was a lampoon circulating at Court entitled 'A song made of My Lady Castlemaine Touching her Growing out of Favour'. Rochester wrote:

The Cootes black and white, Clanbrazil and Fox,
Invade us with impudence, beauty, and pox.
They carry a fate which no man can oppose,
The loss of his heart, and the fall of his nose.

He continued to attend the Lords in his usual desultory fashion. All his life he had viewed politics with complete detachment. The political background of the period was extraordinarily complex and involved the English and the French plotting against the Dutch. Their plans were well advanced, as were the King's own intentions to undermine Parliament. By the spring of 1670, Andrew Marvell, who was an eminent statesman as well as a poet, was able to say that no king since the conquest had been so absolutely powerful as Charles II.

In May 1670, Madame, his sister, paid a long-awaited visit to England. Charles was at loggerheads with Parliament, whom he neither trusted nor liked, and he dearly wanted an ally. He decided to enter into a pact with his cousin Louis, whose absolute monarchy he envied when his own was constantly disrupted by an importunate Parliament. Through the spring and summer of 1669 there had been secret negotiations between Charles and Louis with Madame, his sister, as go-between. Her husband, the Duc d'Orléans, tried to stop her but gave in with bad grace when Louis intervened. The Duc was a homosexual who had surrounded himself with a coterie of male lovers. In spite of it, he was obsessively jealous of his wife. His lover, the Chevalier de Lorraine, fanned his suspicions in the hope of driving them apart. The marital difficulties were aggravated when Madame became the chief agent between the English and French Courts. The Duc, who was not in the confidence of either his wife or Louis, became increasingly mistrustful and was annoyed by her secret meetings with the King. He took her into retirement at Saint Cloud. Louis called them back to Versailles; but the Duc, on finding his wife in private conversation with the King, immediately carried her home again. Eventually he was grudgingly compelled to part with her for a few weeks.

During her visit to England the young Princess concluded the pact between Louis and Charles at Dover that she had been sent to negotiate. Although she was seriously ill she wanted to stay and Louis granted her a few extra days in England. It was then that Charles met the woman who was to become his next *maîtresse en titre*, Louise de Kerouaille. He instantly asked his sister to make him a present of her but she refused, protesting that she was responsible to the girl's parents. That, for the time being, was that. Much to the sorrow of her adoring brother, Madame had to leave. Their parting was one of great sadness. There were tears and lingering embraces, almost like lovers. Indeed, she is widely thought by some to have been the only woman that Charles ever really loved.

Shortly after she arrived back in France she died of acute peritonitis following the perforation of a duodenal ulcer. This was the illness that had been troubling her in England. Her husband the Duc and his catamite immediately fell under suspicion of poisoning her, but nothing could be proved. She was in truth extremely ill. Despite her unreliable health she had insisted against her doctor's advice on bathing in the Seine, and on 29 June 1670, after drinking some chicory water, she suffered violent pains and vomiting. She collapsed and died soon after.

Charles broke down with grief. He withdrew to his bedroom, where he lay prostrate with misery for a week. Rochester was kind to him. He did his best to cheer him up and lighten the burden of grief. He wrote to Elizabeth, 'Pray do not take it ill that I have writ to you so seldom since my coming to town. My being in waiting upon the sad accident of Madame's death, (for which the King endures the highest affliction imaginable) would not allow me the time or power to write letters.' After relating the circumstances of the death he concluded:

But I will not keep you too long upon this doleful relation. It is enough to make most wives in the world very melancholy, but I thank you for my cheeses, my sugar of roses, and all my good things.

Pray let it not be necessary for me to put you too often in mind of what you ought not to be less forward in *doing* than I in *advising* [that is, living with his mother]. I hope you will give me no occasion to explain myself for if I am put upon, you will find me very troublesome. I received no letter from 'with an enclosed to your mother', nor do I believe you writ any. Besides, I find by another circumstance that the return of letters between London and Adderbury are very tedious; if you write to me you must direct to Lincoln's Inn Fields, the house next to the Duke's Playhouse, in Portugal Row. There lives your humble servant, Rochester. Pray send me some ale. Send me word, and if it be not as it should be, I'll send another

tarara —

In August of 1670 Barbara Castlemaine was finally pensioned off after two years of mutiny. She was now nearly thirty and still very beautiful, but the brutal truth was that the King's mistresses had to face early retirement. As Dorimant says in *The Man of Mode*, 'A woman's past her prime at twenty, decayed at four-and twenty, old and insufferable at thirty.' She had had countless affairs, which she always indignantly denied, while taking little trouble to hide them. Her lovers had included all manner of persons including the playwright Wycherley, Henry Jermyn, John Churchill, Lord Sandwich, James Hamilton, Sir Charles Berkeley and a kaleidoscope of others, down to Jacob, a rope-dancer, tumbler and gymnast.

Pepys had been besotted by her. As early as 1662 he wrote of walking into Whitehall Garden: 'In the privy gardens saw the finest smocks and linen petticoats of my Lady Castlemaine, laced with rich lace at the bottoms, that I ever saw; and did me good to look upon them.' He would hang around the artist Lely's studio in the hope of glimpsing her portrait. He bought one of Lely's own copies for his private consumption, which cannot have pleased his wife. He recorded a pageant on the river at Whitehall, when the King and his new Queen arrived in a barge under a canopy, with ten thousand richly caparisoned barges and boats accompanying them. There was always music on the water. Charles loved to be surrounded by it wherever he went. But it was in short supply after 1666, when the Court band walked out after several years' non-payment of wages, and the harpist died of starvation. 'But that which pleased me best', said Pepys,

was that my Lady Castlemaine stood over against us upon a piece of Whitehall, – where I glutted myself with looking on her. But methought it was strange to see her and her lord [Castlemaine] upon the same place, walking up and down without taking notice of one another; only, at first entry, he put off his hat and she made him a very civil salute – but afterwards took no notice of one another. But both of them now and then would take their child which the nurse held in her arms, and dandle it. One thing more; there happened a scaffold below to fall, and we feared some hurt but there was none; but she, of all the great ladies only, run down among the common rabble to see what hurt was done, and did take care of a child that received some little hurt; which me thought was so noble.

But the King was tired of the storms and expense and lasciviousness. She had given birth to another child that he refused to accept. For once Jermyn, her lover for many years, was innocent. She had cuckolded him too. John Churchill, later the first Duke of Marlborough, was the father. Burnet, who was an interfering busybody, found out about the affair and told the King. Charles arrived on a visit and Churchill jumped out of the window. When he found out that Barbara had given Churchill £5,000 of his money, he told him sardonically that he forgave him, for he did it for his bread. Barbara flounced off to Paris, where she remained for some time causing trouble.

Rochester celebrated the downfall of his friend and cousin by writing:

Quoth the Duchess of Cleveland to Mistress Knight,
'I'd fain have a prick, but how to come by 't?

I desire you'll be secret, and give your advice,
Though cunt be not coy, reputation is nice.'

'To some cellar in Sodom your Grace must retire,
There porters with black pots sit round a coal fire.
There open your case, and your Grace cannot fail
Of a dozen of pricks, for a dozen of ale.'

'Is't so?' quoth the Duchess. 'Aye by God' quoth the whore.
'Then give me the key that unlocks the back door –
For I had rather be fucked with porters and car-men,
Than thus be abused by Churchill and Jermyn.'

It was a jovial end to a charming relationship. There is an early story that when Barbara was descending from her carriage Rochester tried to kiss her and she knocked him down. While still on the ground he declaimed:

By heavens! 'twas bravely done
First to attempt the chariot of the sun
And then to fall like Phaeton.

When she was in mid-career, he wrote:

When she has jaded quite
Her almost boundless appetite...
She'd still drudge on in tasteless vice
As if she sinn'd for exercise.

For a year or so Nell Gwyn ruled supreme, though not alone. There were others: Winifred Wells, whose comportment was compared to a goddess and her face to a sheep; Mrs Knight, mentioned in the poem above, who sang beautifully on the stage; Mary Killigrew, the widowed Countess of Falmouth, who subsequently married Lord Buckhurst; and Elizabeth Countess of Kildare. There was also little Jane Roberts, the daughter of a parson. Jane was an especially sweet-natured girl and one of the Court's outstanding beauties, but one of the less durable of the King's mistresses. At a time when the sovereign was not much involved with her, she and Rochester fell for one another. They both swore undying love and at the time both of them meant it. But Rochester as usual grew bored and left her. He wrote a poem based tongue-in-cheek on Hobbes. The philosopher had written that the past and the future did not exist; the only thing that did was the present. Rochester's answer was the poem 'Love and Life':

> All my past life is mine no more,
>   The flying hours are gone,
> Like transitory dreams given o'er,
> Whose images are kept in store
>   By memory alone.
>
> What ever is to come is not,
>   How can it then be mine?
> The present moment's all my lot,
> And that as fast as it is got,
>   Phyllis, is wholly thine.
>
> Then talk not of inconstancy,
>   False hearts, and broken vows,
> If I, by miracle, can be,
> This livelong minute true to thee,
>   'Tis all that heaven allows.

Jane, broken-hearted, went to the King and begged him to take her back. He agreed without the slightest hesitation. She later died from syphilis, which she might have caught from either of them, or from others. Rochester's appropriation of Jane from the King was not an isolated instance. An anonymous essay claimed after his death that he did it quite regularly, in an 'attempt to cure the King's weakness for women'. The picture of Rochester bravely sacrificing himself on the altar of unchastity is a little too much to swallow.

The peaceful scene was broken as usual by Buckingham. He was indirectly responsible for bringing to England the twenty-two-year-old Louise de Kerouaille, who had caught the King's eye at Dover. Still grieving for his sister, Charles had invited Louise to England as maid of honour to the Queen. Louis XIV encouraged her because he wanted a secret weapon at Charles's Court. The Duke of Buckingham thought the same and undertook the arrangements to bring her over. When inevitably he bungled it, Lord Arlington finished the job. She became one of the King's longest-serving mistresses. At all times she kept an alert eye on the Queen's health. She was the only mistress who stood a serious chance of advancement, French spy though she was. She was very refined and suffered agonies at the hands of Nell Gwyn, who constantly mocked her by emphasising her own humble beginnings. As soon as Louise arrived, Nell had pointed out to the King that there was an act of Parliament forbidding the importation of cows from France.

Louise's round face seemed insipid to English eyes. John Evelyn had been expecting much of 'that famed beauty' and instead found her 'childish, simple and baby-faced'. Charles, however, was deeply smitten. Louise was too clever to indulge herself in the fearsome tantrums of a Barbara Palmer. Instead, she would be unwell or burst into tears. Nelly called her 'the weeping willow'. After so many years of Barbara she was balm to the King's nerves. She was a virgin when she arrived, and it took him a full year to seduce her. Arlington confided to the French Ambassador that the King's ministers were just as eager as their sovereign for the consummation. Although Charles was not disposed to communicate his affairs to his women, they could damage those whom they hated and sabotage much business. It was better for all good servants of the King that he should be attracted to a woman whose temperament was not mischievous. Louise was a lady, they thought, in contrast to the 'comediennes and the like on whom no honest man could rely', through whom the Duke of Buckingham persistently enticed the King away from his Court. Unfortunately Rochester and Louise did not get on.

The King and Louise were staying at Arlington's house at Euston for the Newmarket races when, after a mock marriage arranged by Lady Sunderland, the courtship was happily resolved. According to Evelyn, 'the fair lady was bedded one of these nights, and the stocking flung after the manner of a married bride'. This was the fourth ceremony of marriage that Charles had gone through. Two fake, Frances and Louise, one to the Queen which was genuine, and one of dubious standing with Lucy Walter, mother of the Duke of Monmouth, when he was exiled in France. Charles called Louise 'my dear life', and was ever after devoted to her, on and off. On his deathbed he declared, 'I have always loved her, and I die loving her.' He was not prepared to go as far as fidelity, but she remained his wife in all but name. Her rooms, which were far finer than the Queen's, were dismantled and rebuilt many times at unimaginable expense.

Louise turned out to be as expensive as Barbara, with whom she shared a tendency to gamble and to accumulate jewellery. She made a useful sideline out of bribes from ministers and ambassadors seeking influence with the King. Although her power to promote them was limited, she had the customary power to put poison in the King's ear. The Earl of Danby, the Lord High Treasurer, parted with £55,000 over two years to guarantee her support, even against the French. The King gave her a pension of £10,000 out of the revenues of land in Ireland, and a few years later an annuity of £8,600 out of excise duties. She was given £1,000 a year out of clerical revenues, a shilling on each cauldron of coal shipped from Newcastle, and occasional sums from the Secret Service fund. She made a little pin-money from selling royal pardons, and there were frequent gifts of jewels.

As the money trickled away, the House of Commons became increasingly critical of the King. When he asked for funds, MPs had a shrewd idea of where they were going. In 1673, when more money was required for the third Dutch war, one of their grievances was the £400,000 that had been squandered since the previous session, much of it on the Duchess of Cleveland and Louise. Charles was already having difficulties because of his suspected pro-French and pro-Catholic leanings, which in turn led to his proroguing Parliament and living for as long as he could on money from other sources. Religion cast a great shadow over the times, which created difficulty for Louise who was not only French but Papist. The people could not or would not pronounce her name correctly, and she became known as 'Carwell'. She was created Duchess of Portsmouth in February 1673 for her loyal services to the monarch. Someone stuck a notice on her apartment door with the couplet: 'Within this place a bed's appointed For a French bitch and God's anointed.' There is no evidence that this was Rochester. He must have been innocent sometimes, but he had been outraged when she was made a duchess. He had a notorious flirtation with her while he was part of her retinue at Bath in 1674, when onlookers were appalled by their behaviour together in the water, and is thought to have written 'A Pastoral Dialogue between Alexis and Strephon' for her, portraying an unfulfilled relationship. The poem ended:

'Tis too true

Change has greater charms than you.
Be by my example wise:
Faith to pleasure sacrifice.

Silly swain I'll have you know
'Twas my practice long ago:
While you vainly thought me true
I was false in scorn of you.

By my tears my heart's disguise
I thy love and thee despise.
Woman kind more joy discovers
Making fools than keeping lovers.

A further tribute to Louise is thought to be contained in 'Draft of a Love Poem':

Hard hearted saint, since 'tis your will to be
So unrelenting pitiless to me
Regardless of a love so many years
Preserv'd 'twix't lingering hopes so many years...

He wrote these little bon-bons to entertain her – more, it seems, out of courtesy than love. There was certainly bad blood between them as early as the same year. He regarded her loyalty, rightly, with deep suspicion. French ambassadors visited her daily and Charles would meet them confidentially in her rooms. Ministers, too, still congregated there. The truth was that, although she had originally been an agent of France, she had realised how well she was doing and had branched out on her own. There was no cause for alarm. The King knew exactly what she was doing but she was adept at putting his point of view to the French and he saw no reason to intervene.

By December of 1670, as Barbara was leaving Court and Louise arriving, Elizabeth Rochester was preparing for her second child, their only son Charles. The baby was of course named after the King, who was to be godfather. At the ceremony on 2 January 1671, the godparents were to be Sir Charles Sedley and Charles Sackville, Lord Buckhurst (later Earl of Dorset), who represented the monarch. Those two wretches, whose last recorded public appearance together on the balcony of Oxford Kate's got them stoned for blasphemy and buggery by an outraged mob, were to undertake the unfortunate child's moral guidance and renounce the world, the flesh and the Devil on his behalf.

In December, Buckhurst wrote to Rochester at Adderbury. He announced that the King had, by appointing him proxy, been graciously pleased to make him his lieutenant-general against the Devil. He would begin his 'march' on Thursday. In the meantime, however, he was resolved to be discreet so that the Devil, vigilant as he was, should not suspect that he, Buckhurst, was at odds with him. It was with some unwillingness, he confessed, that he began a war against a Prince of Darkness whom he had served so long. He hoped that 'peace would be secured by war' and that this momentary dispute between the Prince of Darkness and himself would ensure abiding harmony thereafter. Meanwhile he would, of course, obey his sovereign.

His 'march' was delayed by a Parliamentary scandal. In the course of a debate about the government's proposal to tax playhouses, Sir John Coventry, the Member for Weymouth, had asked 'whether the King's pleasure lay among the men, or the women, that acted'. This lack of tact was resented in certain quarters. On 21 December, on his way home from supper, he was dragged out of his carriage by a gang led by one Sir Thomas Sandys. They tied him up and sliced his nose to the bone. On hearing of it, the Commons was outraged and debated a bill for banishing the wrongdoers. It was eventually decided, drafted, read, revised and forgotten. For the time being, however, the drama required Buckhurst's attention, and he ended his letter with an apology for leaving little Lord Wilmot at the mercy of the Devil for so long – though it was a danger of which, he pointed out, neither child nor father had the slightest comprehension.

Savile wrote to say how sorry he was to have missed the christening, but, now that Rochester was staying so much in the country with his wife, he presumed that they would all be furnished with similar solemnities at least once a year. He hoped that he would be able to attend the next one.

For many years Rochester's amorous powers had been failing. The reasons were many: mercury poisoning causes impotence, as do the later stages of syphilis. All the curses he had called down upon his recalcitrant member eventually arrived to plague him. Persistent over-indulgence in wine played its part. He had sobered since his five years' constant revelry, though by no means completely. His visits to London were always celebrated with drinking on a massive scale, and when he was in the country he tippled his way methodically through his cellar.

Dear Savile,

Do a charity becoming one of your pious principles, in preserving your humble servant, Rochester from the imminent peril of *sobriety* – which, for want of good wine more than company (for I drink like a hermit betwixt God and my own conscience) is very like to befall me. Remember what pains I have formerly taken to wean you from your pernicious resolutions of discretion and wisdom.

. . .

Dear Savile, as ever thou dost hope to out-do Machiavel or equal *me*, send some good wine! So may thy wearied soul at last find rest, no longer hovering 'twixt th' unequal choice of politics and lewdness! May'st thou be admired and loved for thy domestic wit; beloved and cherished for thy foreign interest and intelligence.

Rochester

There came a time when he could see only too clearly the way his amorous career was going. 'The Disabled Debauchee' was written with a laugh and a flourish but it was prophetic, and Rochester knew it. In one of its early copy-texts the poem was entitled 'Upon his Lying and Could not Drink' and was clearly meant to be a reflection on himself, however many others might have qualified for the privilege. He wrote in heroic stanzas, a style reserved in the seventeenth century for works of an epic character. It was typical of his work that the style that he selected was in itself an irony. If he wanted to make a profound observation, he was equally likely to choose a frivolous style. The poem is a parody of Davenant's 'Gondibert' and also perhaps Dryden's 'Annus Mirabilis'. It concludes ('nice' here means bashful):

> Should any youth (worth being drunk) prove nice,
>   And from his fair inviter meanly shrink,
> 'Twould please the ghost of my departed vice,
>   If at my counsel he repent and drink.
>
> Or should some cold-complexioned sot forbid,
>   With his dull morals, our bold night alarms,
> I'll fire his blood by telling what I did,

When I was strong and able to bear arms.

I'll tell of whores attacked, their lords at home,
   Bawds' quarters beaten up, and fortress won,
Windows demolished, watches overcome,
   And handsome ills by my contrivance done.

Nor shall our love-fits, Chloris, be forgot,
   When each the well-looked link-boy strove t'enjoy,
And the best kiss was the deciding lot
   Whether the boy fucked you, or I the boy.

With tales like these I will such thoughts inspire,
   As to important mischief shall incline.
I'll make him long some ancient church to fire
   And fear no lewdness he's called to by wine.

Thus statesman-like I'll saucily impose,
   And safe from danger valiantly advise,
Sheltered in impotence, urge you to blows
   And being good for nothing else, be wise.

This masterly work that spoke so sadly of so much was a visible footprint on the road to final despair. He did not fail to see the irony of the situation. He was a sick man now, and getting worse, without any clear idea of what was wrong with him. In retrospect, there can be little doubt. In identifying his final illness, the concession must straight away be made that *ex post facto* diagnosis is notoriously difficult even for the most specialised of medical experts. Diagnosing syphilis is hard enough even in the case of a living patient. It became known to doctors as 'the great mimic', 'the Proteus of diseases', because of its ability to imitate the symptoms of other ailments. Nevertheless, there is irresistible evidence that it was what killed Rochester. He was known to have had the 'pox', though in those days the pox meant both syphilis and gonorrhoea. The difference between the two was unknown. It was no secret that he had received treatment in 1669 at a notorious quacksalver's in Leather Lane. The disease was incurable. It would never have left him. It would not necessarily have killed him, but his health would later have been bound to deteriorate. His physical and mental stability were beginning to collapse by 1671.

Syphilis was a comparatively new and mysterious disease. Columbus' sailors acquired it in Haiti and imported it into Europe. The island was inhabited by the Arawak Indians. They were friendly and generous, and gave the visitors freely of everything they had, including tobacco, their women and the pox. Columbus, who died in 1506 with syphilitic visions that he was an ambassador of God, described them as a 'most loving people'.

The endemic strain in Haiti was only a mild form of the disease, a minor infection of the skin to which the Indians had built up a resistance. Columbus' sailors, being new to the contamination and having sex with five or six Arawak women a night, managed to develop a superinfection many times more deadly than the original. On the voyage home there were constant complaints of rashes and ulcers, but no one guessed the truth. Columbus made no mention of it in any of his dispatches, for fear of discouraging his supporters. By 1493, the crew had made their way to Barcelona. They left a trail of disease across Europe. Within a year, the first epidemic had broken out in Barcelona. Over twenty thousand people needed treatment.

The bacterium treponema pallidum is known as a 'spirochaete' because it looks and behaves like a corkscrew. It bores its way into the bones, the tissues and the skull. The sailors carried their spirochaetes to Naples, where the army of King Charles VIII of France received them. After the customary rapine, fifty thousand men recruited from Germany, Switzerland, France and Russia were sent home thoroughly infected. Voltaire remarked, 'France didn't lose all she had won in this campaign. She kept the pox.'

Thus syphilis became known to the Italians as the 'French disease', to the French as the 'Neapolitan disease', the Germans and the English called it the 'French pox', the Portuguese called it the 'Castilian disease', the Persians called it the 'disease of the Turks', and the Turks called it the 'Christian disease'. The Poles blamed it on the Germans, the Russians blamed it on the Poles, the Arabs blamed it on the Jews who had been expelled from Spain, and the Hindus blamed it on the Europeans. The Chinese blamed it on the Portuguese and the Japanese blamed it on the Chinese. The Dutch called it the 'Spanish disease', the Indians the 'Portuguese disease', and Captain Cook was pained to discover that the Tahitians called it the 'British disease'. The affliction was not called 'syphilis' until 1530, when a famous doctor–poet,

Fracastorius, wrote a poem on the subject. He dreamed up a myth that Syphilus, a swineherd, cursed the sun for the heat that was killing his animals. The gods struck him down with his eponymous infection.

The name came into common usage only in the nineteenth century; until then syphilis and gonorrhoea had been universally known as the 'pox'. Originally the disease was accompanied by dramatic symptoms, starting with an ulcer on the mouth or the sexual organs, then rashes, pains and gummy tumours the size of eggs all over the body. It ate away the lips, the nose, the throat and the tonsils. The sufferer's face became a foul mess. A man's scrotum could fall off. As generations passed the symptoms became less gruesome and, by the same token, far less noticeable. The disease grew more insidious until after two centuries it became difficult to recognise at all. No one was aware of the tertiary stages. A further difficulty in identifying the organism was that it could not be stained for inspection under a microscope. Most bacteria absorbed dyes readily and the colour allowed them to be compared with the substance containing them. Treponema pallidum remained invisible.

Syphilis is initially a mild disease; later it becomes chronic. There are no acute stages in its progress. If untreated its duration is marked by years rather than days. There is the primary stage, a local disturbance at the point where the spirochaetes entered the body. In the secondary stage, weeks or months later, there is a general but mild disturbance of the body, while the spirochaetes are invading all parts of their new home, accompanied by physical symptoms such as a more or less severe rash. Finally, when the bacteria have infiltrated the entire body, they slowly concentrate in various organs and cause irreversible damage. This is the last, tertiary stage of the disease, inducing blindness, personality changes, insanity and death. The victim becomes irritable and depressed. His mind is fogged. There is epigastric pain, nausea and vomiting. Bladder and colonic problems such as incontinence and ulcers occur. Muscles atrophy. Hips, knees and ankles are afflicted by advanced osteoarthritis. Tertiary syphilis may take many years to arrive and many more to kill.

Some sectors of society – the Church, the many remaining Puritans and the mercantile middle classes – regarded the pox with contempt as a suitable punishment for sin. However, most regarded it as an everyday hazard that carried little or no stigma. Syphilis was a major reason for the wearing of wigs, which became so popular among the upper classes throughout Europe in the 1600s. Henry VIII had died of it. His body is said to have exploded while lying in state. Both the disease and the treatment caused the hair to fall out. Mary Queen of Scots wore a wig because she was bald from syphilis. So did Queen Elizabeth I; either she was not a Virgin Queen, or she inherited the disease from her father – as, it is thought from her portraits, did her sister Mary. Ivan the Terrible of Russia is thought to have suffered from neurosyphilis, which intensified his insane cruelty. Harry Savile, of course, had it, and Jane Roberts died of it. Etherege caught it, and Rochester soothed him with the epigram:

> Gentle Sir George keeps to himself his Miss
> For who the devil would meddle with his?
> So have I often seen a country clown
> By spitting in the posset make't his own.

Louise de Kerouaille caught the pox. The King gave her some drops and was claiming credit for her recovery. It was all credit to him that she became ill in the first place, since it was he who gave her the disease. She told her confessor, who promised the Virgin Mary on her behalf that in the event of recovery she would have 'no more commerce with that known enemy to virginity and chastity, the Monarch of Great Britain. She would return to a cloister in Little Brittany and there end her days.' The King presented her with a magnificent string of pearls to console her. It seems small recompense now, but at the time the whole affair seemed trivial – though not to Louise, who protested volubly. Eventually she was sufficiently calmed by the pearls to forget her threat of chastity.

Despite the disgust of the moral classes, the infection could not be regarded as a disgrace because so many people of high estate suffered from it. Erasmus of Rotterdam observed that a nobleman without the pox was 'ignoble and rustic'. It is not known which disease Louise contracted, syphilis or gonorrhoea, though it is likely to have been the latter. For centuries no one discovered the difference, though in retrospect one can often tell by the effects of the disease. John Hunter, the great Georgian physician, maintained (as had many before him) that the two diseases were simply different manifestations of the same virus. He tried to prove his point by deliberately inoculating his glans penis with pus taken from a patient with gonorrhoea. He developed syphilis. This was deemed proof that the one disease was merely an aggravated form of the other. However, Hunter had overlooked the possibility of a patient contracting the two infections at the same time. His 'discovery' buried the truth for another century until Philippe Ricord, an eminent French physician, isolated the two infections in 1837. Even then, it took many more years for his findings to be accepted.

Syphilis, once isolated, became a *cause célèbre*. Plays and songs were written about it, like Aids today. In 1885, in an obscure Italian play about the disease, the Devil was given this (much emended) speech:

He will look at his body and wonder, 'Is this me?' His hair and his eyelashes and teeth will fall out; his jaws and his joints will become shaky. His skin will be full of holes. He will get sentimental, and start to moralise. He will play with insects in the sunshine, and envy the young trees in the spring. If he is a Protestant he will become a Catholic, and vice versa. His liver and his other organs will be like lead. Then one of his eyes will start to hurt. Three months later it will close. He will begin to shake and burn as though on fire; he will still be able to walk, but he will be looking anxiously to see if his feet are still attached to his body. Soon he will have to stay in bed to keep warm. He will become pious, very pious, ever more pious; he will conceive a love for the prayer book and the Bible. Later, his bones rotting, he will be bedridden, gaping, his mouth open towards the ceiling, wondering what has happened to him, and finally he will die … then his soul will be yours!

It was an eerily exact account of Rochester's last years by a writer who knew about syphilis but nothing of Rochester. (The dramatist received six months' imprisonment for insufficient respect to God.)

8

'Run away like a rascal'
Failing Marriage, Health and Finances

> The indecency of Lord Rochester I shall pass without comment. His
> indecency is protected against the critics as a skunk is protected
> against the hunters. It is safe, because it is too filthy to handle and
> too noisome even to touch.
>
> S. H., *Gentleman's Magazine*, 1851

There was a marked decline in Rochester's health now. In June of
1671 he had to go to Bath. From there he wrote to Harry Savile:

Whether love, wine, or wisdom (which rule you by turns) have the present
ascendant, I cannot pretend to determine at this distance; but good nature,
which waits about you, is my security that you are not unmindful of your
absent friends; to be from you *and* forgotten by you at once, is a misfortune
I never was criminal enough to merit, since to the 'Black and Fair Countesses'
I villainously betrayed your divided heart.

You forgave me upon the first bottle and upon the second, on my
conscience, would have renounced them *and* the whole sex. Oh that *second
bottle*, Harry, is the sincerest, wisest, and most impartial downright friend we
have, tells us truth of ourselves, and forces us to speak truths of others,
banishes flattery from our tongues and distrust from our hearts, sets us
above the mean policy of Court prudence, which makes us lie to one another
all day for fear of being betrayed by each other at night! And, before God,
I believe the errantest villain breathing is honest, as long as that bottle lives.

Rochester's 'second bottle' has become a metaphysic in the philosophy
of intemperance.

Bath had a reputation for curing rheumatism, which syphilis could
cause, but he may have gone nowhere near the waters. There were
other reasons for going to Bath, like the refreshment of a change of
vices. His eyes were suffering badly, and he was growing blind. On an

afternoon in September 1671, he was sitting in Garraway's coffee house, with his friends Sir William Muddiman, Harry Killigrew and others, when he suddenly got up and without any explanation walked out. He posted straight down to the country, and collapsed with eye-trouble.

Sir William wrote to him:

My dear Lord Rochester,

I am very sorry you find your eyes can neither endure wine nor water: I presume Killigrew (whose talent is description) has given you to understand what a dinner and day you lost when you left us at Garraway's. I confess your sudden start surprised me as much as Harry Savile's attempt upon My Lady Northumberland.

Muddiman launched into the discreditable tale of Harry's woeful romance, the definitive version of which is to be found in a letter from the Attorney General, Sir Heneage Finch, to his son. A number of distinguished guests were visiting Lord Sunderland's house at Althorp, including Harry Savile. Harry had long been a companion to Lady Northumberland either because he was a friend of her dead husband, or as a go-between for her and the Duke of York. While they were at Althorp he got a master key from Lord Sunderland on the pretext of wanting to go into the billiard-room (according to another version, he had stolen the bolt of the door). At one o'clock in the morning he got into Lady Northumberland's room in his shirt and nightgown. He knelt by her bedside and told her, 'Madam, I am come with great confusion of face to tell you now, which I durst not trust the light with, the passion with which I serve and adore you.' She panicked and rang the bell, leaped out of bed, ran to another door that Henry was unaware of and escaped barefoot into the gallery. She knocked at a door down the passageway and tried to get into bed with the lady who was staying there, 'leaving H. Savile to meditate how to come off of this adventure'.

He went back to his room and wrote a letter to Lady Northumberland trying to laugh the episode off, suggesting that the house was haunted. She had hardly got enough breath back by morning to tell her tale. When she did, there was a general meeting of everyone in the house and Harry realised that the place was getting too hot for him. He sneaked down to the stables and fled. When Mr Russell, the Countess's brother-in-law, heard about it he decided to make it a matter of family honour, and with a group of men pursued the culprit to London. He was nowhere to be found. Some thought that he had gone to France, so Mr Russell followed. Luckily Harry remained out of sight, but every genteel person in town was disgusted with him and thought that he should be caught and punished. Since the débâcle, the ladies would not now converse with various gentlemen of doubtful repute, especially Sir Edmund Waller, the sixty-year-old poet and a menace to females, without having their women in the room. It seems a little hard on Sir Edmund, who was not involved in the affair in any way.

Rochester was now shuttling between London and the country. Between bouts of sickness, he had still found the time and energy to get into trouble over a woman. He had recently concluded a sour intrigue with one Meg Foster, who passed herself off at Court as a lady of rank. She had a lethal technique with men that she had learned in her calling as harlot, and seems to have used it successfully on Rochester. He saluted her thus:

> This in my time was so observed a rule,
> Hardly a wench in town, but had her fool.
> The meanest common slut, who long was grown
> The jest and scorn of every pit-buffoon,
> Had yet charms left enough to have subdued
> Some fop or other, fond to be thought lewd.
> *Foster* could make an Irish lord a Nokes...

Nokes was the famous clown of the Restoration theatre.

It is not known exactly what her complaint was. The lady, Meg Foster (if it was she), was after money and had reinforced her demands with the threat of a complaint, presumably for rape. Rochester wrote to his wife who, it seems, had had something to say on the matter:

If you hear not from me, it is not that I want either time or will to write to you, I am sufficiently at leisure and think very often of you, but you would expect an account of what has befallen me, which is not yet fit for you to know, only thus much I will tell you, it was all in vindication of *you*; I am now at Battersea; wonder not if you receive few letters from me, and be satisfied with this, that I think continually of you, and am your

Rochester

'Battersea' was the manor house at Battersea, the home of his uncle and aunt, Sir Walter and Lady St John. He was not a regular visitor and may have been hiding there. Sir William Muddiman wrote in reference to this imbroglio that fate had taken care to vindicate his involvement with the woman, who had been found to be a damsel of low degree. She was not a northern lady, but a mere soldier of fortune. Her uncle was a publican who wielded a 'puissant spigot at Kensington', and she had already been debauched by one Mr Butler. That seems to have been the end of the matter.

Back in London William Wycherley, the playwright, afforded a little light relief when he too became ensnared by Barbara, Duchess of Cleveland and became her lover. Anne Knight, the singer, is said to have lent Barbara her apartment in Whitehall for their meetings. Wycherley had been a member of the Court circle for some years and was a good friend of Rochester's. They shared a predilection for biting satire and the drama. Both had similar tastes in excoriating fops, the smug and the pretentious. Wycherley was worried and uncomfortable, not because of a natural terror of Barbara or of the King, either of which would have been understandable. What terrified him was the prospect of jealousy and reprisals from another of Barbara's former lovers, the Duke of Buckingham, who was also her cousin. Such a reaction would have been quite unreasonable, for the affair had ended years before, but the Duke was not a reasonable man. He had been muttering threats about the affair, which had been passed on to Wycherley. The trembling author went to Rochester and Sedley and begged them to point out to the Duke that he was about to make serious trouble for a man who had never offended him and who had not even the honour to be acquainted with him. When Rochester and Sedley raised the matter with the Duke, his immediate response was that he was not blaming Wycherley in any way. He took exception only to Barbara's behaviour.

Rochester and Sedley argued that putting it about that Wycherley was involved with her might be the undoing of him and that, if it was, he would be causing a disaster to a man whom he would have found extremely entertaining company. They praised Wycherley's conversation so extravagantly that Buckingham, who cared far more for amusement than for Barbara, demanded to meet him. A few nights later when they all dined together, Wycherley was on his best form. The Duke swore, 'By God, my cousin was in the right of it!' Buckingham and Wycherley became lifelong friends, and Wycherley was so grateful to Rochester that he remained under his patronage and a friend for the rest of his life. No one ever really understood what the confrontation was about in the first place.

Meanwhile, all was not well with Elizabeth. She had visited London in March 1671 and been seen at the theatre on the 4th. She was not with her husband. Lady Mary Bertie wrote to a friend relating how she was with Lady Rochester, Lady Betty Howard and Mrs Lee at a play in London, supped at Lady Rochester's and came home shortly before midnight. 'Lady' Rochester's was clearly a different dwelling from 'Lord' Rochester's. The two were now estranged. In view of the husband's penchant for adultery and his refusal to go home, it was hardly surprising. However, in polite society such imperfections were the rule rather than the exception. A more compelling source of disharmony was the malign influence of the mothers-in-law. In particular there was deep animosity between Elizabeth and her mother-in-law, the poisonous Dowager Countess.

Old Lady Rochester was an especially strong-willed, hard and malicious woman. However, mindful of his family duties, and in the most wrong-headed possible way, Rochester was determined that the two should live together in harmony. His wife was a fiery woman and she was equally determined not to get on with a mother-in-law whom she loathed. When Elizabeth was at Adderbury, Rochester took great pains to be elsewhere. In turn Elizabeth took pains to be anywhere that her mother-in-law was not. She would skitter between London, Adderbury and her family home in Enmore in Somerset and Rochester was becoming irked. He wrote to her at Adderbury:

Madam,

I am at last come to Adderbury, where I find none but the housekeeper, the butler and rats who squeak mightily and are all in good health ... Present my humble service to Lady Warre,

Madam,

Your humble servant,

Rochester

156

If you are pleased, I am pleased; were my mother pleased, all were pleased which God be pleased to grant.

    Rochester

He sent her an acid note claiming that she had so neatly arranged her movements that until she went where she actually intended going he could not write to her. If she and his mother could only get on as they used to, it would make him very happy. He concluded sarcastically, 'You show yourself very discreet and kind in this and in other matters. I wish you very well, and my mother, but assure you I will be very backward in giving you the trouble of your humble servant.' In other words if she must, she must, but she should not expect to see him at home. Shortly afterwards he wrote to her testily, 'It was the height of compliance forced me to agree your ladyship should come into Oxfordshire. If it does not please you 'tis not my fault, though much my expectation; I receive the compliment you make in desiring my company, as I ought to do; but I have a poor living to get, that I may be less burdensome to your ladyship...'

There were other letters to her, however, that were jovial, and when there was no particular cause for argument they dealt well enough together. She sent him some portraits of her in 1674:

Dear Wife

    I received your three pictures and am in a great fright lest they should be like you. By the bigness of the head I should apprehend you far gone in the rickets, by the severity of the countenance, somewhat inclined to prayer and prophecy; yet there is an alacrity in the plump cheek, that seems to signify sack & sugar, and the sharp sighted nose has borrowed quickness from the sweet-smelling eye; I never saw a chin smile before, a mouth frown, and a forehead mump [grimace]. Truly the artist has done his part, (God keep him humble) and a fine man he is if his excellencies do not puff him up like his pictures; the next impertinence I have to tell you is that I am coming down to you. I have got horses but want a coach. When that defect is supplied you shall quickly have the trouble of

    Yr. humble servant

    Present my duty to my Lady, and my humble service to my sister, my brother and all the Babies.

He sent her a jovial salutation:

> Your husband tight
> Rising to shite
> This song did write
> The last midnight.

A little while later he was dutifully at home with his wife at Adderbury. The whole family, including a number of relations, was present at dinner. Without any prior announcement, just as he had done at Garraway's, he got up, walked out of the room and took his carriage to London. Later he wrote Elizabeth a letter in mock-Biblical style making light of the affair:

Run away like a rascal, without taking leave, dear wife – it is an unpolished way of proceeding which a modest man ought to be ashamed of. I have left you a prey to your own imaginations amongst my relations – the worst of damnations; but there will come an hour of deliverance, till when may my mother be merciful unto you; so I commit you to what shall ensue, woman to woman, wife to mother, in hopes of future appearance in glory.

It was a parody of the burial service: 'We therefore commit his body to the ground, earth to earth, ashes to ashes, dust to dust, in sure and certain hope of the resurrection to eternal life.' It was meant kindly, expressing a little sly sympathy. But even Rochester was unprepared to show open disrespect to his parent, a convention of the time that was immutable. To Elizabeth the arrangement held the same grim foreboding as the tomb itself.

Time passed, with Elizabeth complaining bitterly about her treatment from her mother-in-law, refusing to bow to Rochester's wishes and determined not to make friends with her. She was showing the same rebelliousness that she had shown at the age of fourteen when her family were trying to palm her off with a husband she did not like. She was not prepared to be palmed off with her mother-in-law either. In another attempt to make light of the matter, Rochester wrote her a letter of reproof composed in the owlish form of contemporary philosophical dissertation; but the message that lay beneath was plain:

I cannot deny to you that heroic resolutions in women are things of which I have never been transported with great admiration, nor can be if my life lay on it; for I think it is a very impertinent [irrelevant] virtue, considering how men and women are compounded as heat and cold, so greatness and meanness are necessary ingredients that enter both into the making up of everyone that is born. Now when heat is predominant, we are termed 'hot', when cold is, we are called 'cold'; though in the mixture both take their places, else our warmth would be a burning, and our cold an excessive freezing.

So greatness or virtue, that spark of primitive grace, is in everyone alive; and likewise meanness or vice, that seed of original sin is also; for if either of them were totally absent, men and women must be perfect angels, or absolute Devils, now from the preheminence of either of these quallityes in us, we are termed good or bad.

When such contrarieties resided in one body, they occupied opposite parts, so that 'a heroic head is liker to be balanced with an humble tail'. Not just reason, but experience, had furnished Rochester with many examples of this kind, 'my Lady Morton, Nell, Villiers, and twenty others, whose honour was ever so excessive in their heads, but they suffered a want of it in every other part'.

Thus it comes about madam that I have no very great esteem for a high spirited lady; and therefore should be glad that none of my friends thought it convenient to adorn their other perfections with that most transcendent accomplishment; it is tolerable only in a waiting gentlewoman, who to prove herself lawfully descended from 'Sir Humphrey her great uncle', is allowed the affectation of a high spirit, and a natural inclination towards a gentle converse.

This now is a letter, and to make it a kind one I must assure you of all the dotage in the world, and then to make a kind one, down at the bottom, with a great space between, I must write,

'Madam
I have too much respect for you to come near you whilst I am in disgrace, but when I am a favourite again I will wait on you;'
Your most humble servant
Rochester

But attempts at cajolery were doomed. It was in a mood of exasperation that he wrote, 'The difficulties of pleasing your ladyship do increase so fast upon me and are growing so numerous, that to a man less resolved than myself, it would appear a madness ever to attempt it more. But through your frailties, mine ought not to multiply; you may therefore secure yourself that it will not be easy to put me off my constant resolution to satisfy you in all I can.'

In 1672 Rochester's financial position deteriorated, a direct result of the King's fiscal difficulties. Apart from the massive allowances paid to Charles's mistresses out of French money in the Secret Service account, his Household expenditure was rising towards £200,000 a year. The Duke of Ormonde, the Lord Steward of his Majesty's Household, refused to visit the ladies concerned and made dogged efforts to obstruct the payments that the King wanted to make them. Nevertheless, Barbara and Louise between them received permanent grants from the state Exchequer of more than £45,000 a year.

One result of the secret treaty of Dover in 1670 was that the King was committed to making war on the Dutch. He also wanted Holland's territories, and Dutch ships to fill his coffers. Hostilities – and the third Dutch war – began on 17 March 1672. Bloody battles were fought, but the French were not much in evidence and the English were indifferent. The King needed supplies of money from Parliament to support his war, but, as the alliance had been devised as a secret source of money from France, the treaty had not been disclosed. Thus when he begged for funds his demands were met with suspicion. Parliament feared that he had some ulterior motive, such as the enforcement of absolutism, and kept him very short.

The King retaliated by exercising his power to prorogue Parliament, thereby rendering it ineffectual. By doing so he forfeited even more revenues, which had not yet been voted to him. The desperate remedy was to put a 'Stop' on the Exchequer. The King, together with Thomas, Baron Clifford of Chudleigh, Treasurer of his Majesty's Household, had designed a type of national savings, or state bonds. These were peremptorily cancelled. Andrew Marvell called it the 'Robbery of the Exchequer', and the nation was enraged. Marvell wrote:

> New upstarts, pimps, bastards, whores,
>   That locust-like devour the land,
> By shutting up th' Exchequer doors
>   When thither our money was trepannd,
> Have rendered, Charles, thy restoration
>   A curse and plague unto the nation.

It was the small investors who bore the brunt. John Evelyn referred to it as 'an action which not only lost the hearts of his subjects and ruined many widows and orphans whose stocks were lent him, but the reputation of his Exchequer for ever'.

Two banks were put out of business. The problems created were not solved until the foundation of the Bank of England in the reign of William III. The King had borrowed £1,300,000 from a number of bankers, who were bankrupted as a result. Rochester was a casualty, like all Crown servants. There were a number of money warrants in his favour, authorised in the previous two years, which he had had great difficulty in cashing. The arrears on his annuity as a gentleman of the bedchamber on 18 March 1672 amounted to £3,375 (a sum approaching £200,000 in today's terms). By good fortune Sir Robert Howard, Secretary to the Treasury, was an old friend of Rochester's family, and the Earl had helped Sir Robert in writing his uncompleted play, 'The Conquest of China'. Howard was in a position to help. He wrote to Rochester on 29 August, 'I will with as much speed as I can endeavour to serve you in the particulars of your wages and pension. I cannot promise so directly as I wish, for the King's affairs are at this time very pressing, but I will do all that is possible to assure of the truth of what I profess to be so really.' Clifford, Treasurer of the King's Household, was also a friend. The Earl had no qualms over lobbying for money. He met with a well-intentioned but futile response. Clifford replied that he had always been delighted to help, and that day they had put in for £500 for him. The warrant was to be issued on 9 September. It was then cancelled.

As the year progressed Rochester's health failed apace with his finances. He wrote to Elizabeth:

I recover so slowly, and relapse so continually, that I am almost weary of myself. If I had the least strength I would come back to Adderbury, but in the condition I am, Kensington and back is a voyage I can hardly support. I hope you excuse my sending you no money, for till I am well enough to fetch it myself, they will not give me a farthing, and if I had not pawned my plate, I believe I must have starved in my sickness. Well God bless you and the children whatever becomes of

Your humble servant...

To add to his trials, Elizabeth and her mother-in-law were teetering on the edge of total war. The Dowager had been complaining to her son of some misdemeanour on her daughter-in-law's part. Rochester characteristically did not keep his wife's letters, so the allegation remains obscure. However, Elizabeth kept Rochester's letters, and it is possible to read between the lines. It seems that the old woman had accused her daughter-in-law of infidelity. (In her later years she had as little compunction in accusing her granddaughter's husband of infidelity, forgery and worse when her granddaughter died and left her estate to him.) Elizabeth had found out and was duly enraged, and Elizabeth's rage was a serious matter. Although saintly in her tolerance of her husband, she was not placid. She had never been even-tempered and she died at a young age of apoplexy. Rochester told her that he had not written because it was difficult to know what to say. She should not be too horrified by his mother's thoughts about her. Since they were mere imagination, they would vanish as quickly as they had arrived and he would do his best to see that they did. Meanwhile, she should obey his mother's demand that she join her at Aylesbury.

The Court was in a mess and becoming more and more grossly mismanaged, to the disgust of what were now the older generation of courtiers. Henry Bulkeley, one of Rochester's great friends who became Master of the King's Household, wrote to him:

The fop is the only fine gentleman of the times, and a committee of those 'able statesmen' assemble daily to talk of nothing but fighting and fucking at Lockets, and will never be reconciled to men who speak sense and reason at the Bear or Covent Garden. It is they who are the hopeful sprigs of the nation, whose knowledge lies in their light periwigs and trimmed shoes; who herd with one another not because they love themselves, but understand nobody else; whose honour, honesty and friendship is like the consent of hounds, who know not why they run together but that they hunt the same scent; fellows that would make the world believe that they are not afraid of dying, and yet are out of heart if the wind disorders their hair or ruffles their cravats.

It is not possible to tell how much time Rochester and his wife spent together, but he saw her for a while every September when he went home for the Adderbury Plate, a four-mile race of which he was patron. In the summer of 1672 it is known that Lady Rochester celebrated the birthday of the brother of her friend Lady Mary Bertie at Adderbury 'with great solemnity, causing the bell to be rung and making a great dinner', Lady Mary wrote. 'We concluded it by dancing sixteen dances after supper and because the weather was hot we danced some of them in the forecourt, some in the garden, and the rest in the hall.' From there the Rochesters moved on to Somerset and stayed there for the summer and autumn. In September he was back at Adderbury for the races and his niece Anne Lee was married.

Although his behaviour in the country was priestly by comparison to London, it was not wholly uneventful. He could not restrain himself from occasional disorderly lapses that have become part of the folklore of Adderbury. The tales are still told of how Rochester once went to Barford a few miles to the south-west of Adderbury dressed up as a tinker, probably drunk and bored, and offered to mend all the villagers' pots and pans. Having got hold of them he knocked all the bottoms out. He was caught in the act and put in the stocks. With some difficulty he persuaded a villager to take a note to 'Lord Rochester at Adderbury'. An aeon later his carriage and four arrived; his servants got out, sighed, dug up the stocks and took them home complete with the Earl still in them. The tale ends with his doing the decent thing and sending the people new pots and pans. They still remember too the time that he disguised himself as a tramp. As he was wandering about he met another and asked him where he was going. The man said that he was going to Lord Rochester's but there wasn't much point, for nothing was to be got from him. Rochester joined him on his mission. They went to the house and the Earl secretly warned his servants. They pounced on the tramp and flung him in a barrel of ale. Every time the man put his head up the Earl threatened to bash him. He was there for some time. Then the Earl let him out and having nearly drowned him in beer gave him a good meal and a new suit of clothes. He told him never again to say that there was nothing to be got from Lord Rochester and sent him on his way.

On the credit side, he involved himself in country affairs, a complete contradiction of his known character. In 1672 he was appointed deputy lieutenant for the county of Somerset and, for one whose life was dedicated to frivolity, took his duties most seriously. He was a benevolent landlord and was at the head of a group of gentlemen whose manors adjoined the Chase of Kingswood in the county of Gloucester. It was all a little obscure, but a certain Sir Baynham

Throckmorton, instead of getting a patent for the rangership of the Chase which would have been the normal course, had secured a lease for sixty years of all the King's rights there. This gave him unprecedented powers and Sir Baynham was making the most of them by tyrannising the commoners and cottagers. Though the Earl was far from being the People's Friend, Sir Baynham was the sort of person, and his conduct the sort of conduct, that he could not stand. Rochester and the others regarded it as the responsibility of their rank to see that something was done and they took action to put the errant knight back in his proper place.

Back again in London in March 1673, he quarrelled at Court with Robert Constable, Viscount Dunbar. It is likely that there was a woman involved. Rochester spent much of his time dallying in St James's Park, along with the rest of the beau monde. The Park was magnificent now. A French architect under the direction of Charles's mother had laid it out with a straight ornamental sheet of water 2,800 feet long and 100 feet wide with two short rows of trees radiating from a coppice of limes. On an island in the middle there were exotic birds. Charles loved his park and would go walking with his advisers and courtiers along Constitution Hill (named after Charles's constitution, not Britain's) and played pell-mell there. He launched two gondolas on the canal that had been given him by the Doge of Venice complete with two gondoliers. The men eventually had to go home because they were never paid.

There was another side to the Park, the nocturnal wantonness that Rochester immortalised in 'A Ramble in St James's Park', which he wrote that month. Women, due perhaps to his flagging powers and the evocations of Madam Fourcard's bathhouse, were not receiving sympathetic treatment at the time. But although the poem was written within three years of his mercury 'cure' its tone is so acrid that it can only have been meant for a particular victim. It was not a drunken tirade. He polished his work extensively. Over a period of weeks enough light must have glimmered through the fog of alcohol for him to know exactly what he was saying and to mean it. He said himself that before he could write satire he had to feel personal hatred. He could not do it in cold blood. Perhaps it was an early manifestation of mental imbalance caused either by mercury poisoning or by syphilis. Blindness was now gathering too, and that combined with the sheer power of hatred expressed in the poem produces an effect that seems close to mental illness. If that was indeed his condition, one can only marvel at his lucidity. On the other hand, with Rochester, it could always have been a joke. If it was, it was fearsome:

> Much wine had passed, with grave discourse
> Of who fucks who, and who does worse,
> Such as you usually do hear
> From them that diet at The Bear.
> When I, who still take care to see
> Drunkenness relieved by lechery,
> Went out into St James's Park
> To cool my head, and fire my heart.
>
> But though St James has the honour on't,
> 'Tis consecrate to prick and cunt.
> There, by a most incestuous birth,
> Strange woods spring from the teeming earth:
> Whence rows of mandrakes tall did rise,
> Whose lewd tops fucked the very skies.
> Each imitative branch does twine
> In some love fold of Aretine;
> And nightly now beneath their shade
> Are buggeries, rapes, and incests made...

To 'this all-sin-sheltering grove' flock great ladies and chamber-maids, divines and footmen, 'And here promiscuously they swive'. One of his lovers is seen picking men up in the Park, and the poem concludes with a broadside against female infidelity that is startling in its ferocity ('limed' means pregnant):

> May stinking vapour choke your womb,
> Such as the men you dote upon.
> May your depraved appetite
> That could in whiffling fools delight,
> Beget such frenzies in your mind
> You may go mad for the North wind;
> And fixing all your hopes upon't,
> To have him bluster in your cunt,
> Turn up your longing arse to the air

And perish in a wild despair.

...

But my revenge will best be timed
When she is married, that is: limed.
In that most lamentable state
I'll make her feel my scorn and hate;
Pelt her with scandals, truth or lies,
And her poor cur with jealousies,
Till I have torn him from her breech
While she whines like a dog-drawn bitch,
Loathed and despised, kicked out of town
Into some dirty hole alone,
To chew the cud of misery
And know she owes it all to *me*.

And may no woman better thrive
That dares profane the cunt *I* swive.

He seems to have been more than a little put out by some lady's imperfect standards of behaviour and taste in admirers. Perhaps Viscount Dunbar, a noted thug, was another of his rivals. A duel between the two men was arranged for 25 March but the King put a stop to it through the intervention of the Earl Marshal. Rochester had yet again committed a banishable, indeed imprisonable, crime and one of the few which the King ever took seriously. Mysteriously, far from being caught and punished, he was rewarded. Shortly afterwards, together with the royal pimp, the 'Keeper of the Closet' Thomas Chiffinch, he received the sinecures of the Park of Bestwood and four loads of hay out of Lenton Mead in Nottinghamshire. The gifts were bestowed 'as a mark of the King's favour and bounty considering of his many and faithful services'. In the case of Chiffinch those services consisted of pimping and spying for the King. He was the King's *valet de chambre* and confidential agent. His principal duty was to procure two girls at a time, set up in different houses, one a virgin, the other a whore. Rochester had often accused himself of being no more than the King's pimp, though there is no evidence that he actually was. What he really did for the King can only be guessed at.

His task was to raise the King's spirits when circumstances

demanded. The monarch, in spite of his even temper, was prone to depression. At such times only two men could deal with him, old Tom Killigrew and Rochester. The latter may have done something beyond mere entertainment in return for the rewards that were heaped upon him. It may be that keeping the King informed was part of his services. He certainly had much of interest to relate – not only the intimate secrets of the Court but, from his roaming about the capital, the attitudes of the merchant class as well. This suggestion may be consistent with his possession of a small armoury in Paris.

As usual when things were plodding along quietly he managed to shatter the peace. He always claimed that he could not stand still life. He could be relied on to agitate it, even if only by accident. In January of 1674 Charles asked him to write a poem on the royal mistresses. Mindful of his duty, he set to and did so. For reasons that will shortly become obvious, no one knows which poem it was, but a possibility is 'Signior Dildo'. Ann, duchess of York and daughter of Clarendon, had died in March 1671. The Duke of York, the King's brother James, therefore needed a wife. It was important politically because James, who now seemed certain to succeed to the throne, was a Roman Catholic. The Duke was very susceptible to beautiful young girls. After secret negotiations he was betrothed to marry the fifteen-year-old beauty Mary Beatrice of Modena. On 20 September 1673 there was a proxy marriage in Portugal with Lord Peterborough acting the part of groom. When the news was released, the uproar was fearsome. The King delayed summoning Parliament for a week to give the Duchess time to get to England and consummate the union. Rochester's view was that if it could be celebrated by proxy it could also be consummated by proxy. He wrote an epic that developed into a slur not only on the King's mistresses, but on every other Court lady he could think of. The 'Duchess' in the first stanza refers to Mary of Modena:

> You ladies all of Merry England
> Who have been to kiss the Duchess's hand,
> Say did you lately observe in the show
> A noble Italian called Signior Dildo?
>
> The Signior was one of her Highness's train
> And helped to conduct her over the main,
> But now she cries out, 'To the Duke I will go,

I have no more need for Signior Dildo.'

At the Sign of the Cross in St James's Street,
When next you go thither to make yourselves sweet,
By buying of powder, gloves, essence, or so,
You may chance get a sight of Signior Dildo.

You'll take him at first for no person of note
Because he appears in a plain leather coat:
But when you his virtuous abilities know
You'll fall down and worship Signior Dildo.

My Lady Southeske, heaven prosper her for't,
First clothed him in satin, and brought him to Court;
But his head in the circle he scarcely durst show,
So modest a youth was Signior Dildo.

Lady Southeske was notoriously promiscuous. She was a friend of
Barbara Palmer and had had a notorious affair with the Earl of
Chesterfield, before moving on to the newly married Duke of York.
Her husband was said to have gone out and deliberately caught the
pox, so as to pass it on to the Duke. The affair ended and she passed
it back to her husband. The slander continues:

The good Lady Suffolk, thinking no harm,
Had got this poor stranger hid under her arm:
Lady Betty by chance came the secret to know,
And from her own mother stole Signior Dildo.

Lady Betty was Lady Suffolk's daughter and was renowned for her
sexual virtuosity. The Countess of Falmouth had acquired a slightly
over-ripe reputation, before secretly marrying Rochester's friend
Charles Sackville, Earl of Dorset. She was strikingly beautiful and had
been a contender for Mary of Modena's position:

The Countess of Falmouth, of whom people tell
Her footmen wear shirts of a guinea an ell,
Might save the expense if she but did know
How lusty a swinger is Signior Dildo.

By the help of this gallant, the Countess of Ralph
Against the fierce Harry preserved herself safe:

> She stifled him almost beneath her pillow,
> So closely she embraced Signior Dildo.

The Countess of Ralph was the Countess of Northumberland, Harry Savile's victim on the occasion of his great seduction attempt at Althorp. The 'fierce Harry' is Savile.

> Our dainty fine Duchesses have got a trick
> To dote on a fool for the sake of his prick;
> The fops were undone did their Graces know
> The discretion and vigour of Signior Dildo.
>
> That pattern of virtue her Grace of Cleveland
> Has swallowed more pricks than the ocean has sand;
> But by rubbing and scrubbing so large it does grow,
> It is fit for just nothing but Signior Dildo.

Rochester's next target is the mother of Mary of Modena:

> The Duchess of Modena, though she looks high,
> With such a gallant is contented to lie:
> And for fear the English her secrets should know,
> For a gentleman-usher took Signior Dildo.
>
> The Countess of the Cockpit (who knows not her name?),
> She's famous in story for a killing dame,
> When all her old lovers forsake her, I trow
> She'll then be contented with Signior Dildo.

This could refer to Nell Gwyn, who lodged at the Cockpit, an area of Whitehall Palace, or possibly to Anna-Maria, Countess of Shrewsbury, whom the Duke of Buckingham had installed there after he had killed her husband.

> Tom Killigrew's wife, North Holland's fine flower,
> At the sight of this signior did fart and belch sour;
> And her Dutch breeding farther to show,
> Says, 'Welcome to England, Myn Heer Van Dildo.'
>
> This signior is sound, safe, ready and dumb,
> As ever was candle, carrot or thumb;
> Then away with these nasty devices and show

How you rate the just merits of Signior Dildo.

A rabble of pricks who were welcome before,
Now finding the porter denied 'em the door,
Maliciously waited his coming below
And inhumanly fell on Signior Dildo.

Nigh wearied out the poor stranger did fly,
And along the Pall Mall they followed full cry,
The women concerned from every window,
Cried, 'Oh for heaven's sake save Signior Dildo!'

The good Lady Sandys burst into a laughter,
To see how the bollocks came wobbling after,
And had not their weight retarded the foe
It had gone hard with Signior Dildo.

The craftsmanship is not polished. It may be that of a number of
contributors, probably impromptu, when drunk. If this was indeed the
poem the King commissioned to commemorate his mistresses, it is
noticeable in view of later events that it bears no reference to Louise
de Kerouaille, who was by now firmly poised in the saddle.

There was a more immediate problem. When the moment came to
hand it over, Rochester was not in a state to know precisely what he
was doing. He handed over the wrong composition, a wounding
lampoon on the King himself. Charles was deeply offended. It was an
offensive squib, though not without affection. Rochester was banished
forthwith, something which the Comte de Gramont says happened at
least once a year and was therefore no great novelty. For once the
King was truly enraged, which was surprising, since the poem was
apparently no worse than many others that had readily been forgiven.

In the Isle of Britain long since famous grown
For breeding the best cunts in all Christendom,
There reigns, and oh! Long may he reign and thrive –
The easiest king and best bred man alive.

Him no ambition moves to get renown
Like the French fool, who wanders up and down,
Starving his soldiers, hazarding his crown.
Peace is his aim. His gentleness is such

That as his love is great, he swives as much.

Nor are his high desires above his strength.
His sceptre and his prick are of an equal length,
And she may sway the one that plays with t'other,
And make him little wiser than his brother.
Poor Prince! Thy prick, like thy buffoons,
Will govern thee because it makes thee sport.

'Tis sure he is the sauciest that e'er did swive,
The proudest, peremptoriest prick alive.
Though safety, law, religion, life lay on't,
'Twould break through all to make its way to cunt.

Who restless rolls about from whore to whore,
Grown *impotent* and scandalously poor.
To Carwell, the most dear of all his dears,
The best relief of his declining years,
Oft he bewails his fortune and her fate
Which made her love too well and so late!

For though in her he settles well his tarse,
Yet still his graceless buttocks hung an arse:
This you'd believe had I but time to tell ye
The pains it costs to poor laborious Nelly,
Whilst she employs hands, fingers, mouth and thighs,
Ere she can raise the member she enjoys.

I hate all monarchs with the thrones they sit on
From the hector of France to the cully of Britain.

The 'French fool' is Louis XIV; 'Carwell' is Louise de Kerouaille; 'hector' means bully and 'cully' dupe.

The poem is another of Rochester's less polished works. The rest of it is a pitiless attack on the King's sexual rapacity and is framed around Louise de Kerouaille. Louise was indeed the King's 'dearest of all dears' and he adored her. His pet name for her was 'Fubbs' which meant chubby and he named his yacht *Fubbs* after her. Notwithstanding the occasional hiccough, she was indeed the best relief of his declining years.

Despite Louise's earlier hesitations, she was now ready to love him to the full, and he was incapable of responding with the vigour that he once possessed. Nelly was always on hand for emergencies and it was left, insultingly, to her to get the job done. The King happily put up with criticism of his government of the realm, but this time Rochester had hit his Achilles' heel. He had dismembered the King's sexual prowess, of which he had always been justifiably proud, and his relationship with a mistress whom he adored. The word 'impotent' appears in only one copy-text, and was rapidly changed. For once Charles's sense of humour failed him. Immediate banishment followed and this time it was no mere token. In the endless debate over Rochester's courage, or lack of it, it is easy to forget the fearlessness that was needed to write a broadside like this. It came out by mistake, but these dissidents were usually quickly identified. The King was tolerant and Rochester was lucky, but it should not be forgotten that he was knowingly committing a serious criminal offence.

One of the severest aspects of the Restoration state was its censorship. The Licensing Act 1662 was devised to protect the Church against blasphemy, but it contained a provision against the publication of seditious or offensive books or pamphlets that might tend to the scandal of the government. This section was used to protect the King, his courtiers, his courtesans and corrupt politicians from public exposure of their excesses. Until it was clearly too late, the King was concerned to maintain some tatters of his reputation. He even considered closing down the coffee houses, as they provided such excellent facilities for debating his lapses. Garraway's, Jonathan's, Mann's and Farr's were notorious cradles of sedition, and were patrolled regularly by the King's spies. He did not take action, nor did he prosecute Rochester. He took the realistic view, as he put it, that 'the more you stir a turd, the more it stinks'.

At about the same time Rochester wrote one of his finest poems, a short and enchanting verse, 'To her Ancient Lover'. Middle-aged men love the poem, and women do not. The point of view is that of a loving young girl coaxing life into the flaccid body of a much older man.

> Ancient Person, for whom I
> All the flattering youth defy;
> Long be it ere thou grow old,

Aching, shaking, crazy, cold,
> But still continue as thou art,
> Ancient Person of my heart.

On thy withered lips, and dry,
Which like barren furrows lie;
Brooding kisses I will pour,
Shall thy youthful heat restore.
Such kind showers in autumn fall
And a second spring recall:
> Nor from thee will ever part,
> Ancient Person of my heart.

Thy nobler part, which but to name
In our sex would be counted shame,
By age's frozen grasp possessed,
From his ice shall be released;
And, soothed by my reviving hand,
In former warmth and vigour stand,
All a lover's wish can reach
For thy joy, my love shall teach:
And for thy pleasure shall improve,
All that art can add to love.
> Yet still I love thee without art,
> Ancient Person of my heart.

It is irresistible to imagine that Rochester composed the poem for
Nell to give the King to make him feel a little better about his flagging
powers (*pace* Germaine Greer, who suggests that it may have been for
the wedding feast of his fourteen-year-old niece Anne Lee (Anne
Wharton) in 1673, after Lord Peterborough, thirty-five years her senior,
had debauched her for her money). If it was written for the King, it
would explain why Rochester was so quickly back in favour, and why
he was then presented with a joyous sinecure and the greatest
blessing of his life, his appointment as ranger of Woodstock Park in
Oxfordshire. It was close to Adderbury, though it involved little
increase in contact between him and his wife. He had acquired the
reputation of a dissident and a rebel. He was mutinous and often cruel
to his lackadaisical ruler, but his treatment of the King was not

uniformly hostile. He had cause to love, and did love, the monarch. He wrote him an affectionate address as a prologue to *The Empress of Morocco* by Elkanah Settle which was spoken by Lady Elizabeth Howard on behalf of the female sex.

> To you, Great Sir, my message hither tends
> From youth and beauty, your allies and friends...
> Nor can you 'scape our soft captivity
> From which old age alone must set you free.
> Then tremble at the fatal consequence,
> Since 'tis well known, for your own part, Great Prince,
> 'Gainst us you still have made a weak defence.
> Remember we have eyes, and you a heart,
> Else you may find, too late, that we are things
> Born to kill vassals and to conquer kings.
> But oh! To what vain conquest I pretend
> Whilst Love is our commander, and your friend.
> Our victory your empire more assures,
> For Love will never make the triumph yours.

The Earl was not one for fawning. As Tom Brown, the 'Prince of Grub Street,' wrote, 'All the world knows my Lord Rochester never flattered anybody ... he spared neither prince nor God ...' Rochester said what he meant, though it is noticeable that his compliment is restricted to the King's amorousness. It does not touch on his statesmanship. What he had long yearned for, though, was the rank of keeper of the old royal hunting forest of Woodstock. The jewel that he received from the King, which accompanied the offices of ranger and keeper, was High Lodge. They had been granted in November 1674 to John, Lord Lovelace, MP for Berkshire, but the following February the grant of the rangership was revoked by the King and given to Rochester instead. In May the grant of the keepership was revoked and given to Rochester as well. No doubt the Earl remembered Lord Lovelace, his old contemporary at Wadham College in 1661, with whom he took his degree. There was skulduggery in the background and the appointment was contentious. There was a violent row about it between Lord Arlington and the Earl of Anglesey in the Council, the background of which is lost in the mists of time. Despite it all, Lovelace and Rochester were still good friends in 1676. Indeed,

Lovelace used to visit Rochester at Woodstock and help him get into trouble there, and joined his interests with Rochester later when they were trying to remove the reversion from Rochester's cousin, the Earl of Lichfield. High Lodge, the ranger's official residence, was a plain house at the west end of Woodstock Forest. One can see from an engraving of 1752 that it was Carolean or Jacobean in style, set on two floors, and square, with a tall tiled roof and dormer windows. Surrounded by its own walls and, beyond that, by woodland and fields, it had mullioned windows and a pretty doorway with a small triangular pediment above it. Grants were made to Rochester for its repair in June 1675 and February 1680.

His first expenditure, he decided, like most proud new house owners, was to attend to its decoration. In Rochester's case, according to John Aubrey, this meant 'having a series of lascivious pictures drawn' (Aretine's Postures). The Lodge commanded ravishing views of Oxfordshire, over the great forest walk that runs among the oaks, towards the Cotswolds in the distance. It was a perfect sanctuary. He could not invite his friends home to Adderbury, or, if he did, they had to behave. Much of the time he was not allowed at Court. He was not on harmonious terms with his wife, his wife was at daggers drawn with his mother, and Adderbury was full of family, children and relatives. There had been an increase in numbers. Elizabeth had just had another baby, his second daughter, Elizabeth. She was baptised on 13 July 1674 and turned out to be the prettiest of the girls. She married Edward Montagu, the son of Lord Hinchingbrooke, Rochester's old rival for Elizabeth's hand. She inherited her father's fire and vivacity. She was described as having more wit than her father; she was as generous as she was witty, and as lovely as she was witty and generous. She lived until she was eighty-three. No sooner had Elizabeth recovered from the birth than she was pregnant again. This was to be their fourth and last child, another daughter, Malet, who was christened on 6 January 1675. Malet eventually became Viscountess Lisburne.

High Lodge was close to Woodstock and next to paradise. Rochester had his most trusted servants with him, no wife, no mother, and a constant flow of cronies visiting and bringing their debaucheries with them. Buckingham would arrive with his pack of hounds, 'the best in the country'. They would go hunting for game, animals and women, and Buckingham would pursue his life's goal of ruining his estates. Rochester was fond of falconry and in January 1675 was appointed master surveyor and keeper of the King's hawks. The place became vacant on its surrender by Sir Allen Apsley, his putative parent, and Sir Peter Apsley. According to local gossip Rochester made friends with a number of young ladies who lived in the area. One of them was Nell Browne of Woodstock, who 'though she looked pretty well when clean, yet was a very nasty ordinary silly creature which made people much admire'. Rochester was unaffected by her low beginnings and is thought to have written 'By all Love's Soft, Yet Mighty Powers' for her. Rochester and his friends behaved very much at High Lodge as they would have anywhere else. One tale still to be found in the archives of local folk legend relates how one morning he and his companions met a comely maid taking her butter to market. They bought all her stock, paid her for it and buttered a tree. They were not entirely sober. After they had gone, thinking it a pity to waste it the girl came back and scraped it off. Unfortunately for the girl they saw this and rode back. They turned her upside down and left her there with the butter spread over her bottom.

The goings-on at the Lodge were naturally a matter of absorbing interest, first locally then as far as London, and sometimes across the entire country. As late as 1677 there was a scandal because the 'mad Earl of Rochester' and his evil cronies had taken to running naked races about the grounds of High Lodge. Savile was concerned enough to write to him about the 'scurvy reports of his having stripped himself of prudence as well as his breeches'. Rochester replied, 'For the hideous deportment which you have heard of concerning running naked, so much is true: that we went into the river somewhat late in the year and had a frisk for forty yards in the meadow to dry ourselves.' Then he added, with spirit:

And now Mr Savile, since you are pleased to quote yourself for a grave man of the number of the scandalized, be pleased to call to mind the year 1676 when two large fat nudities led the coranto round Rosamund's fair fountain [in Woodstock Park], while the poor violated nymph wept to behold the strange decay of manly parts since the days of her dear Harry the Second [Rosamund's lover; Rosamund herself was said to have been bled to death there by Queen Eleanor]. Prick, 'tis confessed, you showed but little of; but for arse and buttocks (a filthier ostentation, God wot!) you exposed more of that nastiness in your two folio volumes than we all together in our six quartos. 'Pluck therefore the beam out of thine own eye', etc.

The only person to whom High Lodge was not open was Lady Rochester. Her husband's tact (or fear) restrained him from letting her witness the merriment there. In one of her letters she said unhappily that she was at Cornbury Park, the Clarendon family seat close by at Charlbury. She would be not a little rejoiced if he sent to command her to Woodstock when she was so near. Needless to say he did not. In one of his letters to her from High Lodge he wrote, 'I fear I must see London shortly and begin to repent I did not bring you with me for, since these rakehells are not here to disturb us, you might have passed your devotions this Holy season as well in this place as at Adderbury. But, dear Wife, one of my coach mares is dying, or I had sent my coach instead of my compliments...' In other words, he would not be home for Christmas.

His exasperation with marriage prompted 'Against Marriage':

> Out of mere love and arrant devotion,
> Of marriage I'll give you this galloping notion:
> It's the bane of all business, the end of all pleasure,
> The consumption of youth, wit, courage and treasure.
> It's the rack of our thoughts, and the nightmare of sleep,
> That sets us to work before the day peep.
> It makes us make brick without stubble or straw,
> And a cunt has no sense of conscience or law.
> If you'd use flesh in the way that is *noble*,
> In a generous wench there is nothing of trouble.
> You go on, you come off, say, do what you please –
> The worst you can fear is but a disease;
> And diseases, you know, do admit of a cure,
> But the hell-fire of marriage, none can endure.

How the gods must have laughed when he wrote those last two lines.

When he was comfortably tucked up in High Lodge he turned his attentions to satire. His leaning towards pessimistic probing had begun to darken into pervasive misanthropy. His hatred of mankind, however, was always softened by a streak of humour and understanding. Until his last days he was sour, perhaps, rather than bitter. This was his tone in 'Upon Nothing':

Nothing, thou elder brother even to Shade,
Thou had'st a being ere the world was made,
And, well-fixed, art alone of ending not afraid.

Something, the general attribute of all,
Severed from thee, its sole original,
Into thy boundless self must undistinguished fall.

Great Negative, how vainly would the wise
Enquire, define, distinguish, teach, devise,
Did'st thou not stand to point their blind philosophies.

Is or Is Not, the two great ends of Fate,
And True or False, the subject of debate,
That perfect or destroy the vast designs of State –

When they have racked the politician's breast,
Within thy bosom most securely rest,
And when reduced to thee are least unsafe and blessed.

But, Nothing, why does Something still permit
That sacred monarchs should in council sit
With persons highly thought, at best for nothing fit,

While weighty Something modestly abstains
From princes' coffers and from statesmen's brains,
And nothing there like stately Nothing reigns?

Nothing, who dwells with fools in grave disguise,
For whom they reverend shapes and forms devise,
Lawn-sleeves and furs and gowns, when they like thee look wise.

French truth, Dutch prowess, British policy,
Hibernian learning, Scotch civility,
Spaniards' Dispatch, Danes' Wit, are mainly seen in thee;

The great man's gratitude to his best friend,
Kings' promises, whores' vows, towards thee they bend,
Flow swiftly into thee, and in thee ever end.

In the third Dutch war, which ended in 1674, the Dutch were a military failure against the French, the French had proved treacherous in their alliance with the English, the Spanish spun things out for eighteen months before helping the Dutch, and it was widely thought that Britain should never have become involved in the first place.

Although this work has always been treated as a serious display of melancholy, there is, as always with Rochester, the possibility that it was written tongue in cheek. There was a fashion of writing poetry about 'nothing' from the Renaissance onwards. Rochester's 'Nothing' could easily be a satire on these, the twist being in the last three verses, and the preceding philosophical riddles a mere feint.

9

'I came to town late last night'
Elizabeth Barry and Dr Bendo

> Dorset and Rochester and those superior poets who, as they con-
> ceived lewdly, so they wrote in plain English, and took no care to
> cover up the worst of their thoughts in clean linen; which scandalous
> custom has assisted to bury the best performances of that age,
> because blended with profaneness or indecency. They are not fit to
> be read by people whose religion and modesty have not quite
> forsaken them; and which, had those grosser parts been left out,
> would justly have passed for the most polite poetry that the world
> ever saw.
>
> Daniel Defoe, c. 1721

The centre of the social universe was the West End of London. The
town stretched from the old timbered buildings of the City, past the
fields north of Piccadilly, to Westminster and the vast, rambling
Whitehall Palace. Here the King lived, his courtiers courting in glorious
array. Charles was thirty-five now, very tall, very dark and very
amorous. He was always busy, though not with governing his kingdom.
He loved music and always had it played about him. He loved art, and
did his best with limited resources to replace his father's collection of
Renaissance paintings, the best outside Italy, which had been plundered
by the Parliamentarians. His particular affections, however, were for
women and wit. Life was lived at Court at giddying speed. The centre
of the vortex was the theatre. Charles loved to involve himself in the
drama. He would take an interest in the work of individual writers
and discuss their plays with them. There were of course the actresses:
Nelly, Mistress Knight, the singer, and Moll Davis, who bore him a
child and apparently inspired his love with her touching rendering of
a song, 'My Lodging is on the Cold, Cold Ground'. She performed it
in a play, *The Rival Ladies* by John Downes, who commented that her

performance had raised her from her bed on the cold ground to the bed royal. The theatre and the stews were so well attended, and the Houses of Parliament so poorly, that in 1666 Pepys records the King, needing support in the House of Commons, driven to sending emissaries to the playhouse and the brothels to bid all the Parliament men to go to the Parliament presently.

Performances took place in the early afternoon to catch the natural light, enhanced by chandeliers and footlights. There were gallants posing everywhere, particularly in the actresses' dressing rooms. Gentry sat in the boxes or in the pit. The middle gallery was populated by the merchants and middle classes, with strumpets according to their rank. In the gods there were the riffraff and the trulls. Women of higher standing who wanted to misbehave attended wearing masks, or 'vizards'. Three months after the Restoration Charles had issued patents to Thomas Killigrew and Sir William Davenant to form two licensed theatre companies, the King's Players and the Duke's Players. The King's Players came to rest at the Theatre Royal, Drury Lane in May 1663 and the Duke's Players settled at Dorset Gardens, a fine theatre designed by Wren and opened in 1671. Rochester was heavily involved with both. Louise de Kerouaille set up her own theatre, the Duchess of Portsmouth's Servants, in about 1673, which seems coincidentally to have been the time when she fell out with Rochester.

Another talent that Rochester fostered was Aphra Behn. She was a friend of several of the Merry Gang, in particular Buckingham and Rochester. The Earl used his influence to promote the eccentric playwright, and she in turn adored him for the rest of his short life. She based the hero in her play *The Rover*, and to a greater degree *The Rover, Part II*, on him and beat her breast extravagantly when he died. On his death she wrote of his spirit:

> With the same wonted grace my muse it praised,
> With the same goodness did my faults correct,
> And careful of the fame himself first raised,
> Obligingly it schooled my loose neglect.

She was nineteen at the Restoration, and not long afterwards went to Surinam, where she wrote her best-known novel, *Oroonoko*. On her return to England the King employed her as a spy. Her father was Dutch, and she became involved in the politics of the first Dutch war.

After a brief spell in prison for debt, she set about making a living as a writer and, though much mocked, was a triumphant success. She became known as the female laureate, but her works were racy and exhibited a catholic sexual taste. For the same reason as Rochester, indecency, she fell into oblivion after her death, and has only recently, in the late twentieth century, been swept up on the tide of feminism. She is said to have opened up the world of literature for women.

By 1675 Rochester had taken under his wing the playwright Thomas Otway. He used his influence to get Otway's play *Alcibiades* put on at the Dorset Gardens Theatre in September. Now it was time for Nemesis to join him. She did so in the comely form of Elizabeth Barry. She was the problem to all his answers. In the play a small role, Draxilla, took on an unexpected prominence because of the startling inadequacy of the actress, Elizabeth, who played the part. This was her third attempt. Edward Cole in his *History of the English Stage* comments that she was so bad at acting that 'several persons of wit and quality being at the play and observing how she performed, positively gave their opinion she never would be capable of any part of acting'. It was also considered that she could 'neither sing nor dance, not even in a country dance'.

Rochester was present at the performance. He fell dizzily for her and, overcome by the heat of passion, decided that she could be coached into something special. It was probably a ruse to get her alone for a month or two, but he took a bet with one of his friends that in less than six months he could turn her into the finest player on the stage. This was what she became. She was transfigured into the outstanding actress of her century. The achievement may say much about Elizabeth Barry's character; it says a great deal about Rochester's. It reveals his instinctive feeling for drama. This was the man who roamed in disguise; who could write poetry dressed in anyone's boots; who could rub shoulders with a beggar or a king; who could trick God. It also shows an utter determination against all odds to finish a task that he had started.

It was perhaps the closest brush of his life with real passion. It was the only love that he ever truly felt and it had to be paid for. Elizabeth was an actress to whom there could be no one more vulnerable than an actor, for actors fool themselves and also one another. As a specimen Elizabeth was no great beauty. She was described as a fine creature but not handsome, her mouth opening most on the right side which she strove to draw the other way, at times composing her face as if sitting to have her picture drawn. She was middle-sized and had darkish hair, light eyes and dark eyebrows and was 'indifferently plump'. Where she came from nobody knew. She was said to have been a servant of a Lady Shelton in Norfolk. Having been a servant was no great disgrace. It was the common fate of unmarried daughters of respectable families with little money. Her father, Robert Barry, was said to be a Royalist barrister and by repute she had been given a good education by Lady Davenant, a relative of Sir William Davenant, proprietor of one of the theatres.

Rochester was trapped. He had been leading a cheerful life with another actress, Mrs Boutel, who was celebrated for her interpretation of tragedy. Her special role was Cleopatra in Dryden's *All for Love*, which was very intense. She was immediately forgotten in favour of the unimpressive Barry. But the latter was said to have exquisitely charming conversation, an expressive face and a graceful manner. She was, if anything, *jolie laide*, and could charm without mercy. She was strong minded and determined, which Rochester found irresistible, and she was bad tempered, demanding and hard, which excited him all the more. She was mercenary and eventually gained a nasty reputation for making use of any man who could advance her career and prospects. Tom Brown, the Grub Street hack, said of her, 'Should you lie with her all night, she would not know you the next morning, unless you had another £5 at her service.' Even twenty years later it was said that the 'slattern Betty Barry was still a very hopeful whore at thirty-eight and would choose the highest bidder'. After Rochester's death the poet Robert Gould wrote:

> Who counts her sins may as well count the stars;
> So insolent! It is by all allowed
> There never was so base a thing, so proud:
> Yet covetous, she'll prostitute with any,
> Rather than waive the getting of a penny;
> For the whole harvest of her youthful crimes
> She hoards, to keep herself in future times,
> But by her gains now she may then be fed,
> Which in effect's to damn herself of bread.

Yet in her morals this is thought the best;
Imagine then the lewdness of the rest.

The bewitched Earl laboured with her at High Lodge, where he had taken her for his course of instruction. He worked on her speech and comportment and taught her to express the meaning of what she was saying rather than just declaiming the words. At that time sonorousness was the essence of drama, involving a painstaking repertoire of gestures, vocal gymnastics and sufficient power to talk over the constant hubbub. She learned to express feeling.

Rochester's method must have anticipated Chekhov and Stanislavsky by nearly three centuries. Colley Cibber, who later became Poet Laureate, said that she developed a presence of 'elevated dignity, her mien and her motion superb and gracefully majestic, her voice full, clear and strong, so that no violence of passion could be too much for her and when distress or tenderness possessed her, she subsided into the most affecting melody and softness. In the art of exciting pity she had a power beyond all the actresses I have yet seen, or what your imagination can conceive. In scenes of anger, defiance or resentment, while she was impetuous and terrible, she poured the sentiment with an enchanting harmony.' Rochester had made her work hard for it. He would make her rehearse a role thirty times on the stage, twelve of them in full costume, an approach that was quite unheard of at the time. He overlooked no detail, no look, no movement. Even her page was instructed to manage the train of her dress so as to give every step a peculiar grace. The first part for which she was trained was the Little Gypsy in *The Rover*, the comedy by Aphra Behn, but the first triumph was as Isabella in *Mustapha* by Otway. Her lover brought the King and the Duke and Duchess of York to see her, and the theatre shook with applause. Her subsequent career was triumphant and she became the foremost actress in the realm for the rest of the seventeenth and the early eighteenth century.

Rochester, wisely, was never quite sure of Elizabeth. She was as promiscuous as he, and jealousy and mistrust can be felt like an itching sore in his poetry of the time. As a result, his love letters and poems to her tended to hedge slightly.

My dear mistress has a heart,
Soft as those kind looks she gave me

When, with love's resistless art
   And her eyes, she did enslave me.
But her constancy's so weak,
   She's so wild and apt to wander,
That my jealous heart would break,
   Should we live one day asunder.

Melting joys about her move,
   Killing pleasures, wounding blisses,
She can dress her eyes in love
   And her lips can arm with kisses;
Angels listen when she speaks,
   She's my delight, all mankind's wonder;
But my jealous heart would break,
   Should we live one day asunder.

This is said to be one of the most perfect poems that he wrote, but it betrays his misgivings. There was a flurry of letter writing.

Dear Madam,

You are stark mad, and therefore the fitter for me to love; and that is the reason I think I can never leave to be

Your humble servant...

Madam,

Your letter so transports me that I know not how to answer it. The expressions are so soft and seem to be so sincere that I were the unreasonablest creature on earth, could I but seem to distrust my being the happier.

Madam,

So much wit and beauty as you have should think of nothing less than doing miracles, and there cannot be a greater than to continue to love me. To pick out the wildest and most fantastical odd man alive, and to place your kindness there, is an act so brave and daring as show the greatness of your spirit and distinguish you in love, as you are in all things else, from womankind.

Here's a damned impertinent fool bolted in that hinders me from ending my letter. The plague of – take him and any man or woman alive that take my thoughts off of you.

Then the worm of doubt began to gnaw:

There is now no minute of my life that does not afford me some new argument how much I love you. The little joy I take in everything wherein you are not concerned, the pleasing perplexity of endless thought which I fall into wherever you are brought to my remembrance; and lastly the continual disquiet I am in during your absence, convince me sufficiently that I do you justice in loving you so as woman was never loved before.

'The pleasing perplexity of endless thought' suggests that he is worrying about her sincerity. Othello's poison was in the vein, though it took another two years to prove fatal. The tone of his letters gradually changed.

You are the most afflicting fair creature in the world and however you would persuade me to the contrary, I cannot but believe the fault you pretend to excuse is the only one I could ever be guilty of to you. When you think of receiving an answer with common sense in it, you must write letters that give less confusion than your last. I will wait on you, and be revenged by continuing to love you when you grow weariest of it.

Thomas Otway unfortunately chose this moment to fall in love with Elizabeth too. Rochester has gone down in history as the blackhearted aristocrat who ground the face of the innocent playwright into the dirt and finally ruined him. As usual, with Rochester's reputation, there is no evidence at all. Otway was certainly in love with the actress. It is painfully apparent from his later correspondence. There is no sign that he was ever rewarded with anything more than complete indifference, but he was taking a dangerous risk. As Rochester had demonstrated to the luckless Miss Goditha Price, when crossed he could be merciless.

The history was that in 1675, on Rochester's recommendation to the Court, Otway's *Alcibiades* was produced at the Dorset Gardens Theatre, starring Mrs Barry. For the next two years Otway, while dedicating his work to the Earl, was secretly yearning for his mistress. In the winter of 1675, in the lengthy 'Allusion to Horace' which mocked most of his literary contemporaries, Rochester wrote almost parenthetically while abusing Dryden for populism:

'Tis therefore not enough, when your false sense
Hits the false judgment of an audience

186

Of clapping fools, assembling a vast crowd
Till the thronged playhouse crack with the dull load;
Though even that talent merits in some sort
That can divert the rabble and the Court,
Which blundering Settle never could attain,
And puzzling Otway labours at in vain.

It was little enough to cause resentment in the most sensitive artist, especially when compared with what he had to say about all the others. Although *Alcibiades* was not a roaring success, Rochester recommended Otway's second attempt, *Don Carlos*, to the King and the Duke of York in June 1676; and the third attempt, *Titus and Berenice*, was dedicated to Rochester himself in 1677.

In May of 1678 Otway was granted a commission in the army and went soldiering in Flanders. Rochester was said to have forced him into it. The playwright returned in the spring of 1679, scabbed and lousy, and wrote 'The Poet's Complaint to his Muse', which contained the words:

The first was he who stunk of that rank verse
In which he wrote his *Sodom* farce,
A wretch whom old diseases did so bite
That he writ bawdy sure in spite
To ruin and disgrace him quite.

This was a reference to Rochester's play *Sodom*, which is so appalling that faint-hearted critics cannot believe that it came from the same pen as 'To her Ancient Lover'. The full title was *Sodom, or the Quintessence of Debauchery by E of R Written for the Royal Company of Whoremasters*. One can glean an idea of its obscene pyrotechnics from the stage direction to the opening of the second act: 'Six naked women and six naked men appear, and dance, the men doing obeisance to the women's cunts, kissing and touching them often, the women doing ceremonies to the men's pricks, kissing them, dandling their cods, etc., and so fall to fucking, after which the women sigh, and the men look simple and sneak off.'

Sodom bears a striking resemblance in form, though not content, to *Valentinian*, a rather serious play that Rochester based on John Fletcher's work of the same name. It contained a covert attack on the King to show support for Rochester's friend Buckingham, who had been dismissed from all his offices in 1674 for appealing against Charles's policies to the House of Commons without the permission of the King or the Cabal or the House of Lords. *Sodom* looks like another case of the poet satirising himself, though it was probably more a satire on Dryden. It was rumoured to have been 'performed at Court'. If it was, the cast must have been relieved that there was no second house. It was almost certainly a private joke for the King and his cronies, perhaps performed as a 'closet drama' (in a reading).

There was undoubtedly a lengthy courtship of Mrs Barry by Otway. He wrote a series of passionate letters to her, most of which were dated after Rochester's death. William Oldys wrote caustically, 'That language of doting madness and despair, however it may succeed with raw girls, is seldom successful with such practitioners in that passion as Mrs Barry, since it only hardens their vanity. For she could get bastards with other men, though she would hardly condescend to grant Otway a kiss, who was as amiable in person and address as the best of them.' The playwright fell into a decline and finally died in abject poverty. Having been given a guinea for bread when he was destitute, the first mouthful killed him. The long dead Rochester was as always blamed.

On 25 June 1675 once again Rochester went too far. The King, we know, was a lover of clocks. In the Great Privy Garden at Whitehall he kept his favourite, which was thought to be the most remarkable clock in all Europe. It was a type of sundial and had been designed by Franciscus Linus, a learned Jesuit, and bore little resemblance to the ordinary appliance with gnomon and dial. It was an elaborate set of chronometers. It was perfectly accurate and phallic in shape. A group of the Ballers including Rochester, Buckhurst, Fleetwood Shepherd, Lord Middlesex, Lord Sussex and Harry Savile had been drinking all night with the King. They were on their way to their respective lodgings through the Privy Garden and still had sufficient clarity of vision to notice the clock in the dark. In a matter of seconds the device had disintegrated. Rochester was the ringleader – shouting in a drunken lapse into metaphysics, 'What, dost thou stand here to fuck time?' Others shouted, 'Kings and Kingdoms tumble down and so shall thou.'

The incident has been cited, together with Rochester's many offences against the King, to suggest that he was fundamentally republican. Lines from his poetry such as 'I hate all monarchs with the thrones they sit on, From the hector of France to the cully of Britain' are relied on in support. In fact, Rochester was virtually apolitical, despite a tendency towards whiggishness as he grew older. He loathed politicians (and priests) impartially, together with all other forms of authority. After his death, his friend Robert Wolseley wrote:

He had a wit that was accompanied with an unaffected greatness of mind, and a natural love to justice and truth; a wit that was in perpetual war with knavery, and ever attacking those kind of vices most such as tended to the prejudice of public bodies, and were of a common nuisance to the happiness of humankind. Never was his pen drawn except on the side of good sense, to stop the progress of arbitrary oppression and beat down the brutishness of headstrong will. If he did not take such care of himself as he ought, he had the humanity however to wish well to others, and I think I may truly affirm he did the world as much good by a right application of satire, as he hurt himself by a wrong pursuit of pleasure.

When the King heard about the sundial he did not find it easy to see the joke. He loved drinking himself and tippled constantly, but he was seldom out of control. He had a sneaking affection for his crapulous courtiers, but could never quite see how drunkenness itself explained inexplicable behaviour. Rochester was now twenty-eight and old enough to know better. He had alienated Cleveland, who mattered little. Nell Gwyn was impossible to offend. But he had upset Louise de Kerouaille, who had little humour and who had taken violent personal offence at one of Rochester's misdemeanours. She had been stirring up trouble for him for some time. Rochester once again withdrew to the countryside.

One of the effects of rustication was to give him time to write poetry; another was to give Elizabeth Barry time to misbehave in London. The third was to give Louise de Kerouaille an opportunity to make more mischief for him. She was simmering because of some slight or plot of which he seems genuinely to have been unaware. To Rochester, what was happening was an outrage. He was accused of having written 'Portsmouth's Looking Glass':

Methinks I see you newly risen

189

> From your embroidered bed and pissing,
> With studied mien, and much grimace
> Present yourself before your glass...

There followed an extensive list of male lovers, few of whom had anything to do with Louise. The innocent Rochester, the all-purpose culprit, got the blame. In 1677, when he was dining in an eating house in the Mall, the French cook was stabbed in another room. It was rumoured that he was to blame. He wrote in desperation to Harry begging him to get his brother, Lord Halifax, to stifle the lie when it reached him, because once it got as far as York the truth would not be believed for another three years. Shortly after his death, Samuel Woodforde wrote in his 'Ode to the Memory of the Right Honourable John Lord Wilmot, the Earl of Rochester':

> Madness and follies, which howeer begun,
> Were not by Rochester sustained alone,
> Though he almost alone the burden bore
> (Beside the monstrous pack, which *were* his own).

He had *not* written 'The History of the Insipids'. He probably wished that he had. Many considered it the best satire on Charles's reign. It was blamed on Rochester, and some of it bears his unmistakable stamp, but the perpetrator was either Andrew Marvell or John Freke.

> But, Charles what could thy policy be,
> To run so many sad disasters
> To join thy fleet with false D'Estrées,
> To make the French of Holland masters,
> Was't Carwell, brother James or Teague
> That made thee break the triple league?
>
> By the Lord Mayor and his grave coxcombs,
> Freeman of London Charles is made;
> Then to Whitehall a rich gold box comes,
> Which was bestowed on the French jade.
> But wonder it should be so, Sirs,
> When monarchs rank themselves with grocers...

It was a wounding poem, more so because it was true.

Admittedly, it was Rochester who had, in a moment of thoughtless levity, transformed a popular street ballad of the period,

> When first I bid my love good morrow,
>   With tear in eye and hand on breast,
> My heart was even drowned in sorrow
>   And I poor soul, was much oppressed...

into this diaphanous little ditty:

NELL: 'When to the King I bid good-morrow
  With tongue in mouth and hand on tarse,
Portsmouth may rend her cunt for sorrow
  And Mazarine may kiss mine arse.'

PORTSMOUTH: 'When England's monarch's on my belly
  With prick in cunt, though double-crammed,
Fart of mine arse for small whore Nelly
  And great whore Mazarine be damned.'

KING: 'When on Portsmouth's lap I lay my head
  And Knight does sing her bawdy song,
I envy not George Porter's bed
  Nor the delights of Madam Long.'

PEOPLE: 'Now heavens preserve our faith's defender,
  From Paris plots and Roman cunt,
From Mazarine, that new pretender
  And from that politic Gramont.'

'Portsmouth' was Louise. 'Mazarine' was married to the brutish Duc de Mazarin. In 1676 she escaped from him and fled to England dressed as a man. The Duke of York bought her a house, whereon while Louise was still *maîtress en titre* Mazarine became the King's mistress. 'Knight' was the singer and occasional mistress to the King, and Jane Long was an actress and mistress to Rochester's friend George Porter.

The joke may have proved elusive for Louise. The row between her and the Earl began in the summer of 1675 and continued until June 1676. For whatever reason, Rochester was either ill or banished in the country when he heard reports of Louise turning the King and the Court against him. He was already unpopular, terrified and very put out. He bombarded poor Henry Savile with demands to sort it out. At first he remained cool, though isolated and melancholy. He wrote to Harry on 8 June 1675:

'Tis not the least of my happiness that I think you love me, but the first of all my pretensions, is to make it appear that I faithfully endeavour to deserve it. If there be a real good upon earth 'tis in the name of 'friend' without which all others are merely fantastical. How few of us are fit stuff to make that thing we have daily the melancholy experience. However, dear Harry let us not give out nor despair of bringing that about, which as it is the most difficult and rare accident of life, is also the best, – nay perhaps the only good one.

This thought has so entirely possessed me since I came into the country, (where *only* one can think, for you at Court think not at all, or at least as if you were shut up in a drum – you can think of nothing but the noise made about you) that I have made many serious reflections upon it. I forget that you may impute my philosophy to the dogdays and living alone; to prevent the inconveniences of solitude and many others, I intend to go to Bath on Sunday next...

Your hearty faithful affectionate humble servant

Rochester

If you see the Duchess of Portsmouth very often, take some opportunity to talk to her about what I spoke to you at London.

The affair was not so easily settled, however. Matters took a turn for the worse. In about September 1675 a dejected Rochester wrote from the country to Savile in London: 'That night I received the surprising account of my lady Duchess's more than ordinary indignation against me. I was newly brought in dead of a fall from my horse, of which I still remain bruised and bed-rid, and can now scarce think it a happiness that I saved my neck. What ill star reigns over me, that I'm still marked out for ingratitude and only used barbarously by those I am obliged to?' He was, he said, 'a creature who had already received of her all the obligations he ever could pretend to', so 'why should she take the advantage of a false, idle story [it is unknown what this was] to hate such a man, as if it were an inconvenience to her to be harmless, or a pain to continue just? By that God that made me, I have no more offended her in thought, word or deed, no more imagined or uttered the least thought to her contempt or prejudice

192

than I have plotted treason, concealed arms, trained regiments for a rebellion.' He went on:

I thought the Duchess of Portsmouth more an angel than a woman, and, as this is the first, it shall be the most malicious thing I will ever say of her. For her generous resolution of not hurting me to the King, I thank her; but she must think a man much obliged after the calling of him knave, to say she will do him no farther prejudice. For the Countess of Pembroke [Louise's sister], whatever she has heard me say, or anybody else, of her, I'll stand the test of any impartial judge. 'Twas neither injurious nor unmannerly, and how severe soever she pleases to be, I have always been her humble servant and will continue so.

Rochester then begged Savile 'to talk once more with her [the Duchess], and desire her to give me the fair hearing she would afford any *footman* of hers who had been complained of to her by a less worthy creature – for such a one I assure myself my accuser is.' His letter concluded:

I would not be run down by a company of rogues and this looks like an endeavour towards it. Therefore, dear Harry, send me word how I am with other folks. If you visit my Lord Treasurer name the calamity of this matter to him and tell me sincerely how he takes it. And if you hear the King mention me, do the office of a friend to

    Your humble servant,
      Rochester

Rochester could not afford to offend the Lord Treasurer, who seems to have been dragged into the squabble. He was a good friend and the fount of all money. On the contrary he needed to cultivate him. It is clear that an ill-wisher had accused him of some crime of hand or tongue well beyond his usual level of offensiveness. The Countess of Pembroke, married to the drunken and manically savage Earl, had accused Rochester of slandering her sister. If he did it, he had forgotten it. It is unlikely to have been the references to Louise in the verses for which he was banished, for they were written eighteen months before in early 1674. The whole letter is surprising. It was uncharacteristic of Rochester to grovel for forgiveness. Even if he were innocent, in earlier times he would have cheerfully accepted the blame and done his best to compound it. He had never had the least scruple over maligning the King's mistresses or indeed the King. Circumstances of course had changed. The monarch was getting on in years. He was beginning to enjoy a domestic cosiness with Louise that had inevitably increased her influence on him. But the King knew her hysterical and melodramatic nature, and Louise had said that she would not involve Charles, for which the Earl was abjectly grateful.

It is sterile to speculate over causes when the entire background is a mystery, but throughout the course of this correspondence the intensity of his reaction suggests a certain level of mental imbalance. Perhaps his mind now had begun to deteriorate through illness. It may have been merely a symptom of his loss of favour with the King, something which was his life's blood. The importance of the discord between Rochester and Louise is that Rochester's spirit was beginning to look beaten by the spring of 1676, the date of Louise's departure from Court. He was twenty-nine. Had he been himself he would never have given such a display of self-abasement. It betrayed an almost complete loss of pride. Still, 'All men would be cowards if they durst ...' He next wrote desolately from the country to Savile in London, 'If it were the sign of an honest man to be happy in his friends, sure I were marked out for the worst of men, since no one e'er lost so many as I have done or knew how to make so few,' and he added, 'The severity you say the Duchess of Portsmouth shows to me is a proof that 'tis not in my power to deserve well of anybody, since (I call truth to witness) I have never been guilty of an error that I know to her. And this may be a warning to you that remain in the mistake of being kind to me, never to expect a grateful return, since I am so utterly ignorant how to make it.' He explained:

To value you in my thoughts, to prefer you in my wishes, to serve you in my words, to observe, study and obey you in all my actions is too little, since I have performed all this to her without so much as an offensive accident, and yet she thinks it just to use me ill. If I were not malicious enough to hope she were in the wrong, I must have a very melancholy opinion of myself. I wish your interest might prevail with her, as a friend of hers not mine, to tell how I have deserved it of her, since she has ne'er accused me of any crime but of being cunning; and I told her, somebody had been cunninger than I to persuade her so.

His tone reeks of self-pity and that was not his character. He endured appalling pain from his sickness for many years with great stoicism, and he constantly tolerated libels and groundless aspersions on himself with little more than a resigned sigh. He had spoken to the Duchess about the affair. He was none the wiser, but the accusations of cunning and knavery suggest some more elaborate offence than a mere poetic barb.

In early October 1675, perhaps to demonstrate his displeasure, the King signed a warrant granting the reversion of the rangership of Woodstock Park to the Earl of Lichfield, a cousin of Rochester's married to an illegitimate daughter of the King and Barbara Cleveland. Although this had no effect on Rochester's right to occupy High Lodge, it removed the property from Rochester's heirs on the instant of his death. It was a sinister portent. He and Lovelace both entered caveats, and took the matter to arbitration by the Keeper of the Seal, thus by implication suing the King. His standing at Court was very low indeed. A few months later news was made public that he was dead. He wrote to Harry:

This day I received the unhappy news of my own death and burial. But hearing what heirs and successors were decreed me in my place, and chiefly in my lodgings, it was no small joy to me that those tidings prove untrue. My passion for living is so increased that I omit no care of myself, which before, I never thought life worth the trouble of taking. The King, who knows me to be a very ill natured man, will not think it an easy matter for me to die now I live chiefly out of spite.

Dear Mr Savile, afford me some news from your land of the living; and though I have little curiosity to hear who's well, yet I would be glad my few friends are so, of whom you are no more the least than the leanest. I have better compliments for you, but that may not look so sincere as I would have you believe I am, when I profess myself,

Your humble servant

It was not mere imagination. There really was something unpleasant going on behind his back. Erroneous reports of his death had caused a certain amount of glee. He received support against his enemies from his old friend the Secretary to the Treasury. Sir Robert Howard wrote on 29 February 1676 that, although Londoners might be more interested in bad news than good, he could not believe that they were so stupid as to be oblivious of what they would have lost by Rochester's death. He was delighted that the Earl was alive, and not just because of their friendship; he had to concede that it was also because he could enjoy all the delights that Rochester's doctor had warned the Earl against. He wanted to know when the Earl was coming to town, though it was where the worst men and women censured the best, and where the silent knave was sheltered under the appearance of a sober person. Those who criticised others were like the critics in the theatre, most critical where there was genuine talent and inspired more by envy than by judgement.

Rochester also received support from his friend Henry Bulkeley, a captain in the King's guards and Master of the Royal Household, who wrote, 'Though there is no man living more faithfully concerned than I am at any good or ill that can happen to you, yet I don't wonder you fall into such persecutions as the last, since you live in an age when fools are the most powerful enemies; and the few wise we have either cannot or will not befriend us. My Lord, all I can say is since we who reverence bottle and bold truth are contemned, these creatures have interest [influence] enough to invade our ease and our reputations.' Things had indeed changed since his sparkling years.

The battle with Louise gradually petered out. Rochester wrote to Savile thanking him for his help and apologising for all the trouble to which he had been put. It seems that money had had to change hands, since he added, 'I daily expect more considerable effects of your friendship, and have the vanity to think I shall be the better for your growing poorer.' The affair died with Portsmouth's humiliation at Court. There was an excited fluttering in the diplomatic and ministerial dovecotes with the arrival in London of Hortense Mancini, Duchesse de Mazarin, a niece of the great Cardinal Mazarin. During Charles's exile, marriage between the two of them had been mooted, but since then she had married disastrously elsewhere and separated from her husband. 'An extraordinary beauty and wit, but dissolute,' John Evelyn decided, 'all the world knows her story.' Charles was enraptured and could not see enough of her. The Duchess of Portsmouth was ousted as *maîtresse en titre* by 'Mazarine' and retired to Bath. Rochester charitably wrote to Savile, 'I am sorry for the declining Duchess and would have you generous to her at this time, for that is true pride and I delight in it.' Portsmouth's problems were shared by the King's ministers, who were divided over which mare to back, and by the French Ambassador, who was always trying to assess the relative influence over the King of his various mistresses. Hortense turned out to be as chaste as Charles. When the young Prince of Monaco, an old friend, arrived in London, it was soon apparent that she had taken a new lover. Charles's ardour quickly cooled. Though the two remained on friendly terms, Louise was recalled to office.

Later, when Louise was still in her early thirties and Charles was fifty-three and beginning to feel his age, it was her own wandering eye which caused trouble. She strayed in the direction of another French visitor to England, Philippe de Vendôme. Charles, coming on them abruptly, saw more than he had a mind to see and sent Vendôme on his way. The monarch realised that he could not face life without her. To the horror of his courtiers, from then on he effectively took her to wife, indulging in elaborate displays of public affection. His fabled amorous urges had waned but he still depended as much as ever on the consolation of female company. He divided his attentions between Louise and Nelly. John Evelyn was present at one typical evening at Court at a family scene 'in the midst of the King's natural children, *viz*: the Lady Lichfield, Sussex, Duchess of Portsmouth, Nelly and co., concubines and cattle of that sort, as splendid as jewels and excess of bravery could make them'. Early in 1685, shortly before the King's death, Evelyn witnessed a similar scene: 'I am never to forget the inexpressible luxury and profaneness, gaming and all dissolution, and as it were total forgetfulness of God (it being Sunday evening), the King sitting and toying with his concubines, Portsmouth, Cleveland and Mazarine, a French boy singing love songs. Six days after, all was dust.'

In the spring of 1676 Rochester wrote to Harry, who was now becoming an important diplomat, '... I would be glad to know if the Parliament be like to sit any time, for the peers of England being grown of late years very considerable in the Government, I would make one at the session. Livy and sickness has a little inclined me to policy [politics]. When I come to town I make no question but to change that folly for some less, whether wine or women I know not, according as my constitution serves me.'

Inevitably it came to pass. It was not *a* career that he wanted, only *to* career. In 1677 he attended the House of Lords four times in February, thirteen in March and seven in April, but by May it had tailed off to once in the month. There is a record of the Earl of

Rochester making a very serious speech about the future of the Roman Catholic Duke of York, but it is thought that this was another Earl of Rochester at a later date. There is an alternative legend that he made just one speech. He began, 'My lords, I divide my speech into four parts.' There was a long pause, and he added, 'My lords, if I ever I rise to speak again in this House, I give you leave to cut me in pieces.' Somehow, it is the apocryphal version that bears the ring of truth. 'It is a miraculous thing (as the wise have it) when a man half in the grave cannot leave off playing the fool and the buffoon, but so it falls out to my comfort,' he admitted.

Back in London, ill as he was, he was soon in trouble again. Predictably, he was having problems with Elizabeth Barry.

Madam

If there be yet alive within you the least memory of me, give me leave to assure you I will meet it very shortly with such a share on my side as will justify me to you from all ingratitude. If there can be any addition to one of the highest misfortunes, my absence from you has found the way to give it me in not affording me the least occasion of doing you any service since I left you.

It seems, till I am capable of greater merit, you resolve to keep me from the vanity of pretending any at *all*. Pray consider, when you give another leave to serve you more than I, how much injustice you run the hazard of committing, when it will not be in your power to reward that more deserving man with half so much happiness as you have thrown away upon my worthless self.

Your restless servant.

Then in May 1676 he wrote ominously to her: 'I came to town late last night, though time enough to receive news from the King – very surprising, you being chiefly concerned in't. I must beg that I may speak with you this morning at ten o'clock. I will not fail to be at your door. The affair is unhappy ...' His friends Etherege and Buckhurst both had liaisons with her. No one knows when, though it is thought to have been after Rochester's death, and they were only two of an army. But it was something of that nature that the King imparted to him. At least the monarch was his friend again, even though his mistress was not. He was once again warmed and illuminated in the glow of the Court's favour. He was able to bask untroubled for a whole month, until on 28 June he found himself amid the worst ructions he had ever caused in his life of Misrule.

That Saturday he and a number of the Ballers including Etherege, Captain Bridges, Mr Jephson and Mr Downs had gone to Epsom in Surrey for the races. They drank until Sunday night, when they decided that what they needed most was music. After two days in the village such was their popularity that the fiddlers refused to play. To teach them a lesson the visitors began tossing the fiddlers in a blanket. A passer-by, a barber, heard the noise and went to see what was going on. He was grabbed too. To fob them off, he offered to take them to the prettiest woman in Epsom. The plan was approved and they let him go. He duly led them to the house of the constable.

In those days the village constable was not the professional custodian of the law that we know today. He was an ordinary citizen who had been appointed to the office for a year by the village. His duty was to take charge of the watch and to quell riots and disturbances. It was an honour and a chore, and the quality of the constable varied widely. The Epsom constable answered his door and demanded to know what his visitors wanted. They told him they had come for a whore. He refused to let them in, so they broke down the doors and set about him. He made his escape, got to the watch and called them in. When they arrived armed with half-pikes the Ballers sobered up a little. Etherege addressed the men in honeyed words. He managed to placate them and the constable dismissed them.

But things then got worse. As soon as they had gone, Rochester, who was the most aggressive of the group and looking for trouble, drew his sword on the constable. His friend Downs, in an effort to stop him doing serious damage, grabbed him, and the constable cried out, 'Murder!' The watch rushed back towards Downs's rear, and seeing him involved in the renewed affray assumed he was the aggressor and split his skull with a staff. Rochester and the others ran away into the darkness, probably having no idea of what was happening to Downs in the mêlée. Downs, who was not carrying a sword, picked up a stick and tried to defend himself. The watch attacked him with their pikes, one of which pierced his side. Some days later, he died. Etherege and the others absconded.

The King, who notoriously disapproved of this type of behaviour, was incensed and was determined to make an example of the Earl.

He gave orders for his arrest and contemporary letters show that he had every intention of putting him on trial, probably for murder. Taking part in a riot from which death resulted was technically murder, and the coroner had delivered his verdict accordingly. But Rochester had gone to earth. He could not be found. He was not at his London lodgings, nor at Adderbury, nor at High Lodge, nor at the Court, and he was certainly nowhere near Epsom. Everyone thought that he had escaped to France, but in fact he was only three miles from Court at Tower Hill, masquerading as the 'famous Italian pathologist, Dr Alexander Bendo'.

He had made no effort to blend into the crowds. He was dressed in bizarre oriental clothing, with a false beard, having widely advertised his presence with a handbill. That document alone should have given the game away to anyone who knew him and who was prepared to unravel the deliberately convoluted prose:

To All Gentlemen, Ladies & others, whether of City, Town or Country: Alexander Bendo wisheth all Health and Prosperity. *Whereas* this famous metropolis of England has ever been infested with a numerous company of such whose arrogant confidence has enabled them to impose upon the people either premeditated cheats, or, at best, the dull & empty mistakes of their self-deluded imaginations in physic, chymical and Galenic, in astrology, physiognomy, palmistry, mathematics, alchemy and even Government itself – the last of which I will not propose to discourse of since it no ways belongs to my vocation as the rest do, *which*, thanks to my God I find much more safe, equally honest and therefore more profitable.

Bendo professes to oppose 'those impudent fops whose saucy pretensions have brought such scandal upon their reputations', and offers a paradox: 'I hope you will not think I could be so imprudent that if I had intended any such foul play myself, I should have given you warning by my observations upon others.' He elaborates the conceit: 'Is it my fault if the cheat by his wits makes himself so like me that *I* cannot avoid resembling *him*? Consider, pray, the valiant and the coward ... They are the same in many things, and differ but in one alone. The valiant man holds up his head, looks confidently round about him, wears a sword, courts a lord's wife and owns it. So does the coward. One only point of honour, and that's courage, makes the distinction.' He then teasingly seeks to protect himself against exposure:

I'll only say something to the honour of the mountebank, in case you discover *me* to be one.

Reflect a little what kind a creature 'tis: he is fain to supply some higher ability he pretends to, with craft; he draws great companies to him by undertaking strange things which can never be effected. The *politician*, finding how the people are taken with miraculous impossibilities, plays the same game – promises things which he's sure can ne'er be brought about; the people believe, are deluded and pleased. The expectation of a future good which shall never befall them, draws their eyes off a present evil; thus are *they* kept in subjection, *he* in greatness, wealth and power. So you see the politician is a mountebank in State affairs, and the mountebank is an arrant politician in physic.

That was Rochester's true view of politics. Seven years after Rochester's death, as a New Year's present, an old servant, Thomas Alcock, recounted the details of the adventure in a manuscript book for Lady Ann Baynton, Rochester's eldest daughter.

I wish it were possible for me by this narrative to procure your Ladyship that real mirth and continual hearty laughs this frequently gave us whilst we plied our operations in the laboratory; some stirring an old boiling kettle of soot and urine, tinged with a little asafoetida [a foul-smelling gum resin] and all the nasty ingredients that would render the smell more unsavoury, others tending the fire, some luting [sealing] the retorts, others pounding bricks and scraping powders from them.

Here, one busy calcining [heating] the minerals, there another scumming a crucible; some grinding oils with a stone upon marble till they sweat, whilst the drops from face and nose made the medicine the bigger and consequently more beneficial; others labouring at the pestle & mortar, and all of them dressed like the old witches in Macbeth, whilst the grave and wise, the civil, modest and just pathologist, the noble Doctor Alexander Bendo, in an old overgrown green gown which he religiously wore in memory of Rabelais his master, put on at the reception of his Doctor's degree at Montpellier, lined through with exotic furs of diverse colours, an antique cap, a great reverend beard, and a magnificent false medal set round with glittering pearl, rubies, and diamonds, hung about his neck in a massy goldlike chain of prince's metal [alloy of copper and zinc] (which the King of Cyprus had given him for doing a signal cure upon his darling daughter, the Princess Aloephangina, who was painted in a banner and hung up at his elbow) sat with his scales and weights making up medicines of all sorts and sealing them with his seal of office, giving pretended directions to his operators by his gestures in a language which neither he nor they understood one word of.

Bendo 'also made predictions', wrote Alcock, 'casting nativities, interpreting of dreams, solving of omens, responses to horary questions, illustrations of signs and tokens, judgments upon moles, wens, warts and natural marks, according to their several kinds, and accidental positions in various parts of the naked body'. And 'If modest ladies could not declare their whereabouts without blushing', the Doctor would disguise himself as 'a grave matron' and arrange to inspect the hidden marks. His workers were careful to maintain the illusion:

For though we had Latin, French and Italian to use on occasion, yet since our mystery flourished best under the deep recesses of concealment and secrecy, we of the fraternity kept a perpetual jangling to one another as if we were mighty industrious and intent upon our respective operations, in a jargon of damned unintelligible gibberish all the while, and indeed we judged it not convenient, in our circumstances, to do anything in plain English but laugh. And all this to amuse the gentle spectators whom we freely admitted into our laboratory, that they might see we took pains for what we had and consequently were no cheats, as the apothecaries had endeavoured to represent us.

Bendo accepted payment for his medicines only, 'and by this means reaped a rich harvest of good gold and silver which was cheerfully paid him by his credulous patients with thanks to boot'. His 'affable and communicative advice' he gave for nothing. Eventually, Rochester found himself back in favour with the King. Bendo had served his purpose, and Alcock, who still relished 'out-cheating' the patients, could only lament:

But ah, fading joys! The pleasures we had so long fed on were now become meat for our masters, and the hungry Court could no longer sustain her drooping spirits without the intellectual viands we had hitherto feasted on; and the noble Doctor (with sorrow to his desponding enemies & joy to his triumphant friends) was now called home, who made the quickest voyage from France that ever man did, which was the talk and admiration of the whole town; for those that saw his ostracism cancelled this night at Whitehall, did the very next day see him there in splendour dancing at a ball in as great favour as ever; and nobody knew what was become of the mountebanks.

It was for some time rumoured, Alcock boasts, that the mountebanks 'were an enchanted crew, raised and laid by necromancy; and who so apt to believe this story (think ye) as their credulous patients, which made the twice deluded fools who had furnished themselves with medicines against all accidents whatsoever, throw them now away for fear of witchcraft. The apothecaries really believed that the Devil was run away with them, for it was not known who or what they were till a long time after.'

The enterprise was not mounted on a modest scale. The great Doctor achieved fame throughout the capital. He did not practise his art solely among the artisans of East London. Patients of all ranks travelled great distances. Thus his enemies, who were painstakingly searching London for him, were themselves being palmed off with his revolting specifics. Any waiter could imagine his joy. Rochester was not broken yet. However, his reputation had not survived so well as he. Because of the Epsom affray the old taunt of cowardice was resurrected and once again echoed round Whitehall, while his enemies exulted in an orgy of Schadenfreude. A spiteful little offering, probably the work of one Thomas D'Urfey, went round:

> Room, room for a blade of the town
> That takes delight in roaring,
> Who all day long rambles up and down,
> And at night in the street lies snoring.
>
> That for the noble name of spark
> Does his companions rally;
> Commits an outrage in the dark,
> Then slinks into an alley.

10

'And thus he got the name of Poet Squab'
The Feud with Dryden

Rochester may be signalised as the first thoroughly depraved and vicious person, so far as we remember, who assumed the office of the satirist, – the first, although not, alas! the last human imitator of 'Satan accusing sin'. Here, for the first time, was a man of no virtue or belief in virtue whatever, and whose life was one mass of wounds, bruises, and putrefying sores, – a naked satyr who gloried in his shame, – becoming a severe castigator of public morals and of private character.

The Rev. George Gilfillan, *Specimens with Memoirs of the less known British poets*, 1860

In the course of his career as literary patron, Rochester had picked up, and rapidly put down, Elkanah Settle, one of the least talented of the Restoration tragedians, who scored one success with *The Empress of Morocco* and became insufferably conceited. The Earl of Mulgrave wrote the first prologue to the play. Rochester wrote another that seems to have been used in the second Court performance, which must have created a little tension. He was soon on hostile terms with Settle as well as with Mulgrave and Dryden. He took up the cause of John Crowne, who was good at comedy, had no talent at tragedy and insisted on specialising in the latter. He also took an interest that did not fade in William Wycherley, Thomas Otway, with whom his relationship was bedevilled by Otway's admiration of Elizabeth Barry, Sir Francis Fane, who was not one of his more talented choices, and Nathaniel Lee, who was successful. However, Lee was an alcoholic who suffered from fits of insanity and ended his days in Bedlam (which may explain certain contradictions in his play *The Princess of Cleves*). According to his father, Sir Sydney Lee, Nathaniel had been driven to insanity by his debaucheries in the company of Rochester and other aristocratic patrons. There is no evidence that this is true, but it is inherently likely. The Earl also encouraged the young John Oldham, who likewise swiftly began to ruin his prospects with alcohol. But he pulled out of it in time to form a lofty disdain for his exemplar's habits. Oldham had written a lampoon on him, with the caption: 'A Satyr against Virtue, supposed to be spoken by the Court Hector who demolished the sundial'. Rochester was delighted by it, and sought him out with the intention of advancing his career.

The writer, however, with whom he parted company with true bravura was Dryden. The intimacy ended with Dryden being brutally cudgelled by hired thugs in Rose Alley, off Covent Garden, after the publication of a poem he was thought to have written shortly before Rochester's death. Their friendship had begun more than ten years beforehand in April 1668, when Rochester took a significant role in Dryden's appointment as Poet Laureate.

Dryden was not of aristocratic birth. Rochester was indifferent to breeding, including his own, but Dryden was not. He was deeply conscious of the fact that he had to earn a living and resented the effortless success of wealthy courtiers, who though amateurs could equal and occasionally surpass him. He was sixteen years older than his patron, and ultimately so dominated the literature of his day that the period became known as 'The Age of Dryden'. The son of a country gentleman, he received a classical education at Westminster School. His early poetry was slavishly complimentary to Cromwell; later, after the Restoration, it was slavishly complimentary to Charles II. He made a speciality of writing encomia to the King, and so when Sir William Davenant, the Poet Laureate, who claimed to be the illegitimate son of Shakespeare, died in 1668, Dryden was an obvious candidate. Rochester pointed it out to the King. Dryden wrote grandiose verse with flourishes and rhetoric of the type that moved Rochester to write:

> Have you seen the raging stormy main
> Toss a ship up, then cast her down again?
> Sometimes she seems to touch the very skies
> And then again upon the sand she lies.
> Or have you seen a bull, when he is jealous,
> How he does tear the ground, and roars and bellows?

Or have you seen the pretty turtledove
When she laments the absence of her love?
Or have you seen the fairies, when they sing
And dance with mirth together in a ring?
Or have you seen the daughters of Apollo
Pour down their rhyming liquors in a hollow
Cane in spongy brain, congealing into verse?
If you have seen all this – then kiss mine arse!

Dryden was prepared to sacrifice almost any principle to keep his finances afloat. In his middle years he was found to be studying for holy orders in the Anglican Church, in the hope of getting an appointment in a university. Long after Rochester's death, when the Catholic James II succeeded to the throne, Dryden joined the Catholic Church in the hopes of securing his position. Unfortunately the scheme failed, for in 1688 James II abdicated in favour of the Protestant William of Orange, and Dryden lost the laureateship to Shadwell.

In 1673 in his dedication of *Marriage à la Mode*, Dryden wrote an embarrassingly servile paean to the twenty-six-year-old Rochester:

I have so much of self-interest, as to be content with reading some papers of your verses without desiring you should proceed to a play, with the common prudence of those who are worsted in a duel, and declare they are satisfied when they are first wounded. Your Lordship has but another step to make, and from the patron of wit you may become its tyrant and *oppress* our little reputations with more ease than you now *protect* them.

He continued to develop the theme and amplified it with a letter in May 1673: 'I find it is not for me to contend any way with your Lordship, who can write better on the meanest subject than I can on the best ...' and much more, omitted on the grounds of taste. The Earl detested fawning, and the sly dig that Dryden was taking at him for his amateur efforts will not have escaped his notice, but he recognised the Laureate's talent and put up with it. In 1674, when Settle printed *The Empress of Morocco*, he included in the dedication a quite gratuitous attack on Dryden.

Dryden retaliated against Settle in a pamphlet that he had written together with Crowne and Shadwell:

From breath of *fools* thy commendation spreads,
Fame sings thy praise with mouths of loggerheads.
With noise and laughing each thy fustian greets
'Tis clapped by squires of empty headed cits.

'Breath of fools' and 'commendation', though referring directly to the philistine merchant classes, also included by implication his patron Rochester. Whether he saw Rochester as the influence behind Settle's attack is unclear; but after this a certain frost began to chill relations between Dryden and the Earl. An abortive duel between Mulgrave and Harry Savile, who had joined in the vendetta on the side of his old friend, sharpened the nastiness of the general mood. They had been having supper with the King at the Treasurer's. Harry laid about Mulgrave so viciously that the King told him to leave. Mulgrave challenged him the next day. Rochester, naturally, was to have been Harry's second, but the duel was stopped, and Harry was consigned to a period of disgrace.

In June 1674, in his poem 'Timon', Rochester took an amiable swipe at a number of poets, including several of his friends and Dryden:

Mine host, who had said nothing in an hour,
Rose up and praised *The Indian Emperor.*
  'As if our old world modestly withdrew,
  And here in private had brought forth a new.'
There are two lines! Who but he durst presume
To make the old world a withdrawing room,
Whereof another world she's brought to bed!
What a brave midwife is a laureate's head.

The Indian Emperor was one of Dryden's plays. Rochester turns a couplet from the play into one of his habitual snipes at Dryden for aiming his work at the common people, instead of the literati in the drawing room. Dryden was sensitive about it, and resented such criticism from amateurs.

Matters came to a head soon afterwards. Occasionally the Court at Whitehall would perform specially written masques that were a form of spectacle in which masked courtiers danced and acted. It was the privilege of Dryden as Laureate to write them. In 1675, however,

Rochester is said to have used his influence with the King to commission *The Masque of Calisto* from John Crowne instead of Dryden. It was not true, and Crowne said so, but Rochester's reputation had swung into action. As is clear from his preface Crowne was deeply embarrassed. He was a friend of Dryden and had no wish to upstage him. He protested, 'Had it been written by him to whom the double right of place and merit, the honour of the employment belonged, the pleasure had been in all kinds complete.' *The Masque of Calisto* was not an unqualified success. The problem was how to write a play featuring the Princesses of York, Mary and Anne, aged twelve and nine respectively, on a very delicate subject. Moreover, as neither of them could make themselves heard, their voices had to be supplemented by two professionals, Moll Davis and Mrs Knight. As both of those ladies had had affairs with the King, the rehearsals vibrated with tension. Crowne in his preface wrote modestly:

But you will be disappointed, you will find nothing here to answer the swelling expectations. How it happens to be so, it is enough to tell you that it was written by me, and it would be very strange if a bad writer should write well; but, which was as great an unhappiness, I had not time enough allowed me to muster together, on so great an occasion those few abilities I have.

I was invaded on the sudden by a powerful command to prepare an entertainment for the Court, which was to be written, learnt, practised, and performed in less time than was necessary for the writing alone. For my subject I had but some few hours allowed me to choose one. I, resolving to choose the first tolerable story I could meet with, unhappily encountered *this* where, by my own rashness and the malice of fortune, I involved myself before I was aware, in a difficulty greater than the invention of the philosopher's stone, to write a clean, decent, and inoffensive play on the story of a *rape*.

Afterwards the frost spread to relations between Dryden and Crowne. People noticed that Dryden only ever complimented Crowne when Crowne's plays failed. He would concede that his rival had some genius but he always qualified it by adding that Crowne's mother and his own father were '*very*' well acquainted'.

In July 1675 Etherege joined the roughhouse with *Ephelia to Bajazet*, a satire on Mulgrave, who had become Dryden's new patron in 1673–4.

As we have noted, the name stuck for many years. The poem was an offensive work in which Ephelia reproaches Bajazet for his infidelity. Rochester then concocted Bajazet's (Mulgrave's) arrogant reply to Etherege's poem. He called it 'A Very Heroical Epistle in Answer to Ephelia', with the note 'Dol-Common being forsaken by my Lord All-Pride, and having written him a most lamentable letter, his Lordship sends her the following answer'. In fact, though it purported to be addressed to Dol Common, a noted whore, it was really meant for someone else, probably an old flame of Rochester's, Mary Kirk. He satirised Mulgrave's notorious conceit over his accomplishments as lover, soldier and poet. 'My Lord All-Pride' or 'Monster All-Pride' were also names with which Rochester had christened him at Court because of his haughty and self-satisfied demeanour. The poem ends with a snide reference to an embarrassing affair in which Mulgrave had been made to appear ludicrous, his affair with Mall Kirke, one of the Duchess of York's maids of honour. The Duke of Monmouth, the King's illegitimate firstborn, was a rival for Mall's affections. In September 1674, as Mulgrave was sneaking out of the lady's lodgings, Monmouth had him arrested as an intruder by the guard and thrown in gaol for the night. When Mall gave birth to a boy nine months later, Mulgrave was blamed, though he was by no means the only contender. Captain Percy Kirke, the girl's brother and a ruffian, played the injured relative and called Mulgrave out. The duel took place and Mulgrave was severely wounded, providing a source of innocent delight for his peers.

The friendship between Rochester and Dryden collapsed completely in 1675 when Dryden's *Aurengzebe* (a heroic play about the Mogul Emperor of India) was dedicated to Rochester's old enemy Mulgrave. In another sideswipe at amateur writers, Dryden accused them of fawning to men of real talent against whom they were powerless. They quoted professionals' work when they were present and, when they were absent, stole it. They were hostile to men of lesser talents whom they could crush. Like the Dutch navy they would run away if they were outgunned, but commit murder if they could do it in safety. Dryden's accusing Rochester of fawning caused widespread merriment.

The Earl retaliated with 'An Allusion to Horace', a long poem detailing his opinions of most of his contemporaries, especially Dryden, most in less than complimentary terms. The 'Allusion' was written some time before 4 April 1675, at about the time of his twenty-eighth birthday. It is not a translation, but an adaptation of the tenth satire of the first book of Horace. It was not considered plagiarism to adapt the classical masters; if it was done with ingenuity and skill the result was greatly admired. The convention continued throughout the seventeenth and eighteenth centuries. The poem contains an almost complete account of Rochester's literary precepts which, naturally, were infinitely variable. It opens with an attack on Dryden and Mulgrave ('foolish patron'). It should be borne in mind that at this time Dryden had not yet written any of his great works.

> Well sir, 'tis granted I said Dryden's rhymes
> Were stolen, unequal, nay dull many times:
> What foolish patron is there found of his
> So blindly partial to deny me this?
>
> But that his plays, embroidered up and down
> With wit and learning justly pleased the Town
> In the same paper I as freely own:
> Yet having this allowed, the heavy mass
> That stuffs up his loose volumes must not pass...

Although he denied it Dryden had always yearned to be one of the Gang. He longed to join in the patrician revelry but never quite managed to fit. He was older than the Wits and his struggles to emulate them with oaths and cumbersome obscenities were mockingly received. Their disdain embittered him all his life. Rochester writes spitefully:

> Dryden in vain tried this nice style of wit,
> For he, to be a tearing blade thought fit;
> But when he would be sharp, he still was blunt,
> To frisk his frolic fancy, he'd cry 'cunt';
> Would give the ladies a dry bawdy bob,
> And thus he got the name of Poet Squab.

A 'dry bob' is an orgasm without emission. He proceeds 'To search and censure Dryden's works', and pronounces:

To write what may securely stand the test
Of being well read over thrice at least,
Compare each phrase, examine every line,
Weigh every word, and every thought refine;
Scorn all applause the vile rout can bestow
And be content to please those few who know.

Can'st thou be such a vain mistaken thing
To wish thy works might make a playhouse ring
With the unthinking laughter, and poor praise
Of fops and ladies, facetious for thy plays?
Then send a cunning friend to learn thy doom
From the shrewd judges in the drawing-room.

I've no ambition on that idle score,
But say with Betty Morris, heretofore
When a Court Lady called her 'Bulkeley's whore':
'*I* please one man of wit, am proud on't too,
Let all the coxcombs dance to bed to you.'

The next lines were an opening salvo on Mulgrave's crony, Sir Carr
Scrope, a poet noted for his lack of both talent and beauty. He suffered
from conceit, a squint and unpleasant habits in bed.

Should I be troubled when the purblind knight
Who squints more in his judgment than his sight,
Picks silly faults, and censures what I write?
Or when the poor-fed poets of the Town
For scraps and coach-room cry my verses down?
I loathe the rabble...

'Poet Squab' became Dryden's nickname at Court. He was so peeved
by it that Shadwell was moved to write:

He huffs and struts, and cocks an hundred ways,
And damns the Whigs 'cause they did damn his plays.
So raging once 'twas thought himself had stabbed
'Cause Rochester baptised him 'Poet Squab'.

Scrope retaliated with a spirited but anonymous piece, 'On the
Author of a Play called Sodom', in which he called Rochester 'a weak

feeble strainer at mere ribaldry'. Rochester's 'Allusion' is a plea for artistic integrity and criticises the temptation to play to the gallery into which Dryden above all was wont to fall. It is written coolly, there is no heat in its barbs. It is a justifiable work of criticism of contemporary artists and its judgements are impartially distributed between enemies and friends alike. It was later criticised by Alexander Pope for its occasional imperfect rhymes and assonances and lapses in versification, but Rochester's aim was not to produce highly polished work. He regarded glossy writing as mere slavish conformity to precept, calculated to please the public, and valueless as a result. He had no desire to please anyone save the few whose judgement he valued. He meant his work to be read quickly, and a little roughness here and there was of no significance. Whatever Pope had to say about it, the 'Allusion to Horace' is said to have been an important influence on Pope's own development. Robert Wolseley said of Rochester, 'As nothing is more disagreeable either in verse or prose than a slovenly looseness of style, so on the other hand too nice a correctness will be apt to deaden the life, and make the piece too stiff; between those two extremes is the character of my Lord Rochester's poetry to be found.'

Rochester was not fond of critics, despite having distinguished himself as one of them. In his epilogue to *Circe*, a tragedy by Charles D'Avenant (the twenty-one-year-old son of Sir William), he distinguishes those who 'from wit have this *true* maxim got That 'tis still better to be pleased than not' from the malicious critics who 'agree To loathe each play they come and pay to see'.

> The first know 'tis a meaner part of sense
> To find a fault, than taste an excellence;
> Therefore *they* praise and strive to like
> While *these* are dully vain of being hard to please.

In spring 1676, after the publication of the 'Allusion to Horace', Dryden had been seen looking down in the mouth in Will's coffee house. Savile wrote to Rochester warning him that Dryden was displeased with him. Rochester replied:

You write me word that I'm out of favour with a certain poet whom I have ever admired for the disproportion of him and his attributes. He is a rarity which I cannot but be *fond* of, as one would be of a hog that could fiddle or a singing owl. If he falls upon me at the blunt [fencing foil] which is his very good weapon in wit, I will forgive him if you please and leave the repartee to Black Will with a cudgel.

And now dear Harry if it may agree with your affairs to show yourself in the country this summer, contrive such a crew together as may not be ashamed of passing by Woodstock. And if you can debauch Alderman Georgy [the King's nickname for the Duke of Buckingham], we will make a shift to delight his gravity.

Buckingham's 'gravity' was ironic of course. The passage about the cudgel was another irony, but one that badly misfired. It returned to haunt Rochester later.

Shortly afterwards Scrope took his turn with 'In Defence of Satire', a sour and unfair reference to the Epsom incident and the Bendo masquerade.

> He who can push into a midnight fray
> His brave companion, then run away,
> Leaving him to be murder'd in the street,
> Then put it off with some buffoon conceit;
> This is he you should beware of, all,
> Yet him a pleasant witty man you call.

This was too much for Rochester. He retaliated with 'On the Supposed Author of a late Poem "In Defence of Satire"':

> To rack and torture thy unmeaning brain
> In satire's praise, to a low, untuned strain,
> In thee was most impertinent and vain:
> When in thy person we more clearly see
> That satire's of divine authority,
> For God made one on man when he made thee.

He refers to Scrope as 'an ass, prodigious and refined. A lump deformed and shapeless ... Harsh to the ear and hideous to the sight', one:

> Who needs will be an ugly *beau-garçon*,
> Spat at and shunned by every girl in town;
> Where dreadfully, love's scarecrow, thou art placed
> To fright the tender flock that long to taste;

> While every coming maid, when you appear,
> Starts back for shame and straight turns chaste for fear.

The remark about 'ugly *beau-garçon*' was particularly unkind. Nell Gwyn, in her only surviving letter, complained that the Pall Mall was now a dismal place to her since she had utterly lost Sir Carr Scrope, never to be recovered again. He had told her that he could not live always at this rate and had begun to be a little uncivil, which she would not put up with from an ugly *beau-garçon*. Naturally this had been circulated at Court and had become a source of unholy joy.

Scrope was not prepared to take it lying down. He replied with the succinct rejoinder:

> Rail on, poor feeble scribbler, speak of me
> In as bad terms as the world speaks of thee.
> Sit swelling in thy hole like a vex'd toad,
> And full of pox and malice spit abroad.
> Thou can'st hurt no man's fame with *thy* ill-word;
> Thy pen is full as harmless as thy sword.

It was almost a knockout blow. Rochester of course spat back. Scrope had written a love song of which he was rather proud to Mistress Carey Frazier, with whom he was having an affair. He had declared, 'I cannot change as others do Though you unjustly scorn,' insisting, 'No, Phyllis, no, your heart to move A surer way I'll try'. Rochester suggested an improved version that included the lines:

> I swive as well as others do,
>   I'm young, not yet deformed,
> My tender heart, sincere and true,
>   Deserves not to be scorned.
> Why Phyllis then, why will you swive
>   With forty lovers more?
> Can I (said she) with nature strive,
>   Alas I am, alas I am a whore.

For the sake of completeness, he wrote a short tribute to the girl friend Carey Frazier too. She was a maid of honour to the Queen and daughter of the King's surgeon, Alexander Frazier, who was renowned for his skills as an abortionist and venereologist and whom Rochester had satirised as 'that learned physician' several years before. Carey was mistress of the Earl of Mulgrave and was reported to be pregnant by Sir Carr Scrope. She was ambitious to become the King's mistress, failed and eventually married a Viscount Mordaunt.

> Her father gave her dildos six;
> Her mother made 'em up a score:
> But she loves nought but *living* pricks,
> And swears by God she'll frig no more.

Out of the whole glorious, disgraceful brawl Rochester retaliated with the most memorable thrust of all. It was distilled essence of John Wilmot. He had his portrait painted by an eminent Dutch artist, Jacob Huysmans. It is a picture of a beautiful but slightly tired-looking Earl. He is not visibly affected by the ravages of disease and debauchery, but Huysmans's popularity depended much on his ability to show his subjects in the best possible light. Rochester is gorgeously arrayed in silk and satin, holding between right thumb and forefinger a wreath of laurel. He is dangling it disdainfully over the head of a monkey, which is sitting on a pile of books tearing blank leaves out of them and proffering them, crumpled, to the Earl. The work is a mocking inversion of a fashionable allegory of the period that has a monkey sitting at the feet of Academia 'reading' a book. The monkey represents blind imitation and Dryden had a reputation for plagiarism, hence: 'Well sir, 'tis granted I said Dryden's rhymes Were stolen, unequal, nay dull many times...'

There is a further subtlety. Rochester's greatest criticism of Dryden had always been that he prostituted his gifts for money. Pietro Aretino, who wrote the famed volume on sexual positions on which Barbara Villiers was so expert, also wrote a book, *Reasonings*, a satire on the world of letters. He dedicated it to his pet monkey, which he referred to as a great 'master'. He acknowledged that his only reward from his patron would be that it would bite him. He called on the monkey to take away his book and tear out the leaves, for all great lords who were patrons did so and then used them to wipe their arses. Aretino claimed that he was as respected by his monkey as the Muses were by the patrons whom they chased with their skirts raised.

Rochester had helped procure the Laureate's crown for Dryden and is making it quite clear in the painting that if he wished he could remove it again. It is generally thought that he is placing the crown on the monkey's head, but looked at closely the laurels are pointing in the wrong direction. If he continued with the movement the laurels would come to rest on the monkey's head back to front, upside down and across his eyes. Thus the Earl is either about to miscrown Dryden, or he is removing the crown, or he is just dangling the crown over the poet's head. Whichever interpretation is correct, it is most insulting. In 1676 Dryden's poem 'The Answer to the Satyr' was published anonymously, throwing the same insult back and addressing Rochester as 'Lord Monkey' and 'Your Monkeyship'.

On 1 November 1677 Savile wrote to Rochester, 'And now I am upon poetry, I must tell you the whole tribe are alarmed at a libel against them, lately sent by the post to Will's coffee house. I am not happy enough to have seen it but I hear it commended and therefore the more probably thought to be composed at Woodstock.' In his reply Rochester did not claim authorship: 'For the libel you speak of upon that most unwitty generation, the present poets, I rejoice in it with all my heart and shall take it for a favour if you will send me a copy. He cannot want wit utterly that has a spleen to those rogues, though never so dully expressed.'

This may have been a reference to 'A Session of the Poets', which announced that Dryden was retiring from poetry and becoming a priest so that he could get a post as a don at Oxford. It dismisses the claims of a series of contemporaries to replace him and is variously attributed to Rochester, Buckingham, Rochester and Buckingham together, and Elkanah Settle, who was the victor in the poem. Alternatively the verses in question could have been 'An Advice to Apollo,' which praised Rochester and Dorset, scorned Scrope and Mulgrave, and was probably written by Buckingham. Whoever was responsible, the fight had now become a free-for-all, with the factions becoming ranged in two opposing rabbles.

In early 1678, Rochester fired off both barrels of his literary fowling piece, one at Mulgrave, the other at Scrope. For Mulgrave, he wrote 'My Lord All-pride', which begins: 'Bursting with pride, the loathed impostume swells, Prick him, he sheds his venom straight, and smells.' (An 'impostume' is an abscess.) He charges Mulgrave with raking 'Among the excrements of others' wit, To make a stinking meal of what they shit,' and with turning to jest 'what is best In others'. He ends with:

> Go where he will, he never finds a friend,
> Shame and derision all his steps attend.
> Alike abroad, at home, i'th' camp and Court,
> Knight o'th' Burning Pestle, make us sport!

For Scrope he composed 'On Poet Ninny', sneering that 'never satire did so softly bite':

> Born to no other but thy own disgrace,
> Thou art a thing so wretched and so base
> Thou canst not e'en offend, but with thy face...

He sets Scrope apart: 'There are some modish fools we daily see, Modest and dull – why they are wits to thee!'

In 1678, Dryden published *All for Love*, a tragedy based on Shakespeare's *Antony and Cleopatra*. In the preface he wrote that poetry, as a picture of nature, must generally please. But that did not mean that all parts of it must please every man. A witty man whose taste was confined only to comedy should not judge tragedy. A man who loved tragedy should understand its merits. Otherwise he could not be a critic, only a blind admirer. Poets were satirised and censured. Men of pleasant conversation with a passing fancy and a smattering of Latin were keen to stand out from the herd through their poetry. Was it not a pathetic affectation to expose their own ignorance and needlessly display their nakedness to public view? They should be happy with their good luck, sit down quietly on their estates and realise that they could not expect the same approval from sober men that they were given by their flatterers after the third bottle. It was an open and public attack on Rochester that was bound to attract retribution. It is amusing to compare it with the sycophancy that he had poured on the Earl when he needed him.

In October 1677 Rochester was feeling the strain of illness and unpopularity. As the anonymous author of the preface of Rochester's play *Valentinian* wrote:

> [He] advised young sighing fools to be more pressing,
> And fops of forty to give over dressing.

By this he got the envy of the age,
No fury's like a humbled blockhead's rage...

He had failed to reckon the price of writing satire. He wrote from Woodstock to Savile in London:

Though I am almost blind, utterly lame, and scarce within reasonable hopes of ever seeing London again, I am not yet so wholly mortified and dead to the taste of all happiness not to be extremely revived at the receipt of a kind letter from an old friend who in all probability might have laid me aside in his thoughts, if not quite forgot me by this time. I ever thought you an extraordinary man and must now think you such a friend who, being a courtier as you are, can love a man whom it is the great mode to hate.

He should have remembered his own words – 'For wits are treated just like common whores, First they're enjoyed, and then kicked out of doors.'

The next round in this bare-knuckle brawl was the publication by Mulgrave in 1679 of the *Essay on Satire*. Although the piece was truly written by Mulgrave, the general opinion, especially that of the victims, was that it was really written by Dryden. He undoubtedly wrote certain passages. It was a lengthy work. Turning to Rochester the writer announces:

Rochester I despise for his mere want of wit,
Though thought to have a tail and cloven feet,
For while he mischief means to all mankind,
Himself alone the ill effects does find.

He says his words are false, his wit affected, his targets missed. What is more, 'To every face he cringes while he speaks, But when the back is turned the head he breaks.'

Rochester was mildly amused. On 21 November 1679, back in London and mortally ill, he wrote to Harry, who was now a diplomat in Paris:

I have sent you herewith a libel in which my own share is not the least. The King having perused it is no ways dissatisfied with his. The author is apparently Mr Dryden, his patron, my Lord, having a *panegyric* in the midst, upon which happened a handsome quarrel between his Lordship and Mrs Bulkeley at the Duchess of Portsmouth's. She called him the hero of the libel and complimented him upon having made more cuckolds than any man alive, to which he answered she very well knew *one* he never made nor never cared to be employed in making. 'Rogue!' and 'Bitch!' ensued, till the King, taking his grandfather's character upon him, became the peace-maker. I will not trouble you any longer, but beg you still to love

Your faithful humble servant...

Mulgrave's poem had been also spiteful about Louise and Nell Gwyn ('Nor shall the royal mistresses be named, Too ugly, or too easy to be blamed' and so on).

The King was 'in no way dissatisfied with his share', because he was an easygoing monarch with a rich sense of humour. Nell Gwyn shared the same generosity. Louise did not, and from this derived the quarrel Rochester reported to Harry. The *Essay on Satire* was read at her house and it was noted that it was offensive about all the courtiers except Mulgrave, about whom the only 'criticism' was excessive adultery ('His patron, my Lord, having a *panegyric* in the midst'). He was therefore under deep suspicion. However, he was thought not to have had the skill to accomplish it himself, which by necessity implicated Dryden. Indeed, the end savours overwhelmingly of the Laureate's style. Then Mulgrave arrived with the King at the house, which belonged to Louise's brother, the Earl of Pembroke. Henry Bulkeley's wife called out a cheery greeting with a passing reference to his cuckold-making. Mulgrave was not keen to be accused in front of his victim Louise, and snapped back that the one man he was most unlikely to cuckold was Mr Bulkeley. Mrs Bulkeley was so enraged that she wanted her husband to demand satisfaction. The King, with the experience of years of mollifying enraged mistresses, managed to smooth her ruffled feathers and the fuss died down.

On 23 December 1679 Dryden was set upon near Will's coffee house in Rose Alley, off Covent Garden. Three thugs abused him, calling him a son-of-a-whore, and beat him with cudgels, badly injuring him. The *London Gazette* carried notice of a reward of fifty pounds for the capture of the guilty and promised a pardon if the informer was a participant. It remained unclaimed. The broadsheet *Domestic Intelligence* called it 'a *feminine* if not *popish* vengeance', in a clear pointer to Louise Portsmouth. Narcissus Luttrell wrote in 1679, ''Tis thought to be done by order of the Duchess of Portsmouth, she being abused in a late libel called an "Essay upon Satire", of which Mr Dryden is suspected to be the author.'

However, there was Rochester's letter written in spring 1676: 'I will forgive him if you please and leave the repartee to Black Will with a cudgel.' Everyone knew about the long-standing feud. Everyone knew about the letter. There were several schools of thought: the Rochester, the Portsmouth and those who subscribed to both, insisting that they were jointly responsible. A further faction, very likely the correct one, backed the Earl of Pembroke. He was Louise's brother-in-law and had himself been mildly maligned in the poem, which had been first been read out at his house. Moreover, the Earl was a savage. In 1677 he had nearly killed his opponent in a duel. In 1678 he was tried and condemned for manslaughter after a drunken scuffle but was pardoned. In 1680 he killed an officer of the watch while out drinking. John Aubrey tells how he kept greyhounds, mastiffs, some bears and a lion, and 'a matter of 60 fellowes more bestiall than they'. He was accused in an anonymous poem, which concludes:

> Pembroke loved tragedy, and did provide
> For butchers' dogs, and for the whole Bank-side.
> More could I say; but care not much to meet
> A crab tree cudgel, in a narrow street.

No one ever found the answer, but as always the presumption of guilt in favour of Rochester went into operation, leaving another cloud over his long career of disrepute. Dryden supporters still blame him. It is not that he was incapable of such an act, but it did not suit his style. The relevance of the letter is minimal, having been written some three years before the event. It is difficult to say how seriously either Rochester or Dryden took their squabble. Rochester's attitude is probably best summed up in his letter to Harry, 'He is a rarity which I cannot but be *fond* of, as one would be of a hog that could fiddle or a singing owl.' Dryden made reference to his old enemy many times after his death, and always in kindly terms.

Not so Mulgrave, of course, who continued to write offensive poetry about him long after he was buried, and to malign him to anyone who would listen. The body was hardly cold when Mulgrave was spitting out venom on 'Such nauseous songs as the late convert made Which justly call this censure on his shade.' The fact that his enemy was dead was no hindrance. After all, they had dug up Cromwell in order to hang him. He maligned his old foe to Alexander Pope. In fact he later commissioned Pope to rewrite his *Essay on Satire* for republication. Pope promptly deleted the passage condemning Rochester's poetry. At the end of 1682 the Earl of Mulgrave was deprived of his offices and forbidden the Court for renewing his suit to the Duke of York's second daughter, Princess Anne. She was now seventeen, he was thirty-four and had been in love with her for years. He asked Aphra Behn, the celebrated poetess, to write a poem of vindication and pleading as though from himself to Anne. Showing at least a glimmer of a sense of humour, he had the work entitled 'Bajazet to Gloriana'.

11

'Dissolve thy sunbeams, close thy wings'
Lovesick

Rochester's poetry is the poetry of wit combined with the love of pleasure, of thought with licentiousness. His extravagant heedless levity has a sort of passionate enthusiasm in it; his contempt for everything that others respect almost amounts to sublimity. His poem upon Nothing is itself no trifling work. His epigrams were the bitterest, the least laboured, and the truest that ever were written.

William Hazlitt, 1818

Throughout these last years Rochester's private war was being fought on several fronts. He was taking a severe battering from both his wife and his mistress. In the early summer of 1676, he had been giving unsatisfactory service to Barry, apparently by failing to get her a part in which she could show off her new skills. He was also in trouble with her for wandering. He wrote forlornly:

I assure you I am not half so faulty as unfortunate in serving you. I will not tell you my endeavours nor excuse my breach of promise, but leave it to *you* to find the cause of my doing so ill to one I wish so well to. But I hope to give you a better account shortly. The complaint you spoke to me, concerning Miss—, I know nothing of, for she is as great a stranger to me as she can be to you. So, thou pretty creature, farewell.

'Miss—' may have been a reference to Elizabeth Boutel, with whom Rochester had been dallying when he met Barry. Later, when the two ladies appeared together in *The Rival Queens*, Barry was called on to feign an assault on Boutel. When the moment arrived Barry played her part with 'such vivacity', as one critic described it, that the dagger went through Boutel's stays and a quarter of an inch into her body. It bore every appearance of a grudge fight over the poet, but some thought that the matter had nothing to do with Rochester and arose out of an argument between the two over the use of a particular costume in the wardrobe. The cause could as well have been either grievance, they being of equal gravity.

While Rochester was back in London languishing in the toils of his mistress, old Lady Rochester was spending more and more time with the dissident Elizabeth. The Dowager had lost the Ditchley Estate in 1677 to her grandson, Sir Edward Lee, when he married at the age of fourteen. The house was Lee property and not hers, so she moved to Adderbury. This meant that Elizabeth was no longer chatelaine of her own household and also that she now had her mother-in-law's unremitting company. Apart from her complaints about Elizabeth to her son, she complained to Elizabeth about her son, his dogs, his children and his experiments in chemistry of which, like the King and his friend Buckingham, he had an extensive knowledge. He was also a close acquaintance with M. Rabell, a noted French apothecary. Rochester wrote ironically to his wife, 'The last letter I received from your honour was something scandalous, so that I knew not well how to answer it. 'Twas my design to have write to my Lady Ann Wilmot [his daughter] to intercede for me, but now with joy I find my self again in your favour, it shall be my endeavour to continue so; In order to which very shortly I will be with you.' He added, 'In the meantime my Mother may be pleased to dispose of my children, and my chimists, and my little dogs and whatever is mine as she will; only if I may have nothing about me that I like, it will be the cause of making the felicity of waiting on her befall me very *seldom*.'

Rochester had been at Adderbury when his mother moved in. Elizabeth was staying well out of the way at Enmore. He wrote to her from Adderbury, telling her that his mother was 'now resolved against ever moving from hence' and preparing her 'for a remove first hither, and afterwards as fate shall direct which is the true disposer of things, whatever we attribute to wisdom or providence. Be therefore in readiness upon the first notice from me, to put that in execution which I shall first inform you. Let me have an answer and dispatch this messenger quickly.'

He was determined that the two should get on, however deeply they detested one other. In his will he made them joint guardians of his son Charles until the boy should attain twenty-one, 'for the better assurance of a happy correspondency between them'. This was conditional on his wife remaining unmarried and 'living friendlily' with his mother. If she decided to marry or wilfully removed herself from his mother, her guardianship would determine. On one occasion when his wife was staying at Enmore, Rochester was given the job of looking after Charles at High Lodge. The boy fell ill, so he sent him back to Adderbury where he could be looked after by the Dowager rather than by Elizabeth, and set off for London. His wife was incensed. She wrote to him complaining. He replied, 'It were very unreasonable should I not love you whilst I believe you a deserving good creature. 'Twas very well for your son, as ill as you took it, that I sent him to Adderbury, for it proves at last to be the King's Evil [scrofula] that troubles him, and he comes up to London this week to be touched...'

He took the young Viscount to the King. It was not a casual affair. Scrofula is tuberculosis of the bones and lymphatic glands and especially afflicts children. It was called the King's Evil in the belief that it could be cured by the Sovereign's touch. The ceremony was first practised by Edward the Confessor and reached a peak during the Restoration. The first thing that Charles had done when he gained the throne in 1660 was to renew the custom. Between 1660 and 1682 he touched over 90,000 sufferers, more than ever before or since.

The practice still existed a century later when Dr Johnson was touched for the same complaint by Queen Anne. The disease, usually caught from cows with bovine tuberculosis, was highly debilitating. It affected the eyesight badly and the limbs became uncoordinated. Sufferers were often thought to be mentally retarded. The ceremony was religious and was carried out once a quarter in London at the Banqueting Hall or anywhere that Charles happened to be, including Newmarket. The King would appear and two ministers began the prayers. The formal pleas from the supplicants were read, then the patients were led one at a time into the King's presence and knelt before him. He would touch them with both hands on the part affected. After more prayers they were formally presented, for the King to place blue ribbons round their necks carrying gold medallions stamped with his image.

The King was not the only person who claimed to accomplish the cure. There were also commoners, in particular an Irishman called Valentine Greatrex, who touched hundreds of sufferers including Flamsteed, the Royal Astronomer. Charles, in his usual sporting and scientific fashion, was not in the least put out by this trespass on his historical function. He was so interested that he invited Greatrex to Court in 1666 to demonstrate his powers but was unimpressed. The King's own efforts for the young Lord Wilmot were little more successful. The boy, one of the handsomest children in the realm, remained in feeble health and died shortly after his father.

Rochester's correspondence with his wife became perceptibly more irritable. Probably because of his obsession with Barry, matters at home were deteriorating. Sir John and Lady Warre, his wife's step-parents, spent a good deal of time in London. Lady Warre wasted no time in letting Elizabeth know about her handsome son-in-law's vagaries. She had tried to prevent the marriage in the first place, had been frustrated and was implacable. Elizabeth herself would write the sort of restrained letter of suffering that was nicely calculated to make him feel bad. She complained, 'If I could have been troubled at anything when I had the happiness of receiving a letter from you, I should be so because you did not name a time when I might hope to see you: the uncertainty very much afflicts me,' and confidently predicted that 'you will find so much business as will not allow you to come into the country'. This letter elegantly concluded, 'Therefore pray lay your commands upon me what I am to do, and though it be to forget my children and the long hopes I have lived in of seeing you, yet I will endeavour to obey you, or in the memory only torment my self, without giving you the trouble of putting you in the mind there *lives* such a creature as your faithful humble wife.'

Rochester was self-centred but he was neither cruel nor even unkind, and this type of reproach was most effective. His only recourse was to turn and snap, 'My most neglected wife, Till you are a much respected widow, I find you will scarce be a contented woman and to say no more than the plain truth, I do endeavour so fairly to do you that last good service, that none but the most impatient would refuse to rest satisfied'. He believed he knew who was stirring things up: 'What evil angel enemy to my repose does inspire my Lady Warr to visit you once a year and leave you bewitched for eleven months after? I thank my god that I have the torments of the stone upon me (which are no small ones) rather than that unspeakable one of being an eyewitness to your uneasinesses.' Even so, he claimed to be baffled by Elizabeth's wretchedness:

Do but propose to me any reasonable thing upon Earth I can do to set you at quiet, – but it is like a mad woman to lie roaring out of pain and never confess in what part it is. These three years have I heard you continually complain – nor has it ever in my power to obtain the knowledge of any cause to be confident I shall not have the like affliction three years hence.

But that repose I owe to a surer friend than you; when that time comes you will grow wiser though I fear not much happier.

The three years of bitterness seem to have coincided with his affair with Barry. Rochester was genuinely in love with his mistress, a situation not within the Rake's Handbook, and impossible for him to cope with. His plight is echoed in Etherege's *Man of Mode*. In an aside, Dorimant laments, 'I love her and dare not let her know it. I fear she has an ascendant o'er me and may revenge the wrongs I have done her sex.' But then he summons the nerve to declare himself to Harriet, 'Think of making a party, madam; love will engage' – only to provoke her sarcastic rejoinder: 'You make me start! I did not think to have heard of love from *you*.' He insists, concedes that he used to laugh at love and demands to be heard. But when Harriet mockingly invites him to begin Dorimant protests, 'That the company may take notice how passionately I make advances of love and how disdainfully you receive 'em?' Unanswerably, she retorts, 'When your love's grown strong enough to make you bear being laughed at, I'll give you leave to trouble me with it. Till when, pray forbear, sir.'

Rochester was fatally smitten. He wrote his most passionate verse to Elizabeth Barry. In this poem, he sees his wretched self reflected in his loved one's eyes:

> While on those lovely looks I gaze,
>   To see a wretch pursuing,
> In raptures of a blessed amaze
>   His pleasing happy ruin:
>
> 'Tis not for pity that I move,
>   His fate is too aspiring;
> Whose heart broke with a load of love,
>   Dies wishing and admiring.
>
> But, if this murder you'd forgo,
>   Your slave from death removing,

Let me your art of charming know,
    Or learn you mine of loving.

But whether life or death betide,
    In love, 'tis equal measure;
The victor lives with empty pride,
    The vanquished dies with pleasure.

He took a number of Francis Quarles's passionate expressions of abasement before God and turned them into a no less abasing cry to his mistress. He succeeded in changing a minimal proportion of the original words, while turning their entire meaning on its head:

Why do'st thou shade thy lovely face? Oh why
Does that eclipsing hand of thine deny
The sunshine of the sun's enlivening eye?

The poem continues with this lyrical conceit – 'Thou art my light, if hid how blind am I. Thou art my life, if thou withdraw I die' – until its final, hopeful entreaty:

Dissolve thy sunbeams, close thy wings and stay.
See, see how I am blind and dead, and stray.
Oh thou that art my life, my light, my way.

Then work my will if passion bid me flee.
My reason shall obey. My wings shall be
Stretched out no further than from me to thee.

It undoubtedly amused Rochester, with its frisson of blasphemy, to take a famous work of sacred fervour and profane it. It is ironic that it resulted in his most passionate outpouring of romantic love. Now that Barry was back in the theatre and rapidly advancing in her career, her independence of Rochester was growing, and his drinking and moods were becoming intolerable. She was as incapable as he was of fidelity, and she was quite happy to use her body to further her ambition. But she had no compunction in complaining bitterly of her lover's tendency to wander. He was still a spectacularly handsome young man. It would have taken superhuman self-discipline, a quality for which he was not noted, to resist the constant temptation that women still presented. He remonstrated with her: 'My visit yesterday was intended to tell you I had not dined in company of women. Were men without frailties, how would you bring it about to make 'em love you so blindly as they do? I cannot yet imagine what fault you could find in my love-letter. Certainly 'twas full of kindness and duty to you, and whilst these two points are kept inviolable, 'tis very hard when you take anything ill.' He wanted to soothe her:

I fear staying at home so much gives you the spleen, for I am loth to believe 'tis I. I have therefore sent you the two plays that are acted this afternoon. If that diversion could put you into so good a humour as to make you able to endure me again, I should be very much obliged to the stage. However, if your anger continue, show yourself at the play that I may look upon you and go mad. Your revenge is in your own eyes and if I must suffer, I would choose that way.

Rochester convinced himself, as lovers do, that the jealousy he felt and the bitter quarrels were merely symptoms of a good relationship. It led to 'The Mistress', one of his finest, most forlorn works.

> An age in her embraces past,
>   Would seem a winter's day
> When life and light, with envious haste,
>   Are torn and snatched away.
>
> But oh how slowly minutes roll,
>   When absent from her eyes
> That feed my love, which is my soul,
>   It languishes and dies.
>
>   . . .
>
> Nor censure us, you who perceive
>   My best-beloved and me
> Sigh and lament, complain and grieve,
>   You think we disagree.
>
> Alas! 'Tis sacred jealousy!
>   Love raised to an extreme;
> The only proof 'twixt her and me,
>   We love, and do not dream.

Rochester had a shrewd idea of what she was up to with her coterie of admirers and hangers-on. He knew only too well the dissipated life that actors led and the temptations with which they constantly presented one another. He had led the same life himself for years, faced the same temptations and never failed to surrender. He made a desperate effort to woo her away from the profession:

> Leave this gaudy gilded stage
>> From custom more than use frequented,
> Where fools of either sex and age
>> Crowd to see themselves presented.

Elizabeth Barry had become pregnant by Rochester in April 1677. The little girl was born in mid-December. The Earl had been marooned at High Lodge since about August, very ill and unable to get back to London, and he wrote solicitously, 'Your safe delivery has delivered me too from fears for your sake, which were, I'll promise you, as burdensome to me as your great-belly was to you. Everything has fallen out to my wish, for you are out of danger and the child is of the soft sex I love. Shortly, my hopes are to see you, and in a little while to look on you with all your beauty about you.' He was anxious to seem helpful too: 'Pray let nobody but yourself open the box I sent you; I did not know but that in lying in you might have use of those trifles. Sick and in bed as I am, I could come at no more of 'em; but if you find 'em, or whatever is in my power of use to your service, let me know it.'

Harry wrote to congratulate him, and to tell him that a friend of Barry's (Nell Gwyn) had been complaining to him about how poor she was, and criticising Rochester for his 'want of either generosity or bowels toward a lady who had not refused him the full enjoyment of all her charms'. But, apart from his box of presents, he had little with which to be generous. He made a little extra from his sinecures, but his only personal income came from his £1,000 per annum as gentleman of the bedchamber. This was seldom if ever paid. He was fending off a pack of creditors with excuses gilded by his famously lyrical voice. 'His tongue', it was said, 'would tempt the angels to a second fall'; not, however, his tradesmen. They were pursuing him to the source by petitioning the Lord Treasurer, who administered the King's obligations. It was at this juncture that he found out that his lover had acquired another protector.

There followed a crescendo of abuse. We know only what Rochester had to say, since Barry alone kept the letters. It is not difficult to imagine their context, however. Suspicion has been cast on their authenticity, they not being in his own hand and Barry not being thought above manufacturing them for profit. However, they all have the ring of truth; some of them are so agitated as to be barely comprehensible.

Barry was accusing him of hating her, avowing her regret that she had ever fallen in love with him. He demanded that she give him proof that their relationship was over. She was making the memories of their love so agonising that he might as well hate her: 'I can never forget how very happy I have been, but the love that gives *you* the torment of repentance on your side, and *me* the trouble of perceiving it in the other, is equally unjust and cruel to us both, and ought to die.' And 'Anger, spleen, revenge and shame are not yet so powerful with me as to make me disown this great truth, that I love you above all things in the world. But I thank God I can distinguish, I can see very *woman* in you, and from yourself am convinced I have never been in the wrong in my opinion of women... It seems, as you excel in everything, you scorn to grow less in that noble quality of using your servants [admirers] very hardly.'

He concluded the correspondence with the most bitter poem that he ever wrote:

> 'Tis not that I am weary grown
> Of being yours, and yours alone;
> But with what face can I incline
> To damn you to be only mine?
>   You whom some kinder power did fashion,
>   By merit and by inclination,
> The joy at least of one whole *nation*.

Then he delivered the *coup de grâce*. He took the little girl away from her mother, purportedly because she was not suitable to look after her. Whether or not this was a mere pretext, one cannot tell. It was undoubtedly true that Barry was not the motherly sort and did not live a maternal life. Apart from her unstable temperament, she led a wholly random existence as she strove to become the diva of the seventeenth-century stage. His last letter said, tersely, 'I am far from delighting in the grief I have given you by taking away the child; and you, who made it so absolutely necessary for me to do so, must take that excuse from me for all the ill nature of it. On the other side, pray be assured I love Betty so well that you need not apprehend any neglect from those I employ, and I hope very shortly to restore her to you a finer girl than ever.' But he was unable to resist a little moralising: 'In the meantime you would do well to think of the advice I gave you, for how little show soever my prudence makes in my own affairs, in yours it will prove very successful if you please to follow it. And since discretion is the thing alone you are like to want, pray study to get it.'

Barry quickly returned to the stage. For a while parts were in short supply, possibly as a result of the withdrawal of Rochester's support. She had affairs with her cousin, Henry St John, and with countless others and was pursued unsuccessfully by Otway. When Rochester died he left their child, who was named Elizabeth Clarke, an annuity of £40 for life, secured on the manor of Sutton Malet. The little girl died in 1691 when she was fourteen and was buried at Acton. Her mother joined her there twenty-two years later in 1713, the greatest actress of her time. She took the lead in plays by Congreve, Vanbrugh, Otway, Lee and Dryden. Her most acclaimed roles were those on which she played the heroine opposite a character modelled on Rochester. She was 'Mrs Loveit' in *The Man of Mode* by Etherege, Hellena in Aphra Behn's *The Rover*, La Nuche in *The Rover, Part II* and the Princess of Cleves in Lee's play of the same name.

By the time the affair ended in 1678, Rochester was thirty-one and close to death. He had been declining since his visit to Madam Fourcard's establishment in 1669. There had been a period when his health was severely affected by the ingestion of huge quantities of mercury. After that he never truly recovered and his correspondence shows his life gradually ebbing towards his final extinction. The first suspicion that all was not well had been in June of 1671, when he went to Bath. It was a visit he was to make yearly. He may have been there for a number of reasons; Bath was a popular social gathering place and its waters were taken for generally improving the health. In addition he always needed to importune the Lord Treasurer, who lived there. But it was also a place where syphilitics could obtain treatment to loosen their limbs. One of the disabilities that Rochester suffered was arthritis. Shortly afterwards his friend John Muddiman was saying (as we have seen), 'I am very sorry you find your eyes can neither endure wine nor water,' on the occasion when he walked out of Garraway's coffee house. It happened again at home in early 1672. That year was a bad year. In September he wrote to his wife that if he had not pawned his plate he believed that he would have starved in his sickness. In the autumn he suffered his extraordinary reaction to the Louise quarrel.

By the spring of 1676 sickness had a little inclined him towards politics. He knew that there was no great time left to make amends for his wasted life. It should be borne in mind that whenever he was seriously ill he became penitent, lamenting his misdeeds and promising to reform if he survived. Then, as soon as he was well enough, he would lapse into his old way of life. He wrote, 'This is the season of tribulation, and I piously beg of almighty God that the strict severity shown to one scandalous sin amongst us may expiate for all grievous calamities – so help them God whom it concerns!' This must have been a reference to the pox, visited upon so many for the sin of fornication. If it was, his insight was in advance of the medical profession by two centuries.

For almost the whole of 1677 he was in the country, too ill to get to London. In October, 'my condition of health alters I hope for the better, though various accidents succeed. My pains are pretty well over, and my rheumatism begins to turn to honest gout, my pissing of blood Doctor Wetherly says is "nothing". My eyes are almost out but *that* he says will not do me much harm, in short he makes me eat flesh and drink diet drink.' (Wetherly, one of the King's physicians, attended Rochester during his last illness and was a witness to his will.) A little later that year he wrote to Elizabeth Barry, who was still his lover, the first letter in which he mentioned his illness to her. 'Madam, this is the first service my hand has done me since my being a cripple, and I would not employ it in a lie so soon; therefore pray believe me sincere when I assure you that you are very dear to me; and as long as I live I will be kind to you. P.S. this is all my hand would write, but my heart thinks a great deal more.'

At about the same time in 1677 Savile wrote to him from London on the first post day since his return from Paris. He would have written anyway, but he was doing so urgently because of a 'scurvy report' of his friend's being very ill. He wanted to know the truth from Rochester, who alone could be trusted to be honest about himself. Everyone else was only too ready to believe and to make up lies about him. Rochester replied that he was almost blind, utterly lame and scarce within the reasonable hopes of ever seeing London again. He signed himself at the end of the letter, in French, 'a tired bugger who all the rest of his wretched life will be your faithful friend and most humble servant'.

Savile replied on 18 November. He was mighty glad to find that a man both lame and blind could be so merry. Rochester answered the compliment:

Harry, you who have known me these ten years the grievance of all prudent persons, the byword of statesmen, the scorn of ugly ladies (which are very near all) and the irreconcilable aversion of fine gentlemen (who are the *ornamental* part of a nation) and yet found me seldom sad even under these weighty oppressions; can you *think* that the having of lean arms, small legs, red eyes and nose (if you will consider that trifle too) can have the power to depress the natural alacrity of my careless soul?

In a letter to his wife that same month he complained of having the torments of the stone upon him. Harry Savile wrote to him suggesting that, as he was now at a better age for writing poetry than he had been before, he should make use of his indisposition to produce some, as he had done during previous bouts of illness. He implies that such occasions had been numerous. Rochester was convinced throughout his last years that his recurring disability was due to kidney stones, with which some of his symptoms were consistent. What they truly betokened was ulceration of the kidneys from syphilis.

When Elizabeth Barry presented him with a daughter at the end of 1677, he was confined to his bed. That December Savile wrote to Rochester from London concerned about his health. He had heard that his friend was coming to town but had now given up hope of seeing him. On the 23rd for some reason Rochester took it into his head to write to his cousin, the Earl of Lichfield, and heir to Woodstock Park, to whom he had so strongly objected when the King made the appointment in 1675.

My dear Lord,

I would not have slipped this opportunity of waiting upon you, but the change of the weather makes it a dangerous journey for a man in no better health than I am. Neither would you condemn the care I take of my self, did you know how kind an uncle and how faithful a servant I preserve for you. The character you have of me from others may give you some reason to consider this no farther than good nature obliges you; but if I am ever so happy to live where my inclinations to you may show themselves, be assured you shall not want very good proof how much the memory of your father [Sir Francis Lee], the favours of my Lady Lyndsey [Lady Lee], (how long-soever past) and to your own merit, can oblige a very grateful man to be faithfully sincerely and eternally, dear nephew,

Your most humble servant

Rochester

The letter is slightly oracular. Lichfield was still a child. He had become a peer on his marriage, at the age of four, to Charles II's illegitimate daughter by the Duchess of Cleveland. Either Rochester was in an unstable mood of affection for his rival, or he was beginning to make his peace with the world, or he was plotting to keep High Lodge for his own son. In June of 1678 there were alarming reports about his health following his departure from London, but it was soon rumoured that he was getting better. For one whose life was characterised by unsteadiness, his long decline was true to pattern. He was throughout subject to sudden remissions, then relapses. The relapses were progressively greater than the remissions.

Savile had been in serious trouble with the King over the Duke of Lauderdale, whom he loathed. The Duke was the Scottish High Commissioner. Out of sheer animosity, Savile voted against him in the House of Commons when Lauderdale was presenting the King's business. Charles was beside himself with rage. When he met Savile going to bed that night he paled, his cheeks and arms trembled and he bellowed, 'You villain! How *dare* you have the impudence to come into my presence when you are guilty of such baseness as you have shown this day? I do now and from henceforth discharge you from my service, commanding you never to come any more into my presence nor to any place where I shall happen to be.' Savile complained to Rochester, 'You can not but have heard the misfortunes that have befallen both my body *natural* and body *politic*, how I have been sacrificed to that filthy dog Lauderdale, and how the return of my venereal pains have thrown me back to dry mutton and diet drink; and whether this *latter* does most afflict the pleasure of my body, or the *former* the pride of my soul, it is hard to determine, but *both together* do for the present make me unhappy enough. How soon His Majesty will deliver me from the one, and Mr Barton [quacksalver] from the other lies in the one's royal breast and in the other's skill chirurgical.'

Deliverance was not long in coming. The monarch's fury as always softened quickly. Henry was soon back in favour and acting as the King's faithful ambassador to France. Rochester, who was at Woodstock, missed him badly. Now his last contact with humanity, the regular reports of excesses at Court, was ended. It was not long before he lost interest altogether. Yet within weeks Will Fanshaw was excitedly telling friends that Rochester had recovered beyond all hazard of a relapse. Fanshaw, who also had syphilis, was Master of Requests and a member of the Court circle. He had had an affair with Lucy Walter, the mistress and reputed wife of Charles II, and later married Lucy's daughter Mary. He had just returned from an 'expedition', possibly either to Bath or to Epsom for the waters. He too was lame with osteoarthritis from the pox and his mouth was distorted by gingivitis from mercury poisoning. Despite the expedition his lameness had not improved and he had just grown scraggier. He had already been described as a 'lean, poverty-stricken courtier'. He had the distinction, it was said, of stinking worse than anyone else at Court. Harry said that he was now 'thinner than Churchill' and was wearing three flannel waistcoats. Savile wrote of him, 'I thought there could be but one lame thing upon earth in perfect happiness and that is Fanshaw,' but, he conceded philosophically, of all men living *he* ought not to mock Fanshaw. There was something in humans that made a man, however badly off, try to find someone even worse off. 'As poor Fanshaw is the only creature upon earth poorer and pockier than myself, he is the only trophy I have in the world.'

Rochester commiserated, reminding Savile of Falstaff: ' "If sack and sugar be a sin, God help the *wicked*", was the saying of a merry fat gentleman who lived in days of yore, loved a glass of wine, would be merry with a friend and sometimes had an unlucky fancy for a wench.' He went further: 'No, dear Mr Savile, forgive me if I confess that upon several occasions you have put me in mind of this fat person, and now more particularly, for thinking upon your present circumstances I cannot but say, if loving a pretty woman and hating Lauderdale bring banishments and pox, the Lord have mercy upon poor thieves and swivers. But by this time all your inconveniences draw very near their end.' For his own part, he said, 'I'm taking pains *not* to die without knowing how to live on when I have brought it about. But most human affairs are carried on at the same nonsensical rate, which makes me think it a fault to laugh at the monkey we have here when I compare his condition with mankind.'

The two friends were in a lugubrious mood of *memento mori*. Both were disillusioned. Rochester was thirty-one. Savile replied, 'I will not say how good a time this is to be in the country, how good a time to be sick, nay how good a time to *die*, for fear you should either think me near *my* end or believe I thought *you* so, and were therefore gathering some philosophical comfort out of Solomon or Seneca or any other who has treated of the vanity of the world.' He was troubled with splenetic vapours that made him dislike the world as much as he had ever previously approved it: 'from the rising of the sun to the setting thereof, I see nothing that pleases my eyes nor hear nothing but what grates my ears. Not being at Court I can send you no news of Ladies; it is none, that Ladies are women and that women are bitches, whom God confound and let every cripple say "Amen".'

He was suffering badly from the pox at the time, and was experiencing the same vindictive revulsion from women as Rochester had. It was remarkable that he referred to 'gathering philosophical comfort out of Seneca', because that was exactly what his friend was doing. Savile next wrote, awash with gloom, on 2 July 1678 from the fearsome Madam Fourcard's in Leather Lane. He had chosen a private spot to sweat in, and finish a long, tedious course of treatment that had been going on for six months. He swore, if he had been asked to choose at the outset between carrying on or apostasy from the Christian Church, devoted worshipper as he was he would have had great difficulty in deciding. It was hardly surprising. The usual course of treatment was more like six weeks, and even then only half the patients survived. Harry must have had a monumental constitution. He not only lived through the ordeal but seems to have been immune to the side effects. 'I confess', he wrote, 'I wonder at myself and that mass of mercury that has gone down my throat in seven months, but should wonder yet more were it not for Mrs Roberts [Jane Roberts, with whom Rochester and the King had both had affairs so many years before], for "behold a greater than I". She is in the same house and we have met here from several corners, as mad folks do in Bedlam.' What Jane had endured 'would make a damned soul fall alaughing at his lesser pain. It is *so* far beyond description or belief that till she tells you herself, I will not spoil her story by making it worse, or by making your hair stand on end – and hinder anything *else* from doing so for a month after so tragical a relation.'

Will Fanshaw had arrived there for treatment too. Although he had the pox worse than the other two, he was trying to pass it off as scurvy out of consideration for his wife. But the truth was, said Harry, that he was a filthier leper than was ever cured in the Bible. Unless there were another miraculous pool of Bethesda, or another saviour, he was the most incurable animal now crawling upon the Earth.

Rochester replied with one of his finest letters, a magical mock romance on Leather Lane:

Were I as idle as ever, which I should not fail of being if health permitted, I would write a small romance, and make the sun with his dishevelled rays gild the tops of the palaces in Leather Lane. Then should those vile enchanters Batten and Ginman [quacksalvers] lead forth their illustrious captives in chains of quicksilver, and confining 'em by charms to the loathsome banks of a dead lake of diet-drink. You, as my friend, should break the horrid silence and speak the most passionate fine things that ever heroic lover uttered, which being softly and sweetly replied to by Mrs Roberts, should rudely be interrupted by the envious Fanshaw.

Thus would I lead the mournful tale along, till the gentle reader bathed with the tribute of his eyes the names of such unfortunate lovers, – and this, I take it, would be a most excellent way of celebrating the memories of my most pocky friends, companions and mistresses.

Wryly he turned to his own condition: 'But it is a miraculous thing when a man half in the grave cannot leave off playing the fool and the buffoon; but so it falls out to my comfort, for at this moment I am in a damned relapse brought by a fever, the stone and some ten diseases more which have deprived me of the power of *crawling*, which I happily enjoyed some days ago.' So he was looking ahead:

And now I fear I must fall, that it may be fulfilled which was long since written for our instruction in a good old ballad,

> But he who lives not wise and sober
> Falls with the leaf still in October.

About which time, in all probability, there may be a period added to the ridiculous being of
Your humble servant...

The lines of verse were adapted and inverted from the famous drinking song by John Fletcher:

> Drink today and drown all sorrow,
> You shall perhaps not do it tomorrow.
> Best while you have it, use your breath,
> There is no drinking after death.
>
> . . .
>
> Then let us swill boys for our health,
> Who drinks well loves the common wealth.
> And he that will to bed go sober,
> Falls with the leaf still in October.

It was the canon by which Rochester had lived.

I 2

'The Devil rages against my son'
Deathbed Repentance

His *sins* were like his parts, all of them extraordinary. He seemed to
affect something singular in his impieties as well as in his writings,
above the reach of other men, – taking as much pains to draw others
in and to pervert the right ways of virtue, as the apostles and saints
to save them that heard them. For this was the amazing circumstance
of his *sins*, that he was so diligent to recommend and propagate
them, like those the Prophet mentions, *Isaiah 3.9. 'who declare their sin
as Sodom, and hide it not, that take it upon their shoulders, and bind it to
them as a Crown'*; framing arguments for sin, making proselytes to it,
and writing panegyrics upon vice; singing praises to the great Enemy
of God, and casting down coronets and crowns before his throne.
Nay so confirmed was he in *sin*, that he lived, and oftentimes almost
died, a martyr for it.

The Rev. Parsons, Rochester's family chaplain, from *A Sermon
preached at the Earl of Rochester's Funeral*, 1680

Savile was sent to Paris by the King to try to soothe a quarrel between
the Duchess of Cleveland and her daughter Ann, Countess of Sussex,
in which both parties were behaving spectacularly badly. He pressed
Rochester to join him there and promised him that a winter at
Montpellier in the South of France would do him much more good
than Adderbury. A few weeks later Jane Roberts died of her illness.
The Rev. Gilbert Burnet, a fashionable and ambitious confessor,
attended her and in the course of his ministrations procured her
repentance and confession. She died begging him to warn the King
against the evils of a dissolute life. Burnet did as he was asked, adding
a few political exhortations of his own, and left the letter at William
Chiffinch's lodgings. When it was handed to the King, he read it twice
and threw it into the fire. It caused a ripple of shock at Court and a

wave of excitement among the clergy. Charles fulminated against Burnet. Rochester asked him why he would 'use a writer of history ill, for such people could revenge themselves'. The King's view was that, while he remained alive, Burnet would not dare to say anything, and when he was dead it would not matter what he said.

While Savile was away Rochester began to brood. He was introduced to Charles Blount, a Deist and admirer of Hobbes. His father Sir Henry was one of the guiding lights of the sect. Charles Blount and the Earl met and corresponded regularly. The Deists believed that God created all things, but they did not believe in his control and care of humanity. All things were imbued with immutable laws, the 'laws of nature', which worked without supervision, allowing God to withdraw into a detached transcendence.

They did not believe in divine revelation. Religious knowledge was born in everyone or could be acquired by reason, but not through revelation or the teaching of any Church. They rejected orthodox Christianity and regarded the liturgical practices of Catholicism as pagan. Mankind had fallen into error through the weakness of human nature, and the conspiracy of priests to deceive it. The Deist God was gentle and benevolent and intended men to be the same.

In December 1678 Blount sent a long letter to Rochester discussing theological matters. It is of great length and obscurity. The prose is so convoluted that it is virtually impossible to follow and the letter as a whole seems meaningless. It purported to be an account of the subversion of Judaism and of the foundation of Christianity. Rochester now had a deep enough interest in philosophy to try to make sense of it. In February 1679 he received a further letter from Blount, who repeated the words of his father, 'The spirit does not remain the same in us, but is constantly renewed like a flame. We are remade every day out of the things that pass through us. We die and are reborn every day and we are not the same today as we were yesterday, and we are unaware of our character changing until we finally perceive that it has done so.' Rochester later seized on this to argue that if the soul changed every day, including the day a man died, it was not amenable to punishment for wrongs done when it was a completely different soul. This proposition made no impression on the next cleric whom he consulted, Gilbert Burnet, who had gained the soul of Jane Roberts for God. Burnet was thirty-six and a learned priest of some influence, who had been sounded out in confidence by Lauderdale as to the King divorcing the Queen on the grounds of barrenness, and was an adviser to the Privy Council. He was appointed chaplain to Charles II and regarded his primary duty as remonstrating with the King for his sinful life. When Charles was dying he was deprived of his chaplaincy for a vigorously anti-Catholic sermon, two hours in length. He fled the country and returned under William of Orange. He became Bishop of Salisbury in 1689 and attended King William on his deathbed.

In London in October 1679 Rochester sent a friend to request the company of Burnet. He had visited Rochester once or twice before, and now the Earl wanted to discuss his thoughts about religion and morality. Burnet was himself something of a heretic in his views. He was a critic of Moses, and sceptical of the Mosaic idea of creation. He also had an almost Deistic idea of nature growing up by itself, as opposed to creation by God. His works were regarded as a grave threat to the Christian view. The conversations went on until the beginning of April of 1680, when Rochester left the city. Burnet, though fashionable, was thoroughly unpopular at Court. It was thought that he was making capital out of his flock by forcing his attentions on them. He was committing the same crime as Clarendon had in trying to persuade the King to take life and his duties seriously. Dorset and Sedley, in particular, stirred up powerful antagonism against him. The courtiers, as their behaviour made only too clear, were mostly unbelievers and Hobbists. They had a deep and abiding mistrust of the clergy that in many cases was wholly justified. They thought that the virtues of truthfulness and charity were conspicuously lacking in the priesthood, and especially in Burnet.

Burnet's description of the events that follow was widely suspected. He had much to profit from the Earl's conversion. It would bring him fame and further his ecclesiastical ambitions. His account of the Earl's confidences, which he claimed the dying man had wanted published, would sell thousands. The book was brought out hastily on Rochester's death. It was a phenomenal success and has been used as an exemplar by the Christian Church for centuries. There was already a large literature of conversion created to win sinners back into the fold centred round 'trite moral judgements, euphoric advice, and self-complacent congratulation in their own rectitude on the ruin of many a dissolute man. It often took the form of a personal account of the tortures of men on their deathbeds, regretting their every deed and crying for mercy' (in the words of John Redwood). Rochester was the *ne plus ultra* – the evangelist's plum. His conversion was the best publicity for Christianity of the century. Repeated editions were produced, including translations into French, Dutch and German until as late as 1876.

Apart from their theological significance, there was a limitless market in the seventeenth century for 'true confessions' of the sort that are as popular now. There was a fashion for 'Newgate biographies', brief life histories, the confessions and dying speeches of malefactors in Newgate Prison. They were hawked in the streets and became best-sellers. A great deal of money could be made. They were procured by a functionary known as the 'Ordinary of Newgate'. He was usually a priest charged with the care of the prisoners' souls, who would supplement his income by inducing condemned men to confess their crimes (and those of others if possible). Threats of hellfire and damnation were the customary inducement. In about 1680 Daniel Defoe is said to have done such work more than once, to his lasting regret. It was a time of war between the forces of Belial and the forces of God. Both sides were heavily represented. The sinners rushed into print just as quickly as the clergy. A collection of obscene works allegedly by Rochester, *Poems on Several Occasions by the Rt. Hon. The E. of R.*, was published in the same year. They were not his work. His family put an advertisement in the *London Gazette*, 'Whereas there is a Libel of lewd scandalous Poems lately Printed, under the name of the Earl of Rochester, Whoever shall discover the Printer to Mr Thom. L. Cary at the sign of the Blew Bore in Cheap-Side ... shall have 5l. reward.' It turned out to be one Will Richards. His fate is not recorded.

Rochester assured Burnet that although he was still an unbeliever he was prepared to change his mind and would be only too happy to be convinced that he was wrong. He was in a low state of health, on the milk diet and apt to fall into fits of agitation. Any mishap weakened him so badly that he thought he was about to die and he believed that, when he left London this time, he would never come back. Even so he went out frequently and was very 'lively', said Burnet. It was his last visit to Sybaris and he was making the most of it. It conjures up a glorious picture of Rochester's utter inconsistency, all day solemnly debating sin and punishment with the vicar, then tottering off to the stews of London to commit a few more while he still had the strength.

In Burnet's *Some Passages of the Life and Death of John Earl of Rochester* he gives a long account of their disputations. He claimed to have reflected very carefully before he put them down in writing so as to ensure that they were as accurate as possible (though, measured in sheer quantity of print, Burnet's thoughts outweigh those of Rochester by about six to one). They discussed morality, natural religion (Deism) and revealed religion, especially Christianity. The Earl expressed remorse for his wicked past, not as an offence against God, only as an injury to himself and to mankind. The two maxims of his belief were that he should do 'nothing to the hurt of any other or that might prejudice his own health'. He thought that all pleasure when it did not interfere with these was to be indulged as the gratification of our natural appetites. It seemed unreasonable to imagine that those appetites were implanted in men only then to be restrained, and this included the free use of wine and women. He accepted that there was a supreme being, for he could not believe that the world was made by chance. He looked on the deity as a vast impersonal force. There should be no religious worship, only a general celebration of the supreme power. All other devotions were the cant of priests pretending that they had the secret of incensing and appeasing God as they pleased. After death, the soul did not dissolve, but he could not envisage the possibility of either reward or punishment. This aspect of his belief is of particular significance, in view of what was to happen later. He thought that heaven was too much for us to attain for our small services and hell was too extreme a punishment for the level of sin that we could achieve. He had once written, 'Our sphere of action is life's happiness, And he that thinks beyond thinks like an ass.' But that was very much how he was thinking now.

Early in the discussions Burnet subtly introduced the concept of hellfire. He said that God rewarded those capable of achieving a more perfect state of conformity to him with happiness after death. It followed that the punishment for the rest was total exclusion, with all the horror and darkness that must ensue. One or other state must come about if the soul remained separate from the body. This was what Rochester could not afford to accept. Echoing Blount, he argued that it seemed more likely that the soul began anew. Burnet disputed that as sheer conjecture and challenged him to produce evidence – an unattractive argument for a theologian to advance. The priest knew perfectly well that they were talking about belief, not proof. He reinforced the message by proclaiming the joys of a good man, particularly as he drew near death, and the horrors of the wicked. Rochester admitted that he would give everything he owned to be able to believe, and gain the consequent support and joy. But why was man not created more disposed to religion and better illuminated by God? He could not understand how there could be corruption in the *nature* of man. Religious revelation was just the shameless cunning of tricksters preying on the simplicity of the gullible. Once misled, believers passed their mistakes on to future generations without contradiction.

A man could not control his beliefs. What help was there for a man who just *could* not accept the truth of Christian teaching? It was not within a man's power to believe what he could not understand. Acquiescing in the mysteries simply made it easy for the trickery of priests, and enabled them to keep the people in subjection. Burnet's answer was that, once the conditions were performed upon which the Lord's promises were made, the reward of resurrection from the dead was *assured* to us. So we had to do our duty in the hope of eternal life that God, who could not lie, had promised. Rochester still had on his mind the events of so long ago, when Wyndham failed to appear after his death as he had promised. Burnet dealt with that problem succinctly by the observation that one like Rochester who had so corrupted the natural principles of truth had no right to expect that such an irregularity should be permitted simply in order to convince him.

The conclusion of their discussions, according to Burnet, was that Rochester was persuaded to see vice and impiety as being as damaging to human society as wild animals on the rampage. He vowed to change his whole way of life, and be 'strictly just and true; to be chaste and temperate, to forbear swearing and irreligious discourse, to worship and pray to his maker', and though he was not yet fully convinced by Christianity he would stop using his wit to run it down, or to corrupt others. Perhaps Rochester did agree this, but he undoubtedly did not mean it. He was capable of humouring the clergy out of mere politeness and admitted having done so when ill before. If it was indeed his settled intention at the conclusion of the first series of discussions, it was wholly inconsistent with the poem that he then wrote for Blount.

On 6 February 1680 he sent him a close translation of the second-act chorus of the *Troades* by Seneca. Although the original thoughts were those of the Roman, Rochester's translation, one of his finest poems, essentially reflected his own beliefs. There could be no other reason for translating it or for sending it to Blount:

> After death nothing is, and nothing, death,
> The utmost limit of a gasp of breath.
> Let the ambitious zealot lay aside
> His hopes of heaven, whose faith is but his pride;
> > Let slavish souls lay by their fear,
> > Nor be concerned which way nor where
> > After this life they shall be hurled.
>
> Dead we become the lumber of the world,
> And to that mass of matter shall be swept
> Where things destroyed with things unborn are kept.
> > Devouring time swallows us whole;
> Impartial death confounds body and soul.
> > For Hell and the foul fiend that rules
> > God's everlasting fiery jails
> > (Devised by rogues, dreaded by fools).
> With his grim, grisly dog that keeps the door,
> > Are senseless stories, idle tales,
> > Dreams, whimseys and no more.

Blount replied with another almost incomprehensible letter, which he referred to as 'an undigested heap' of his father's thoughts. He thanked Rochester for the most incomparable version of Seneca's work and said that it was to some extent a confutation of Seneca, since no less than an immortal mind could have produced it. Rochester's own genius was an unanswerable argument for his immortality. Modern thinkers, he added, held that all our beliefs about the survival of the soul and the consequent series of rewards and punishments must be true because all our laws were based upon them. If men were by nature inclined to be moral, the survival of the soul would not be necessary. But most men were not inclined to be moral, and if they *did* good they did it more out of fear of eternal loss than out of hope of eternal gain. They had therefore proposed virtuous rewards and vicious punishments that were above all terrifying. It was easier to imagine suffering than the good entertainment in Elysium. Considering their proneness to evil, this expedient was profitable to all men. Lawgivers established the immortality of the soul out of a regard not so much for truth as for honesty, hoping to induce virtue in men as a nurse gave her children what she knew was good for them. Thus, beside the authority of the scriptures and the innumerable arguments of philosophy and reason to prove the immortality of the soul, together with its rewards and punishments, the best argument was necessity and convenience. To believe in the immortality of the soul without its rewards and punishments was as irrational and useless as to believe the soul to be mortal. It was a contradictory, vague and pragmatic argument, and definitely not what Rochester wanted to hear. Rochester had always believed in the separateness of the soul from the body, and wished to believe in its immortality, but he was not attracted by the proposition that the system of reward and punishment would then be bound to follow. He knew only too well at which end of that system he was placed. There was no further correspondence between the two men.

In his absorption with metaphysical questions, Rochester was showing a tendency to forget his old friends. In April 1679 Savile sent him a pot of lemon drink recommended as a cooler (a hangover cure) and two bottles of an infusion of maidenhair fern and liquorice root recommended by Nicholas Culpeper for kidney stones. He was sending these, said the kindly Harry, because when he last saw his friend he had seemed so well that he would soon be debauching himself as usual, and would be needing the restoratives. He also sent, to accommodate another vice to which his Lordship was victim, a bottle of wig powder 'to keep the ladies' heads sweet' and a bottle of scent 'to keep their tails straight'. Given Rochester's health and this equipment he would not suggest any further temperance or chastity, which were excellent for regaining the health but superfluous when you had it.

He had been trying to put his friend forward for some state employment. He hoped to see Rochester at Boulogne as part of an expedition that was due to take place. Strangely, Rochester ignored the letter and the presents. His manners were normally punctilious and he was especially attached to Harry. Savile was hurt but could not believe his friend had simply ignored him. He sent another letter, this time one of pained complaint. He hoped that the Earl was not ill or offended, either of which would 'affect him extremely' and added, what was more, 'the small beer in Paris was very bad, and a man could not get a pipe of good tobacco for love nor money'. Rochester's reply was a little distant. ''Tis neither pride or neglect, but idleness on one side, and not knowing what to say on the other, has hindered me from writing to you after so kind a letter and the present you sent me, for which I return you at last my humble thanks.' Perhaps it was his illness; perhaps he was sulking because he had not yet been found a job to do; perhaps he had lost his sense of humour to metaphysics. He was anxious to try out his newly found gravity by involving himself in politics. He wrote a summary to Harry of the complexities of the turmoil current in London over the Popish Plot, popular suspicion of the Catholic Duke of York to be appeased, the bill to exclude York's succession, the King's prorogation of Parliament enraging both Houses and fighting at the Scottish border. 'Thus much to afford you a taste of my serious abilities and to let you know I have a great goggle-eye to business,' he announced. He was desperate to rehabilitate himself.

His moods, always unpredictable, were beginning to swing uncontrollably. He wrote of a state of contentment marred only by ill health (which his wife would doubtless not have recognised):

We are in such a settled happiness and such merry security in this place [High Lodge] that, if it were not for sickness, I could pass my time very well between my own ill-nature, which inclines me very little to pity the misfortunes of malicious mistaken fools, and the policies [politics] of the times which expose new rarities of that kind every day. The news I have to send, and the sort alone which could be so to you, are things worthy of imprisonment which I dare not trust to this pretty fool the bearer.

The 'news' may refer to sexual misbehaviour or to the general atmosphere of treachery in England at the time. His last letter to his friend was equally enigmatic. It was written on 5 April 1680, when he had left London for the last time some three months before he died. It was four days after his thirty-third birthday. He was attending the races at Newmarket and his letter came from Bishop's Stortford – possibly the King's house at Audley End. What had happened in London is a matter for conjecture, but, mortally ill as he was, he was

247

still capable of some activity that was deeply discreditable and had left him subject to blackmail. He wrote:

In my return from Newmarket I met your packet, and truly was not more surprised at the indirectness of Mr P's proceeding than overjoyed at the kindness and care of yours. Misery makes all men less or more dishonest and I am not astonished to see villainy industrious for bread, especially living in a place where it is often so out of sheer high spirits. I believe the fellow thought of this device to get some money, or else he is put upon it by somebody who has given it him already. But I give him leave to prove what he can against me. However, I will search into the matter and give you a further account within a post or two. In the meantime you have made my heart glad in giving me such a proof of your friendship, and I am now sensible that it is natural for you to be kind to me, and can never more despair of it.

No one knows the identity of 'Mr P'. Perhaps it was Paisible, the singer, whom Rochester had recommended to the King. Savile had written, 'I obeyed your commands to his Majesty, who has heard with very great delight Paisible's new compositions, and was not less pleased at all the compliments you bestowed upon him. But I would not have you think he takes so much pleasure in your good wishes as in your good *company* which is so necessary here to dispel the clouds of dullness, that you can not be thought otherwise than a *traitor* to King and country and a most unmerciful *monster* to all your acquaintance, if you come not quickly to town, though upon crutches.' Whoever it was, Savile had helped suppress the attempt. Any further detail can only be imagined, but the obvious inference is some homosexual misdemeanour. Whatever it entailed, the episode shows how swiftly his moods of penitence during illness tended to evaporate on recovery.

He was doing his best to become reconciled with his wife. Now that he had parted from Elizabeth Barry and taken the child away, he was pondering deeply on his life. He had always had a tendency to depression and there was very little left to raise his spirits. He knew that he could not survive long, and he was hearing things from both Blount and Burnet about the hereafter that he did not want to hear. He had always consoled himself with the thought that his sins were not so very serious, and that in any case there was no credible form of retribution. Now he was beginning to get a chill sensation that he had been wrong. It was he who had written the poignant words:

> Then old age and experience, hand in hand,
> Lead him to death, make him to understand,
> After a search so painful, and so long,
> That all his life he has been in the wrong.

In early 1680 he wrote his wife at Adderbury a final letter, of which this is a fragment:

so great a disproportion t'wixt our desires and what it has ordained to content them; but you will say this is pride and madness, for there are those so entirely satisfied with their shares in this world, that their wishes nor their thoughts have not a farther prospect of felicity and glory. I'll tell you, were that man's soul placed in a body fit for it, he were a dog that could count any thing a benefit obtain'd with flattery, fear, and service,

> Is there a man ye gods whom I do hate
> Dependence and attendance be his fate
> Let him be busy still and in a crowd
> And very much a slave and very proud.
> > Cowley

Remember me to my dearest aunt and my good uncle. I would not have you lose my letter – it is not fit for everybody to find.

> Rochester

Your wine was bought last week, but neglected to be sent.

This letter is slightly opaque, not least because half of it is missing. It has been suggested that the absent part must have said words to the effect that 'If there were a deity, he should give us happiness in the next world to make up for our disappointment in this, caused by the disproportion between our desires and what it has ordained to content them, etc.' There was certainly no sign of the contentment that he had described to Harry. He also sent his nine-year-old son his idea of an improving homily.

Charles

I take it very kindly that you write to me (though seldom) and wish heartily you would behave yourself, so that I might show how much I love you without being asham'd. Obedience to your grandmother and those who instruct you in good things is the way to make you happy here and forever. Avoid idleness, scorn lying and God will bless you, for which I pray…

It seems as if, while being dragged towards divine retribution, he was trying to win points for judgement day. He was advocating obedience to the child's grandmother (noticeably, not to his mother), whose religiosity was notorious, and he concluded his exhortations with an invocation upon God and a reference to his prayers. Whatever he may have truly believed, he gave every appearance of having stumbled even further along the path to righteousness than he had promised Burnet, yet within weeks, on the way to Newmarket, he was inveighing against God as enthusiastically as ever.

In March 1680 he performed one of those capricious gestures for which he was notorious. He was involved in another duel. Since the farce with Mulgrave he had accepted a number of challenges but they had always petered out, usually having been prevented by the King. It was the same with this last pitiful spasm of the dying gamecock. He took up the cause of the Earl of Arran. The Earl was in love with a Miss Poulett, but her uncle Edward Seymour, the former Speaker of the House of Commons, forbade the courtship. Arran, who was young and wild, challenged Seymour to a duel but was forced to flee to The Hague. Rochester had spoken out, encouraging Arran and flaying Seymour for his intervention. Seymour called Rochester out. The Earl, sick as he was, took up the challenge and waited for Seymour at the rendezvous by Arlington Gardens for three hours. Seymour did not attend. Lord Conway, another of Miss Poulett's admirers, received a letter from one Francis Gwyn, claiming that Seymour had sent for Gwyn in the morning and dispatched him to Rochester. Rochester agreed to meet the next morning on horseback, with sword and pistol. He explained that he had 'a weakness in his limbs [which indeed he did], but he thought that he could do very well on horseback'. Gwyn suggested that the true reason was that the Earl thought it impossible for all of them to procure horses and equipage in so short a time without causing suspicion and being found out. Gwyn felt strongly that they could have got away with it. Thus one wonders, if Seymour really wanted a fight, why did he not go ahead and find the equipment?

At two o'clock in the morning of the day in question, Seymour's second Mr Collingwood advised him that the King had commanded him not to stir out of his house. Gwyn claimed that Collingwood had already visited Rochester with the same message. That was the excuse for Gwyn's having not gone to Rochester to tell him that they had been stopped. They said that it was because he knew already. Rochester had gone out the next morning, pretending that the King had only commanded him to stay out of any quarrel involving Lord Arran. When he found no one, which he very well knew he would not, said Gwyn, he came back and reported that he had been in the field and Mr Seymour did not appear. 'But that report is long ago stopped and we are at last in a state of quietness,' said Gwyn. Mr Seymour left town the next day. The Court found it easy enough to judge between the two conflicting stories. Lord Conway, the rival, scribbled a note in his own hand with the comment, 'giving an account of Sir Edward Seymour's heroic courage, a pack of the greatest lies that ever was told, for he durst not fight Lord Arran, that was the jest of the Court on that occasion'.

The next month Rochester was at the races at Newmarket. He was with the King and his courtiers, just as in the old days, except that now he was blind and crippled. He was seen with the King, his head and his goblet as ever held high. He returned to Bishop's Stortford, where he received the letter and packet from Savile. He posted to Woodstock and then set out for Enmore. The journey to Somerset was too much. It was hot, and the violent motion burst an ulcer in his bladder. Vast quantities of purulent matter passed with his urine, causing him dreadful pain. He returned by coach to High Lodge, Woodstock and collapsed into the arms of Mr Baptist. Rochester had an extensive knowledge of medicine, which was one of the subjects he had studied while lying fallow in the country. He knew enough about his condition to realise that his chances of recovery were slim. As he lay in his sick bed at High Lodge he was attended by a number of doctors, one of whom was Dr Radcliffe, a renowned drinker and jovial conversationalist, whose attention to the bottle was sometimes at the expense of his patients. Tom Brown had written after the death of the Duke of Gloucester:

> All our complaints we must on Radcliffe spend,
> Who, for his pleasure, can neglect his friend;
> By whose delays more patients sure have died,

Than by the drugs of others misapplied.
Three bottles keep him, and for their dear sake,
Three kingdoms unregarded lie at stake.

There were also Drs Short and Lower from London, and a Dr Edward
Browne.

As the darkness gathered, so did the clergy. Parsons, his mother's
chaplain, arrived at Woodstock on 26 May and remained constantly in
attendance. The Bishop of Oxford visited every week from his palace
six miles away, 'looking on this as a most important piece of his
pastoral care'. Dr Marshall, the rector of Lincoln College and parson
of the parish, was often there. According to Burnet, 'They were taking
care that Rochester might not on terms more easy than safe, be at
peace with himself' (a chilling euphemism). 'These clergymen combined
together to so direct and support the dying man, to make sure that
his repentance was not too superficial, nor on the other hand be out
of measure oppressed with sorrow without hope.' It was a little
premature to be planning the Earl's repentance, which had not yet
occurred, but doubtless they had grounds for confidence. Soon Dr
Price of Magdalen joined the group. The Earl's mother, now sixty-six,
moved in with Elizabeth, the children and old John Cary, who used
to look after the estate. The Dowager and Cary gave the ecclesiastical
team their devout support. While he was lying in his sickbed, the Earl
was constantly pecked like carrion by the nagging of his mother and
a murder of clerics. He was weak and ill, frightened and probably
mentally disordered. Melancholy turned into lacerating sorrow. His
agonies of mind were worse than his physical pain. He was persuaded
that he had not only neglected and dishonoured but also openly defied
his maker and drawn many others in with him. He came to see himself
as being in the greatest possible danger of damnation. At last he had
been made to accept that such a state existed, and from there it was
but a small step to the expectation that, at the age of thirty-three, it
was assuredly awaiting *him*. It was no longer a case, as he once wrote,
of 'Past joys have more than paid what I endure.'

At the end of May or the beginning of June there was a sudden
bolt of revelation. 'The hand of God touched him,' Burnet wrote, 'but
it did not touch him through the rational arguments of a cleric.'
Although Burnet was not anxious to yield credit to another priest,

what he said seems to have been true. The occasion was the reading by Parsons of the fifty-third chapter of Isaiah, describing the Suffering Servant of Jahweh. The chaplain had been trying to reason with Rochester in the same way that Burnet had, and was pointing out to him the passages in the Old Testament that prophesied the crucifixion of Christ as logical proof of its truth. He was reading:

Who hath believed our report? And to whom is the arm of the Lord revealed? For he shall grow up before him as a tender plant, and as a root out of a dry ground: he hath no form nor comeliness; and when we shall see him, there is no beauty that we should desire him.

He is despised and rejected of men; a man of sorrows, and acquainted with grief: and we hid as it were our faces from him; he was despised, and we esteemed him not...

All we like sheep have gone astray; we have turned every one to his own way; and the Lord hath laid on him the iniquity of us all.

In Parsons's version of events, when Rochester heard the prophecy he felt an 'inward force upon him which did so enlighten his mind and convince him that he could resist it no longer: for the words had an authority which did shoot like rays or beams in his mind; so that he was not only convinced by the reasonings he had about it, which satisfied his understanding, but by a power which did so effectually constrain him, that he did ever afterwards as firmly believe in his saviour as if he had seen him in the clouds.' The reference to 'convinced by the reasonings' suggests that Parsons was no keener than Burnet to yield the credit. The transformation was instantaneous and fervent. From that moment, Rochester displayed every sign not merely of religious faith, but of religious mania. Within days he had persuaded his wife to leave the Catholic Church (which he had persuaded her to enter in the first place) and take the Anglican sacraments with him. No one will ever know whether it was cause or mere coincidence that the times were particularly dangerous for Catholics.

John Cary wrote to Sir Ralph Verney, Rochester's old guardian, that he feared the Earl had not long to live. He was now very weak and ill. He was the most altered person, and the most devout and pious he had ever known, and certainly would make a most worthy man if it would please God to spare his life. The most comforting thing was that they could hope that he would be happy in another world, and also that, in the midst of this sorrow, his lady had returned to her first love, the Protestant religion. At the same time his mother wrote to the sister of her first husband, Lady St John, at Battersea:

Sweet sister, It has pleased God to lay his afflictive hand upon my poor son in visiting of him with a sore sickness, and whether for life or death we cannot guess, but he is reduced to great weakness in the outward man. But in the midst of punishment He has remembered mercy and strengthened him in the inward man, to the comfort of me his poor mother. For never in all the former sicknesses he has had did in the last measure work so much upon him to the knowledge and acknowledgement of God, and to repentance of his former life and the sense how he has gone astray, as this doth. I am not able to write you a long letter.

But there was something that consoled her:

I can only say this, that though he lies under as much misery almost as human man can bear, yet he bears his sufferings with so much patience and resignation to God's will, that I confess I take more comfort in him under this visitation than ever I did in all his life before. And though the Lord has been pleased not to work this work upon him till the last hour, yet I have great reason to believe he will find mercy through the merits and satisfaction of Christ, on whom he throws himself for the favour of God. Oh sister, I am sure, had you heard the heavenly prayers he has made since this sickness, the extraordinary things he has said to the wonder of all that has heard him, *you* would wonder, and think that God alone must teach him, for no man could put into him such things as he says. He has, I must tell you too, converted his wife to be Protestant again. Pray, pray for his perseverance, dear sister, and pardon me that I can say no more but to rest...

The Dowager was happier to see her son dying in Christian agony than bursting with atheistical health. He would have difficulty getting into trouble in heaven. 'The extraordinary things that he has said ... no man could put into him ...' make one wonder exactly what he was saying, and how it would have reflected on his mental condition. The Dowager was at extreme pains to refute the widespread claims, of which she was only too well aware, that her son had finally gone mad. On 5 June Burnet wrote to Henry Savile's brother Lord Halifax that he had heard from Will Fanshaw that letters had come from Rochester from which it seemed that by now he must be dead. He had expressed great remorse for his past ill life. He was dying a serious penitent, and professed himself a Christian. Halifax's reaction was to comment drily, 'The world is grown so foolish a thing, that a witty man may very well be ashamed of staying in it.' Burnet was still not rushing to the bedside of the recent convert.

There was a crisis on 7 June and his mother watched him all night. He fought back and again seemed set fair to recover. With this possibility in mind Burnet wrote to Halifax on the 12th saying, somewhat sourly, that he was suspicious that the Earl's penitence would not survive the sickness that had caused it. 'The Earl of Rochester lives still and is in a probable way of recovery, for it is thought all that ulcerous matter is cast out. All the town is full of his great penitence, which by your Lordship's good leave, I hope flows from a better principle than the height of his *fancy*, and indeed that which depends so much on the disposition of the body cannot be supposed very high when a man's spirits were so spent as his were.' Rochester had fought off all Burnet's attempts to show him the way to truth, and had finally succumbed to an insignificant country parson. Burnet seems successfully to have controlled his natural impulse to rejoice. He was well aware that the conversion had sprung from the height of the patient's fancy, his spirits utterly spent, and that genuine recantation depended entirely on the health of the body.

The rumours of Rochester's insanity were spreading apace. His mother wrote to Lady St John, 'He continues weak, but is sometimes better than he is others. The greatest comfort he enjoys is his sleep, and that he does much. He has a kind of hectic [agitated] fever upon him, as the doctors call it, which is not at all times, for sometimes his temper is good outwardly, but the doctor says he is hot inwardly; yet I cannot think it, because he is seldom dry.' She reported that 'He drinks ass's milk and it digests well with him, and some other spoon-meats, but he takes no broths made with meat for fear of heat. He spits mightily within these two days, which some say is good for him, but I find all evacuations weaken him. I confess I cannot discern amendment in him yet, but as long as life is we have hopes.' It was the state of his mind, and the state of his soul, that concerned her most:

I thank God his sense continues very well and when his strength will give him leave, expresses himself with great devotion upon the account of his former ill life. With great humility he lays himself low before the throne of grace, begging favour and pardon from God, acknowledging himself the greatest of sinners. Truly, sister, I think I may say without partiality that he has never been heard say, when he speaks of religion, an unsensible word, nor of anything else.

But one night, of which I writ you word, he was disordered in his head, but then he said no hurt, only some little ribble rabble which had no hurt in it. But it was observed by his wife and I particularly, that whenever he spoke of God that night, he spoke very well and with great sense, which we wondered at. Since that night he has never had a minute of disorder in his head: that was almost a fortnight ago. This last night, if you had heard him pray, I am sure you would not have took his words for the words of a madman, but such as come from a better spirit than the mind of mere man. But let the wicked of the world say what they please of him. The reproaches of them are an honour to him and I take comfort that the Devil rages against my son: it shows his power over him is subdued in him, and that he has no share in him.

The Dowager was sure that the Devil exerted influence through certain of her son's friends: 'Many messages and compliments his old acquaintance send him, but he is so far from receiving of them that still his answer is, "Let me see none of them, and I would to God I had never conversed with some of them." One of his physicians, thinking to please him, told him the King drank his health the other day. He looked earnestly upon him and said never a word, but turned his face from him. I thank God, his thoughts are wholly taken off from the world and I hope, whether he lives or dies, will ever be so.' Then she exclaimed, 'But they are fine people at Windsor, God forgive them! Sure there never was so great a malice performed as to entitle my poor son to a lampoon at this time, when for aught they know, he lies upon his death-bed ... I do believe, if any has reported that he should speak ridiculous, it has been the *popish* physician who one day listened at the door whilst my son was discoursing with a divine. But my son spoke so low that he could hear but half words, and so he might take it for nonsense, because he had a mind so to do.'

On 15 June Cary felt hope that Rochester was on the mend again.

'Many changes he meets withal, pretty good days succeed ill nights, which help to keep up his spirits, but he is very weak, and expresses himself very good.'

The Court, which was gathered at Windsor, wanted to satisfy its curiosity about the state of Rochester's brain. It is apparent from his mother's last letter that some wit had circulated a lampoon about him, presumably commenting on his sanity. Will Fanshaw was sent down to see how he was. As the Dowager put it bitterly, 'The fine people at Windsor sent down a spy to report.' She knew that the spy was a friend of her granddaughter's husband, whom she loathed. When Fanshaw arrived and was ushered in to see his old friend, Rochester looked at him and said, 'Fanshaw, think of God, let me advise you, and repent you of your former life, and amend your ways. Believe what I say to you. There *is* a God, and a powerful God, and he is a terrible God to unrepenting sinners. The time draws near that he will come to judgement with great terror to the wicked, therefore delay not your repentance. His displeasure will thunder against you if you do; believe me, do not defer the time. You and I have been long acquainted and done ill together.' He added, aside, 'I love the man, and speak to him out of conscience for the good of his soul.' Fanshaw said not a word. He was aghast and seen to be trembling as he left the room. Rochester asked, 'Is a gone? Poor wretch, I fear his heart is hardened.' Before making his way back to Windsor, Fanshaw made the suggestion to those present at High Lodge that the sick man 'should be kept out of melancholy fancies', for which the Dowager never forgave him. One of the doctors, Dr Short, sighed and said that he himself could do Rochester no good, but that the Earl had done him a great deal. On his death the doctor joined the Catholic Church. Rochester's caution to Fanshaw of a God terrible to unrepenting sinners, and his thunderous displeasure for failure to repent, reveals exactly what was on his mind. There *was* future life, and ineluctably there *was* future punishment, but not for the Earl of Rochester if he could find some way of avoiding it.

By 19 June, though in a relapse and slightly feverish, he was sleeping well. The terrible pain had faded and he was gaining a little strength. His mother wrote the tale of Fanshaw's visit to Lady St John. She concluded with a note, 'You must not let Fanshaw know what I have told you. I thank God my son continues at all times very devout, ever since God struck him with a sense of his sins. He is very tender and fearful, but it does not carry him to despair. He is sensible the satisfaction of Christ is his comfort, and relies wholly upon Christ's merits for his salvation. This day has not been so good a day with him as yesterday. He has had some faint fits.'

On 25 June, three weeks after his apotheosis, Rochester received a letter from Burnet. The priest bashfully did not want to publish the Earl's reply because it contained a compliment to himself so far above his merit, and not very well suiting with Rochester's condition. In his account Burnet removed the part that embarrassed him. This is the original letter:

My most honoured Dr Burnet,

My spirits and body decay so equally together that I shall write you a letter, as weak as I am in person. I begin to value churchmen above all men in the world (and you above all the churchmen I know in it). If God be yet pleased to spare me longer in this world, I hope in your conversation to be exalted to that degree of piety that the world may see how much I abhor what I so long loved, and how much I glory in repentance in God's service. Bestow your prayers upon me that God would spare me, (if it be his good will), to show a true repentance and amendment of life for the time to come; or else if the Lord pleaseth to put an end to my worldly being now, that he would mercifully accept my death bed repentance and perform that promise he hath been pleased to make, that at what time soever a sinner doth repent he would receive him.

Put up these prayers, most dear doctor, to almighty God for your most obedient and languishing Servant.

The letter itself was not in Rochester's hand, but his mother's and the signature was almost indecipherable. His mother said, though, that he had dictated every word. He was still scared that his renunciation was inadequate. He produced ever more spectacular displays of remorse. He wanted to tie God down to the contract of which Burnet had spoken, genuine contrition in exchange for a ticket to heaven. A cynic's suspicions would be intensified by the convert's scrutiny of the Prayer Book – 'looking', in the words of a great actor, 'for loopholes'. The last words of the letter are from Ezekiel: 'At what time soever a sinner doth repent of his sin ... I will put all wickedness out of my remembrance, saith the Lord.' They did not appear in that form in the then current Prayer Book of 1662, or in the 1611 Bible. They were only to be found in the superseded 1604 version of the Prayer Book.

On 26 June the Dowager made another determined effort to proclaim her son's sanity. 'I am sure, dear sister, 'tis your desire to hear some time how my poor weak son does. He gives us little hopes of his life, his weakness increasing so much. But as his outward man decays, I thank God his inward increases and strengthens. For he is very pious and devout, and willing to resign himself into the arms of his saviour, when God pleases to take him.' She had heard that 'Mr Fanshaw reports my son is mad, but I thank God he is far from that. I confess for a night and part of a day for want of rest, his head was a little disordered but it was long since Mr Fanshaw saw him. When he reproved him for his sinful life, he was as well in his head as ever he was in his life and so he is now, I thank God.' She was sure, she said, that 'if you heard him pray you would think God has inspired him with true wisdom indeed, and that neither folly nor madness comes near him. I wish that wretch Fanshaw had so great a sense of sin as my poor child has, that so he might be brought to repentance before it is too late; but he is an ungrateful man to such a friend. Dear Sister, pray for us...'

On 2 July Rochester dictated what became known as his 'dying remonstrance' and signed it in the presence of his mother and the chaplain. It was written 'for the benefit of all those whom I may have drawn into sin by my example and encouragement'. It declared that 'from the bottom of my soul I detest and abhor the whole course of my former wicked life'. To underline it, he sent for all the servants, including the pig boy, to hear the declaration read. By this time hope of recovery was again fading. He was getting no stronger, and his flesh was badly wasted. There were fears of consumption, though his lungs were still good. He was sleeping a great deal and 'his head, for the most part, is very well', said his mother. 'He was this day taken up and set up in a chair for an hour, and was not very faint when he went to bed. He does not care to talk much; but, when he does, speaks for the most part well. His expressions are so suddenly spoken that many of them are lost, and cannot be taken; yet I believe some part of what he has said will be remembered.' She told her son that Fanshaw had said that he hoped the Earl would recover and abandon the principles that he now professed. He answered, 'Wretch, I wish I had conversed all my lifetime with link-boys rather than with him and that crew, such I mean as Fanshaw is. Indeed I would not live to return to what I was for all the world.' On 8 July Lady Sunderland wrote to Lord Halifax that there was no hope for Rochester: 'He has ulcers in two places. He sees nobody but his mother, wife, divines and physicians.'

In his ever more urgent quest for heavenly reassurance, Rochester recruited another ecclesiastic, Dr Thomas Pierce, chaplain to the King. Dr Pierce was in charge of the Private Oratory at Court, where Rochester may have met him, and he visited the Earl during his last illness. The tone of the Earl's letter reveals his desperation:

My indisposition renders my intellectuals almost as feeble as my person, but considering the candour and extreme charity your natural mildness has always showed me, I am assured of a favourable construction of my present lines, which can but faintly express the sorrowful character of a humble and afflicted mind, and also those great comforts your inexhaustible goodness, learning and piety, plenteously affords to the drooping spirits of poor sinners, so that I may truly say, holy man!

To you I owe what consolation I enjoy in urging God's mercies against despair, and holding me up under the weight of those high and mountainous sins my wicked and ungovernable life has heaped upon me. If God shall be pleased to spare me a little longer here I have unalterably resolved to become a new man, as to wash out the stains of my lewd courses with my tears and weep over the profane and unhallowed abominations of my former doings; that the world may see how I loathe sin and abhor the very remembrance of those tainted and unclean ways I once delighted in – these being, as the apostle tells us, the things whereof I am now ashamed. Or if it be His great pleasure now to put a period to my days, that He will accept of my last gasp, that the smoke of my deathbed offering may not be unsavoury to His nostrils and drive me like Cain from before His presence.

He needed Pierce's help:

Pray for me, dear Doctor, and all you that forget not God, pray for me fervently. Take heaven by force, and let me enter with you as it were, in disguise, for I dare not appear before the dread majesty of that Holy One I have so often offended. Warn all my friends and companions to a true and sincere repentance today, while it is called today, before the evil day comes and they be no more. Let them know that sin is like the angel's book in the Revelations, it is sweet in the mouth but bitter in the belly. Let them know that God will not be mocked, that He is a Holy God and will be served in holiness and purity that requires the whole man and the early man. Bid them make haste, for the night cometh when no man can work. Oh that they were wise, that they would consider this and not, with me, with wretched me, delay it until their latter end! Pray, dear sir, continually pray for your poor friend,

Rochester

It was an extraordinary effusion. It may or may not have been the work of a sane man but there can be no doubt that it was the work of a terrified one. On 20 July Burnet arrived at Woodstock. He had taken his time in coming, having delayed for some three weeks. He explained that he had felt 'to come so far before would have been a presumption, when the Earl was already in such excellent hands'. Having received the letter he did not think that there was any danger of a sudden change so he put off visiting him. It is perhaps an unworthy thought that, having tried long and hard to procure the repentance of the sinner, he may have been less than ecstatic when the sinner succumbed to a country chaplain. It may be that this was what moved him, immediately on hearing of the change, to express doubt about its genuineness. When he did arrive, Mr Baptist announced his arrival to the Earl, who thought that his servant was talking about someone completely different, a quack who had been offering to cure him and in whose ministrations he was not interested. It took some hours to sort the matter out. Burnet uncomfortably blamed the misunderstanding on the fact that Mr Baptist was French and had failed to follow what he said. The servant had lived in England for many years, spoke English and knew perfectly well who Burnet was. The one who did not was Rochester himself, who was now close to death and, it seems, losing his sanity. Burnet consoled himself with the thought that it was all for the best, for he would have been no use anyway to a man so ill.

That first night the patient was raving and convulsed. He was given laudanum and after some hours' rest calmed down. According to Burnet the fit did not return. When he finally awoke and recognised Burnet, Rochester was pathetically grateful. He launched into a diatribe against himself. Thinking over his past life, he was distraught at having so offended his maker and dishonoured his redeemer. He described the horrors he had gone through, and told him how much he wanted to call on God and his crucified saviour to have mercy, for he believed that he had sincerely repented. He was calm now after several weeks of storm. His spirits were low, and his strength spent. He insisted many times that Burnet pray with him. He was very anxious to know the priest's opinion of deathbed repentance. Burnet told him that before he could give him any decision he would have to hear a detailed account.

Though almost too ill to speak, Rochester retraced his footsteps on his road to Damascus. He said that he had had the passage in Isaiah read to him so often that he knew it by heart. Thus he fed back to Burnet the faith through both reason and revelation that Burnet himself had originally prescribed. He talked of his happiness at receiving the sacrament and his even greater joy at procuring his wife to receive it with him. He admitted that he had been instrumental in procuring her communion with the Church of Rome, so that it was one of the profoundest joys in his sickness that he had undone the damage for which he was responsible.

Throughout his illness he showed great tenderness to his wife. She had put aside his mistreatment of her and become deeply concerned for him. He was brave in his pain and in one of the worst bouts professed that he willingly submitted to it. He looked up to heaven and said, 'God's holy will be done, I bless him for all he does to me.' He asked Burnet to give his former friends a number of improving messages. He told him to publish anything about him that might help to reclaim others and he prayed to God that, as his life had done so much injury, his death might do some good. He pressed Burnet for his true opinion about the looming state of eternity. The priest's response was that, though the promises of the Gospel all depended upon a real change of heart and life, the indispensable condition was that it appeared in our *lives* that our hearts are changed. He said this knowing that Rochester could look forward to no such life in which to atone. Burnet was not making it easy, but then Rochester was not Burnet's conversion. The repentance of most dying men was like the howling of a condemned prisoner for pardon, the priest observed, which came not from a sense of his crimes but from the horror of approaching death, and there was little hope for such regrets as those. On the other hand if the mind of a sinner, even on his deathbed, had truly altered and turned to God, so great was the Lord's mercy that even in that extreme case he would receive him. Rochester assured him that his mind was *entirely* turned and, though horror had given him his first awakening, it was now grown into a settled faith and conversion.

Burnet knew of the widespread view that Rochester had lost his mind. He said afterwards that the obstacle to accepting his reformation was deciding how much of it was due to disease and the fact that his spirit was so utterly crushed; but he said that all the time he was with the Earl after the first night there were no ravings, and insisted that Rochester's thoughts and his memory were perfectly clear. He called often for his children, his son and three daughters, and spoke to them with such feeling that it could not be expressed in writing. He called Burnet to look on them all and said, 'See how good God has been to me in giving me so many blessings, and I have carried myself to him like an ungracious and unthankful dog.' What most impressed the priest was that Rochester had stopped swearing, something that he normally did about every three minutes. On one occasion he referred to 'that damned fellow' who had kept him waiting. He hurriedly apologised. 'Oh, that language of fiends which was so familiar to me, hangs yet about me; sure none of them has more deserved to be damned than I have done!' he whimpered and humbly asked God pardon for it. He asked Burnet to talk to the fellow and ask his forgiveness. Burnet said it was unnecessary, as indeed it was; it is an interesting example of the extreme level of religious fervour that he now displayed.

He was in constant pain and passing water that contained purulent matter, but he did not complain. He thought that he had a stone in his passage but it was searched and none was found. His illness drained the whole substance of his body, until there was nothing left but skin and bone. His hinder parts began to putrefy from bedsores. One night he had a good night's sleep, and became pathetically excited by the hope of recovery, but the truth was that laudanum had been administered without his knowledge. One wonders how much laudanum had been given to him without his knowledge before. It was a remedy to which doctors very quickly resorted. Laudanum was a tincture made from opium and spirits of wine. It was effective in lifting the mood and relieving pain, but not in clarifying the brain.

Burnet decided to leave on Friday, after four days. The dying man begged him in desperation to stay, but on Saturday 24 July at four in the morning the cleric left. He later explained, 'That day there appeared no symptoms of present death and a worthy physician then with him told me that an accident might carry him away on a sudden; yet without such a thing happening he might well live some weeks more.' He bade him no farewell. 'I durst not take leave of him for he had expressed so great an unwillingness to part with me the day before that if I had not presently yielded to one day's stay, it would like to have given him some trouble; therefore I thought it better to leave him without any formality.' Some hours later Rochester asked for the priest. When he was told that he had gone he was deeply distressed and said, 'Hath my friend left me? Then I shall die shortly.' After that he spoke only once or twice. For the rest of the time he lay there in silence. Once his family heard him praying. On Monday, at about two o'clock in the morning, he died, broken by disease and by the well-intentioned. He was thirty-three, the same age as Jesus Christ when he was crucified.

Burnet concluded that Divine Goodness had taken pity on the dying man. It had seen the sincerity of his repentance, but could not spare him to suffer future temptations that he would be powerless to resist. It would have been a very unhelpful piece of propaganda for the Church if, after all the furore, the deathbed repentance turned out to be meaningless. Had Rochester been an unknown ploughman, one suspects that the Church's readiness to accept his conversion might have been more elusive. 'Now', Burnet announced, 'he is at rest, and I am very confident enjoys the fruits of his late but sincere repentance. But such as live, and still go on in their sins and impieties, and will not be awakened neither by this nor the other alarms that are about their ears are, it seems, given up by God to a judicial hardness and impenitency.' He concluded his account with a protracted crow over those who still engaged in sin, threatening them with all sorts of punishments in this world and the next and holding Rochester up as one of the lucky ones.

On 9 August the Earl, at the risk of deconsecrating the church, was buried beside his father in the vault under the north aisle of Spelsbury

Church. (His father had finally come home, though only when long dead.) There was no monument or inscription, only Anthony Wood's elegy, 'In this vault also lies buried John Earl of Rochester. This John made a great noise in the world for his noted and professed atheism, his lampoons and other frivolous stuff; and a great noise after his death for his penitent departure.' Before he died he asked his mother to burn his trunkful of papers and obscene pictures. She enthusiastically obeyed. They included a number of works and his memoirs, a 'History of the Intrigues of the Court of Charles II,' written in letters to Harry Savile. It was probably the fate of all his work in his own hand. For this atrocity, a wit of a later age remarked, 'Her soul is now burning in heaven.'

In his will he appointed his mother and his wife trustees, the trusteeship to last only so long as his wife should remain unmarried and 'friendlily live with my mother'. If she remarried or wilfully separated herself from the Dowager, her trusteeship would automatically determine. He left an annuity of £40 secured on the manor of Sutton Malet to Elizabeth Clarke, his daughter by Elizabeth Barry. His trustees were his mother, his wife, John Cary, Sir John St John, his uncle Sir Richard Hoe and the questionable Sir Allen Apsley. He left Robert Parsons the parsonage of Charlench, and Mr Baptist, who was witness to a codicil, received all his clothes, linen and other personal possessions.

13

'This is the season of tribulation'
Syphilis and Conversion

He well repents that will not sin, yet can;
Deathbed sorrow rarely shows the man.

Nathaniel Lee, The Princess of Cleves, 1681

The likelihood that he died of syphilis is very high. Rochester's symptoms and background disclosed by correspondence and witnesses were as follows: in October 1669 he was infected with the pox and under mercury treatment at Madame Fourcard's bathhouse in Leather Lane. For years he displayed symptoms of kidney stones that were never there. This was established on his deathbed. Almost any part of the body may be infected and almost any chronic disease may be imitated. The kidneys and bladder are two prominent points of attack. Given that he had had syphilis, there was a high probability that it would return to kill him. When he died he had had a number of bladder ulcers which burst and were poisoning him. Vast quantities of purulent matter passed with his urine, causing him dreadful pain. In June of 1671 he went to Bath. He had arthritis. In the same year he suddenly walked out of Garraway's coffee house, so badly was he suffering from his eyes. This may have been due to photophobia caused by mercury poisoning, but his sight became consistently worse and a similar event happened when he walked out of his home in early 1672. He could not take either wine or water. The eyes are one of the areas favoured by the spirochaete.

In September 1672 he told his wife that Kensington and back was a voyage that he could hardly manage, possibly due to osteoarthritis. Syphilis can attack the heart, like any other organ. His constant weakness and sudden remissions and relapses could have been due to the aorta going into a state of aneurysm, with valve leakage preventing the heart pumping efficiently, causing heart failure. The spirochaetes would invade the small arteries and cause persistent inflammation. In the limbs this would cause arthritis and muscle wastage. Rochester was afflicted throughout his body. 'I am in a damned relapse brought by a fever, the stone and some ten diseases more which have deprived me of the power of *crawling* ...' The multiplicity of ailments from which he thought he was suffering points unmistakably to one.

Mucous membranes, skin and bones were common sites of attack. The flesh would be eaten away and the muscle wasted. 'Can you think of having lean arms, small legs, red eyes and nose?' he asked Harry. 'His flesh was badly wasted,' said Burnet. 'His illness drained the whole substance of his body, until there was nothing left but skin and bone.' Organs could be affected either directly or indirectly through pressure from grossly swollen scar tissue. His lungs were involved. When he was dying, he was subject to frequent fits, and he had difficulty breathing. 'He spits mightily within these two days.' In October 1677, he was confined to his bed and was too ill to provide for Elizabeth Barry and the baby. He was almost blind, utterly lame and 'scarce within the reasonable hopes of ever seeing London again'. Theories about his death from debility brought about by general depravity or, more specifically, alcohol are unlikely to be correct. He was undoubtedly a drunk, as were his friends, but they drank on binges. Although he made himself ill through drink it was not the slow, steady, secret pickling of the irredeemable alcoholic. We know from Sir Robert Howard's letter that his doctor had some stern things to say, but Rochester never came anywhere near the level of alcoholism that would have killed him. He never displayed symptoms of liver damage, or of amnesic syndrome (Korsakoff's syndrome) which affects alcoholics, nor was there any sign of delirium tremens, and his drinking grew less with time.

No doubt his binges were of little help, but what happened was no less than was to be expected. He had caught syphilis. It appeared to have gone away, but it had not. It returned to haunt him. It rotted his body and probably also his mind. The odds in favour of syphilis being the cause of death are very strong. Perhaps the most telling point was what Rochester himself, with remarkable insight, said to Harry: 'This is the season of tribulation, and I piously beg of almighty God that the strict severity shown to one scandalous sin amongst us may expiate for all grievous calamities – so help them God whom it concerns!' He had had severe trouble with his eyes for nearly ten years, and he was virtually blind by the time he died.

It was widely thought that he was insane: 'those whom the gods wish to destroy, they first make mad'. Did he have *neuro*syphilis? Was neurosyphilis the road to Damascus?

It had been suspected from the beginning of the sixteenth century that syphilis caused insanity, but the theory was always rejected as inconsistent with the doctrine of the four humours, which had dominated medicine for centuries. Alfred Fournier discovered the truth at the end of the nineteenth century. At the conclusion of his observations he was able to claim that 'the nervous system is the victim par excellence of tertiary syphilis'. His exposition was still not accepted and the argument continued for another twenty years until 1913, when it finally prevailed. Until then syphilis tended to be ignored or shrugged off, as it had been in previous centuries. Delius, Nietzsche and Baudelaire caught it. It was even thought to be a source of artistic inspiration. When Guy de Maupassant, who died insane from neurosyphilis, first contracted the pox in 1877, he was delighted:

I have been taking mercury and potassium iodine for five weeks and I feel very well on it. My hair is starting to grow again and the hair on my arse is sprouting. I've got the pox! At last! Not the miserable clap, no – no – the great pox, the one that Francis I died of. The pox in all its majesty and I'm proud of it, by God. Now I don't have to worry any more about catching it. I screw the street whores, and then I tell them, 'I've got the pox.'

In about 1880, at the time when the medical argument about neuro-syphilis was still raging, he began to experience his first bouts of insanity. When asked if he had ever had the pox, he laughed. 'Oh, yes, all the children's diseases. Everyone gets it when they're young but for ten years I haven't had a trace of it. I have been free of it for a long time now.' He was wrong.

During the advanced stages of syphilis, between 20 and 40 per cent of patients suffer invasion of the central nervous system, and almost all of these develop persistent active infection (neurosyphilis). Neu-rosyphilis falls into two common classifications, tabes dorsalis (locomotor ataxia) and general paresis (general paralysis of the insane), which involves deterioration of personality, delusions, convulsions, dementia and total insanity. In tertiary syphilis colonies of spirochaetes burrow into the tissues and destroy them. As they heal, scars replace them. If brain tissue is destroyed, principally the cerebral cortex, it can no longer function normally and insanity results. Paresis comes at a time when all other symptoms of the disease have long since passed. The sufferer loses his appreciation of reality. Behavioural changes suggest psychosis, a mental disorder characterised by delusions, hallucinations, personality changes, confusion, dementia, loss of memory and emotional instability. In the final stages, seizures occur. If not properly treated, paretic neurosyphilis is fatal. Diagnosis can be extremely difficult. The clinical symptoms are consistent with a wide range of neurological and neuropsychiatric syndromes.

If a substantial proportion of syphilis sufferers contract neurosyphilis, the chances are similarly high that Rochester did too. For most of the last period of his life he appears to have been lucid, though more erratic than usual in his behaviour. He had always been prone to melancholy, but his depressions became worse until they were almost constant. Time after time in his letters he complains of his misery and of his loneliness in a hostile world. The world was not as hostile as he thought and after his death there was a flood of eulogy, not all of which was born of the principle *de mortuis nil nisi bonum*.

His peculiar letters, for example the letter to his cousin the Earl of Lichfield, and his last letter to Dr Pierce, were more than mere caprice; as was his startling reaction to the disagreement with the Duchess of Portsmouth. It is difficult to fathom how he came to ignore and eventually find himself unable to think of anything to say to Harry Savile, his closest friend of all: 'idleness on one side, and not knowing what to say on the other, has hindered me from writing'. The changes in his personality were marked. His involvement in the duel with Seymour was eccentric, even for Rochester. It may have sprung from a misguided impulse to redeem his reputation for courage before he died, but that was not something that had bothered him for years. His violent swings of religious belief with his wife, with Blount and Burnet, and apostasy in between, were not wholly accountable. As his health deteriorated, even before his final collapse he had regular seizures (episodes of 'hectic fever'). Some telling points emerge from the accounts of Burnet and the Dowager. Their determined efforts to insist that he was perfectly sane may not have been merely a response to rumour; they may have been a response to palpable fact. There were similar assertions in Robert Parsons's funeral sermon. Such protestations alone are an argument in favour of what they were intended to disprove. 'He was disordered in his head, but then he said no hurt, only some little ribble rabble which had no hurt in it.' 'If any has reported that he should speak ridiculous, it has been the *popish* physician, who one day listened at the door whilst my son was discoursing with a divine.' 'I confess for a night and part of a day for want of rest, his head was a little disordered.' 'He does not care to talk much; but, when he does, speaks for the most part well. His expressions are so suddenly spoken that many of them are lost, and cannot be taken; yet I believe some part of what he has said will be remembered.' Burnet's self-effacing desire not to publish the Earl's letter because it contained a compliment to himself in it 'so far above his merit, and not very well suiting with Rochester's condition' makes one wonder to what 'condition' he refers. Burnet had heard the rumours that Rochester had lost his mind. Then there was the absurd 'misunderstanding', when he had no idea who Burnet was. That night the patient was raving, and had a convulsion. He was given laudanum and after some hours' rest he calmed down. There is only one witness on the other side – biased, but no more so than others, and that was Fanshaw, who had an extensive knowledge of the disease. He knew Rochester very well. He had no doubt about what he saw. He was quite genuine when he made the suggestion to those gathered at High Lodge that the sick man 'should be kept out of melancholy fancies'. His friend's personality changes, emotional instability, hallucinations, confusion and seizures all serve to confirm that opinion.

Rochester's apotheosis could well have been induced by insanity. Neurosyphilis can produce powerful religious feelings. It may be that with or without mental illness the situation was complicated by the presence of laudanum. The Earl was being treated with the drug, and probably had been for years. In the later stages it was being administered without his knowledge. It was a popular specific. It took effect instantaneously and could cause delusions. According to Thomas de Quincey in his *Confessions of an English Opium Eater* it can produce an 'Opium Paradise', a divine state where religious fantasies, views of Jerusalem, the sound of anthems and visions of death and hell are conjured up. It is well known that Coleridge used it to produce hallucinations, as did certain of Rochester's contemporaries such as

Shadwell, the playwright. It was powerful, composed of thirty grains of opium with a fluid ounce of alcohol. Four grains of opium could be lethal to a person who was not accustomed to it.

But whether he was sane or insane, drugged, drunk or sober he could not have escaped the effect of his circumstances. He was weakened, demoralised, ill, confused and frightened. He was the subject of constant pressure from the ecclesiastics and tirelessly reminded of the consequences of impiety. All his life his simple philosophy was that the soul did not dissolve after death, but he did not believe in rewards and punishments. By the time the blinding flash came, he had been well prepared to greet it. Burnet admitted that he had warned him many times to expect hellfire. The priest had also supplied him with a detailed blueprint for the mental contortions that followed. Never mind that he was incapable of belief through reason; through revelation God could awaken a capacity in men's minds to understand in a way that other men could not. The reward of resurrection from the dead was *assured* once certain conditions were performed. We therefore had to do our duty, in the hope of eternal life. God had promised, and God could not lie. At the time those arguments had little effect on Rochester, but they would not have been forgotten.

When he was dying the clergy descended upon him. They were there to apply pressure, however Burnet liked to phrase it. The Earl later admitted to Burnet that at the beginning his conversion was caused by horror. Both Blount and Burnet had spoken of eternal punishment. He was battered remorselessly by the nagging of the ecclesiastics and his mother. His mother told of how he grovelled before the throne of grace, begging favour and pardon from God. What was in his mind is clear from the way he advised Fanshaw that there was a powerful God, and a God that was terrible to unrepenting sinners. The time drew near that his friend would come to judgement, with great terror to the wicked, and he should not delay his repentance. If he did, God's displeasure would thunder against him. He wrote his letter in panic to Dr Pierce, 'I dare not appear before the dread majesty of that Holy One I have so often offended.'

Without wishing to weary the reader with amateur psychology, a great deal of help can be derived from William Sargant's book *Battle for the Mind: A Physiology of Conversion and Brainwashing*. Much of what Sargant has to say is based on the experiments of Pavlov, the great

Russian neurophysiologist. Everyone has heard of Pavlov's experiments on dogs and how he induced them to salivate at the sound of a bell, but what is not so widely known is that Pavlov was not a psychiatrist or a psychologist, but a neurophysiologist. His discipline was the investigation of the physical structure of the brain and its alteration. He achieved it by producing nervous exhaustion. The experiments on dogs were widely applied to human beings and led to the technique known dramatically as 'brainwashing'. Putting the drama to one side, it was so effective in procuring admissions, true or false, that after 1955 confessions are believed to have been ruled inadmissible in Russian courts. The technique has developed into what is now called 'behaviour therapy'. Pavlov found that, given the right conditions of isolation, questioning and treatment, every human must sooner or later submit. He also discovered that when that happened the brain's chemistry had been physically altered. The organ had been induced to function in a different way. Pavlov showed by repeated experiments how a man could be conditioned to hate what he had previously loved, and love what he had previously hated.

Similarly, one set of behavioural patterns can be replaced by another that altogether contradicts it. It is not done by persuasion alone but also by imposing intolerable strains on a normally functioning brain. The purpose is to induce anxiety if it is not already present. Human beings break down when stresses or conflicts become too great for their nervous system to master. At the point of breakdown their behaviour changes. The amount of stress that a human can cope with varies according to physical conditions. Factors such as fatigue, fever, drugs and glandular changes will cause a lowering of resistance. When the nervous system has been stimulated beyond its capacity ('transmarginally stimulated') there are three distinguishable phases of increasingly abnormal behaviour: the 'equivalent' phase in which the brain gives the same response to both strong and weak stimuli, the 'paradoxical' phase in which the brain responds more actively to weak stimuli than to strong, and the 'ultraparadoxical' phase in which conditioned responses and behaviour patterns turn from positive to negative or from negative to positive.

Once a new behaviour pattern has been acquired, it is very difficult to eradicate. Sargant suggests that this is the explanation for human beings of strong character suddenly finding God or taking up vegetarianism or becoming Marxists. They become fanatics with one-track minds. People become suggestible. They accept as incontrovertible truth whatever they are told, however nonsensical. The required physiological changes in brain function are brought about through repeated psychological stimuli. Patients become highly sensitised to the therapist who causes them repeated emotional upheavals. Psycho-analysts call this 'the formation of positive or negative transference' towards themselves. The patient's tension and dependence on the therapist are greatly increased by fatigue and debilitation resulting from anxiety. Conversion is based upon mental conflict and a feeling of inadequacy. Freud had a psychoanalytic technique whereby for the first months of treatment the patient was made to feel increasing anxiety, humiliation and guilt, so that nothing about his past life seemed satisfactory and all his ideas about himself were contradicted. When he was in a hopeless state, Freud started to restore his self-confidence and reconstruct his world in a new setting. The patient would become completely dependent on the therapist.

The same basic rules apply to the techniques of religious conversion. Preachers disperse and replace 'wrong' beliefs and 'undesirable' behav-iour patterns. They do so in the same way by inducing nervous tension and anger or anxiety. If stress and physical debilitation continue, patterns of thought and behaviour become disrupted and the sug-gestibility of the subject increases. New patterns can then be sub-stituted, or suppressed patterns may be allowed to reassert themselves. By far the most common type of religious conversion is the result of a sudden and intense illumination bursting into the mind, usually after a period of severe emotional stress. William James, a renowned psychologist and brother of Henry James, the novelist, analysed religious conversion as consisting of two elements, an uneasiness and its solution. He wrote:

There are only two ways in which it is possible to get rid of anger, worry, fear, despair, or other undesirable affections. One is that an opposite affection should overpoweringly break over us, and the other is by getting so exhausted with the struggle that we have to stop – so we drop down, give up, and don't care any longer. Our emotional brain-centres strike work, and we lapse into temporary apathy.

John Wesley, the religious leader, gained his reputation through inducing sudden conversions. He attributed the phenomenon to the intervention of the Holy Ghost. It is now thought that his success was due to the correctness of Freud's theories. Wesley's great achievement was the discovery that there was no need to involve the intellect. Beliefs were implanted or eradicated by an overwhelming assault on the emotions. His technique was to create high emotional tension in an audience. He found it easy to convince them that failure to achieve salvation would inevitably condemn them to eternal hellfire. Anybody who left the meeting unchanged and met with a sudden fatal accident would fall straight into the fiery furnace. Fear of everlasting hell, which was quite real in Wesley's own mind, affected the nervous system of his subjects very much as fear had been found to affect Pavlov's dogs. He found particular success in Newgate, where many of the prisoners were about to die.

Wesley realised that conversions in the New Testament had always been sudden. He checked to see if it was the same with his own disciples. He questioned 652 members of his society, who were all without exception quite clear that the change had been instantaneous. An even more effective preacher, the Rev. John Berridge, worked out the mechanics of the process. He had spent eight years trying to reason his congregations into Christianity and never converted one soul. Then he tried hectoring them about hellfire. He was once heard shouting, 'Fall! Why won't you fall! Why don't you fall! Better fall here, then fall into hell!' He had no hesitation in inducing the final state of collapse in his converts. He told them that they were children of wrath under the curse of God and nothing could recover them out of this state but faith in the Lord Jesus Christ. It was an enormous success.

One of Wesley's predecessors was the Rev. Jonathan Edwards, who instituted the 1735 revival and brought God's cheering message to the people of Northampton, Massachusetts. Edwards preached that the world would be converted into a great lake or liquid globe of fire in which the wicked would be overwhelmed. Their heads, their eyes, their tongues, their hands, their feet, their loins and their vitals would forever be full of a glowing melting fire, enough to melt the very rocks and elements. They would be full of the most quick and lively sensitivity to the torments not for ten millions of ages, but for ever. The damned would be tormented in the presence of the glorified saints, who would thus be made more sensible how great their salvation was. Their view of the misery of the damned would double the ardour of the love and gratitude of the saints in heaven. Those whose consciences were awakened were told that there was a saviour who was excellent and glorious and who stood ready to receive them.

In 1835 Charles G. Finney, who had been making mass conversions in the state of New York, published a book on the subject, *Lectures on Revivals of Religions*. He said that the revivalist should never relax the mental pressure on a prospective convert. Once the sense of guilt had been implanted, in order to clinch the matter no concessions of any sort could be made. No sinner ever realised how bad his sins were until he was told in graphic terms. It should be made perfectly clear to him that, if he did not submit soon, his case was hopeless. He had discovered that there was not a case of protracted conversion recorded in the whole Bible. All of them were sudden. He advised taking pains to learn the state of the subject's mind – what he was thinking of, how he felt – and then press that thoroughly. His mind should not be diverted by speaking of anything else. The inquisitors of the Holy Office used the same methods. Suspected heretics were called for preliminary examination and forbidden to tell their families. Once in prison they faced the constant threat of being burned alive, which could be avoided only by a full confession. Yet it had to be a *sincere* confession. They had to believe themselves genuinely guilty of crimes suggested by the inquisitors or invented by their own overwrought imaginations.

It is hardly necessary to underline the similarities of Rochester's situation with those described above. Although he had always had a genuine respect for those who preached morality and practised it, he was a lifetime unbeliever. As death approached he began to yearn for consolation. But he was intellectually honest, at least – a man who loathed hypocrisy and could not bring himself to believe the unbeliev-able. It was anathema to his intellect. He had tried hard but could not be satisfied with the assurances of Blount and Burnet. For a moment, Burnet had him promising to lead a religious life without going so far as actually to believe, but he was one of nature's backsliders. He was soon affirming Seneca. Shortly after that he was declaiming against God again. Suddenly he became dramatically ill. During the following months he saw virtually no one but priests and doctors. The priests never let up in their oppression. The oppression became threats. Rochester was dying and had been for ten years. He was in constant agony, weak, weary, miserable and frightened. The possibility that it was neurosyphilis is strong.

Neither of these factors alone need have caused his conversion, though both would have made a powerful contribution. He was powerless to resist anyway. The succinct theological way of summarising it is 'Man's extremity is God's opportunity.' He knew that the chances of success through remorse were slim. He put everything into making his contrition genuine. He admitted that at the beginning his conversion was caused by horror. Nevertheless the answer to the blunt question 'Was the conversion genuine?' must be a hesitant 'Yes.' If a pretence seems genuine to the pretender, so far as the pretender is concerned it becomes a fact, irrespective of its still being objectively a pretence. If Rochester had really fooled himself, the conversion was genuine, irrespective of the disbelief of others whom he failed to fool. How much it was worth is a different matter. Certainly it did not amount to evidence confirming ecclesiastical doctrine, though it was widely treated as if it did. It was genuine in the sense that confessions proffered by terrified suspects to the Inquisition were genuine. Otherwise they would have no effect. If the time comes when a human has to believe then he will believe. It was another façade, but, as with many of his other pretences, he became wholly absorbed by it. How long it would have lasted if he had recovered is a matter of speculation. Burnet and even Rochester had their doubts, though most of Wesley's disciples, once converted, stayed converted. Both Burnet and Parsons lamented that he did not live on, to turn his great talent to propagating the word of God. Somehow, it is not easy to conjure up the vision.

EPITAPH

NEMOURS: Ha, my grave Lord of Chartres! *Welcome* as health, as wine, and
taking whores! And tell me now the business of the court.

VIDAME: Hold it, Nemours, forever at defiance.
Fogs of ill humour, damps of melancholy,
Old maids of fifty choked with eternal vapours,
Stuff it with fulsome honour. Dozing virtue
And everlasting dulness husk it round,
Since he that was the life, the soul of pleasure,
Count Rosidore is dead.

NEMOURS: Then we may say
Wit was, and satire is a carcase now.
I thought his last debauch would be his death –
But is it certain?

VIDAME: Yes, I saw him dust,
I saw the mighty thing a nothing made,
Huddled with worms, and swept to that cold den
Where kings lie crumbled just like other men.

NEMOURS: Nay then let's rave and elegise together,
Where Rosidore is now but common clay,
Whom every wiser emmet bears away,
And lays him up against a winter's day.

He was the spirit of wit – and had such an art in gilding his failures, that
it was hard not to love his faults: he never spoke a witty thing twice,
though to different persons. His imperfections were catching, and his
genius was so luxuriant, that he was forced to tame it with a hesitation in
his speech to keep it in view – but, oh, how awkward, how insipid, how
poor and wretchedly dull is the imitation of those that have all the
affectation of his verse, and none of his wit!

An 'emmet' is an ant.

This is a passage from *The Princess of Cleves* by Nathaniel Lee, performed in 1681 shortly after Rochester's death. Lee, who according to his father was led astray by Rochester, was an alcoholic who died insane in Bedlam, which does not help to penetrate the opacity of the play. One fact that has never been doubted, though, is that Rosidore is Rochester. He is Rochester's avatar. The character gives every appearance of having been included as an afterthought, and seems to bear no relevance to the action of the play at all. It is not even a true role, since Rosidore makes no appearance except in the mouths of others. The opposite character in the play, the arch-villain Duke Nemours who reforms at the end, also represents Rochester. It is thought that, in Nemours, Lee creates a portrait of what the man was like, and Rosidore is a transubstantiation of his spirit. The same conflict is remarked by Etherege in Dorimant: 'I know he is a Devil, but he has something of the angel yet undefac'd in him.' Lee wrote in the dedication of *The Princess of Cleves*, addressed to Charles Sackville, now Earl of Dorset and Middlesex, 'The play cost me much pains, the story is true, and I hope the object will display treachery in its own colours. But this farce, comedy, tragedy, or mere play, was a revenge [on the public]. For when they expected the most polished hero in Nemours, I gave 'em a ruffian reeking from Whetstone Park' (the brothel area of London, between Holborn and Lincoln's Inn Fields). There was a battle under way between God, represented by the clergy, and the forces of Belial, represented by the King and his Court. In the play, Tournon, the heroine, says to Nemours, 'Go thy ways, Petronius. Nay if he were dying too, with his veins cut, he would call for wine, fiddles and whores, and laugh himself into the other world.' Petronius was a notorious sensualist at the time of Nero, who committed suicide by slashing his veins, then chatting to his friends about trivia while bleeding to death. It was an open sneer at Burnet's claims of Rochester's apotheosis. The forces of Belial simply ignored their friend's rebirth as if it had not happened, or was meaningless if it had.

Aphra Behn also outraged Burnet by ignoring the conversion. In *The Rover, Part II*, a famous courtesan, La Nuche, played by Elizabeth Barry, agrees to run away with Willmore, the Rochester character, without benefit of clergy. Willmore, in Rochester's words, describes marriage as 'formal foppery':

LA NUCHE: Nay, faith, Captain, she that will not take thy word as soon as
the parson's of the parish, deserves not the blessing.

WILLMORE: Thou art reformed, and I adore the change.

Rochester's recantation might as well never have happened. Those
who wished to ignore it, did so. Burnet was so disgusted by Behn's
dogged immoralism that he wrote in a letter to Ann Wharton, a
poetess and Rochester's cousin, 'Some of Mrs Behn's songs are very
tender; but she is so abominably vile a woman, and rallies not only all
religion but all virtue in so odious and obscene a manner, that I am
heartily sorry she has writ anything in your commendation.'

Among those songs was Mrs Behn's elegy on Rochester's death,
which is so ornate that it has been described as a rare example of
English baroque. She was not the only elegist. There were also Thomas
Flatman, John Oldham, Samuel Woodforde, Samuel Holland and Ann
Wharton. The clergy hung out Rochester's tattered soul in hundreds
of improving tracts that appeared over the next two centuries. The
sons of Belial simply shrugged it off. This was a common occurrence
on deathbeds when the clergy were hovering greedily, ready to steal a
soul for God. It was all the more to be expected from a man who
had been drained and incapacitated by sickness for a decade, and had
been seen to have gone mad. In 1682 Thomas Otway, in the bitter
climax to his play *Venice Preserv'd*, has a priest brought to his central
character, Pierre, who is about to be hanged:

PIERRE:　　　You want to lead
My reason blindfold, like a hamper'd lion,
Check'd of its nobler vigour then, when baited
Down to obedient tameness, make it couch
And show strange tricks, which you call signs of faith
So silly souls are gull'd and you get money.
Away, no more: Captain, I would hereafter
This fellow write no lies of my conversion
Because he has crept upon my troubled hours.

John Oldham, who had disapproved of Rochester's excesses, wrote:

If I am reckoned not unblessed in song,
'Tis what I owe to thy all-teaching tongue:
Some of thy art, some of thy tuneful breath

Thou did'st by will to worthless me bequeath:
Others thy flocks, thy lands, thy riches have,
To me thou did'st thy pipe, and skill vouchsafe.

Ann Wharton, his broken-hearted cousin, wrote:

He civilised the rude, and taught the young,
Made fools grow wise; such artful music hung
Upon his useful kind instructing tongue.
His lively wit was of himself a part,
Not as in other men, the work of art.

Voltaire said of him in 1735, 'The Earl of Rochester's name is universally known. Mr de St Evremont has made very frequent mention of him, but he has represented the famous nobleman nothing more than as a man of pleasure, as one who was the idol of beautiful women; but I willingly describe him as a man of genius, and a great poet.'

The words that should have been on Rochester's lips when he faced the abyss had been spoken by him long before. In the *Princess of Cleves*, Nemours says, quoting Rosidore (quoting Rochester):

Thus would I have time roll still all in these lovely extremes, the corruption of reason being the generation of wit, and the spirit of wit lying in the extravagance of pleasure. Nay, the two nearest ways to enter the closet of the gods, and lie even with the fates themselves, are fury and sleep. Therefore the fury of wine and fury of women possess me waking and sleeping. Let me dream of nothing but dimpled cheeks, and laughing lips, and flowing bowls. Venus be my star, and whoring my house, and *Death, I defy thee!*

Perhaps the final elegy should be left to Rochester himself in his own defiant salutation 'To the Post Boy' ('cerecloth' is a bandage impregnated with wax; 'murder' refers to a rumour that Rochester had murdered a whore in her lodgings):

Son of a whore, God damn you, can you tell
A peerless peer the readiest way to Hell?
I've outswilled Bacchus, sworn of my own make
Oaths would fright Furies and make Pluto shake.
I've swived more whores more ways than Sodom's walls
E'er knew, or the College of Rome's Cardinals.

Witness heroic scars, — look here, ne'er go —
Cerecloths and ulcers from the top to toe.
Frighted at my own mischiefs I have fled
And bravely left my life's defender dead.
Broke houses to break chastity, and dyed
That flower with murder that my lust denied.
Pox on it, why do I speak of these poor things?
I have blasphemed my God and libelled Kings;
The readiest way to Hell, boy, quick —

BOY: Ne'er stir,
The readiest way, my lord's by Rochester.

BIBLIOGRAPHY

Quotations of the poetry are taken from the following editions of Rochester's work: Harold Love (ed.), *The Works of John Wilmot, Earl of Rochester* (Oxford University Press, 1999); Paddy Lyons (ed.), *Complete Poems and Plays of Rochester* (Dent, 1993); David M. Vieth (ed.), *The Complete Poems of John Wilmot, Earl of Rochester* (Yale University Press, 1968). Excerpts from Rochester's letters are from Jeremy Treglown's edition, *The Letters of John Wilmot, Earl of Rochester* (Blackwell, 1980). Rochester's spelling throughout has been appropriated by the Author.

PRIMARY SOURCES

Behn, Aphra, *The Rover* (Oxford University Press, 1995).

De Quincey, Thomas, *Confessions of an English Opium Eater* (J. M. Dent & Co., 1821, 1907).

Dryden, John, *The Works of John Dryden* ed. David Marriott (Wordsworth, 1995).

Etherege, George, *The Man of Mode* (Everyman Library, 1994).

Grose, Francis, *A Classical Dictionary of the Vulgar Tongue, 1811* (Digest Books, 1971).

Lee, Nathaniel, 'The Princess of Cleves' from *Four Restoration Marriage Plays*, Book IV, ed. Michael Cordner (Clarendon Press, 1995).

Marvell, Andrew, *The Complete Poems* ed. Elizabeth Story Dunno (Penguin Books, 1972).

Pepys, Samuel, *Diary* (Globe Edition, 1924).

SECONDARY SOURCES

Adlard, John (ed.), *The Debt to Pleasure: John Wilmot, Earl of Rochester, in the Eyes of his Contemporaries and in his own Poetry and Prose* (Carcanet Press, 1974).

Adlard, John (ed.), *The Fruit of that Forbidden Tree: Restoration Poems, Songs and Jests on the Subject of Sensual Love* (Carcanet Press, 1975).

Aubrey, John, *Brief Lives* ed. Oliver Lawson Dick (Secker & Warburg, 1949).

Barrow, Andrew, *The Flesh is Weak: An Intimate History of the Church of England* (Hamish Hamilton, 1980).

Batchelor, John (ed.), *The Art of Literary Biography* (Clarendon Press, 1995).

Brown, James Alexander Campbell, *Techniques of Persuasion: From Propaganda to Brainwashing* (Penguin Books, 1963).

Burford, Ephraim John, *The Orrible Synne: A Look at London Lechery from Roman to Cromwellian Times* (Calder & Boyars, 1973).

Collart and Poitevin, 'La syphilis actualités', *Physiobiologiques* (May 1981).

Duffy, Maureen, *The Passionate Shepherdess: Aphra Behn, 1640–1689* (Cape, 1977).

Farley-Hills, David (ed.), *Earl of Rochester: The Critical Heritage* (Routledge, 1972, repr. 1995).

Fraser, Antonia, *King Charles II* (Weidenfeld & Nicolson, 1979).

Greene, Graham, *Lord Rochester's Monkey* (Bodley Head, 1974).

Gregory, Richard (ed.), *The Oxford Companion to the Mind* (Oxford University Press, 1987).

Gudjonsson, Gisli, *The Psychology of Interrogations, Confessions and Testimony* (Wiley, 1992).

Haggard, Howard Wilcox, *Devils, Drugs and Doctors: The Story of the Science of Healing from Medicine-Man to Doctor* (William Heinemann, 1929).

Hamilton, Anthony, *Memoirs of the Comte de Gramont* trans. Peter Quennell (G. Routledge & Sons, 1930).

Hobbes, Thomas, *Leviathan* ed. Richard Tuck (Cambridge University Press, 1996).

Hobson, J. Allan, *The Chemistry of Conscious States: How the Brain Changes its Mind* (Little, Brown, 1994).

Hua, Huang and Yang, 'Chronic Elemental Mercury Intoxication', *Brain Injury* (May 1996).

Kalant, Harold, *Addiction: Opium Revisited* (Toronto University Press, 1997).

Lamb, Jeremy *'So Idle a Rogue': The Life and Death of Lord Rochester* (Allison & Busby, 1993).

Langauer and Zajac-Nezda, 'Metallic Mercury Poisoning', *Neuralogia Chirurgia Polska* (September 1997).

Magner, Lois N., *A History of Medicine* (Dekker, 1992).

Major, Ralph Hermon, *Classic Descriptions of Disease* (C. C. Thomas, 1939).

Ollard, Richard Laurence, *The Escape of Charles II after the Battle of Worcester* (Hodder & Stoughton, 1966).

Osler, Sir William, Bart., *The Evolution of Modern Medicine* (Yale University Press, 1921).

Petherick, Maurice, *Restoration Rogues* (Hollis & Carter, 1951).

Pinto, Vivian de Sola and Rodway, Allan Edwin, *Enthusiast in Wit: A Portrait of John Wilmot, Earl of Rochester, 1647–1680* (Routledge & Kegan Paul, 1962).

Pinto, Vivian de Sola (ed.), *Poems by John Wilmot, Earl of Rochester* (Routledge & Kegan Paul, 1953).

Porter, Roy, *The Greatest Benefit to Mankind: A Medical History of Humanity from Antiquity to the Present* (HarperCollins, 1997).

Quennell, Peter, *The Pursuit of Happiness* (Constable, 1988).

Redwood, John, *Reason, Ridicule and Religion: The Age of Enlightenment* (Thames and Hudson, 1976, repr. 1996).

Robinson, *John Wilmot, Earl of Rochester* (Clarendon Press, 1995).

Rollins, 'The Effects of Opium Smoking', *British Journal of Psychiatry* (March 1993).

Sargant, William Walters, *Battle for the Mind: A Physiology of Conversion and Brainwashing* (Heinemann, 1957).

Smith, 'Mental Effects of Mercury Poisoning', *Southern Medical Journal* (August 1978).

Thormählen, Marianne, *Rochester: The Poems in Context* (Cambridge University Press, 1993).

Vieth, David M., *Attribution in Restoration Poetry: A Study of Rochester's Poems of 1680* (Yale University Press, 1963).

Wain, John (ed.), *The Oxford Library of English Poetry*, 3 vols (Oxford University Press, 1986).

Wedgwood, Dame Cicely Veronica, *The Great Rebellion* (Collins, 1955, 1958).

INDEX